EPISTLE TO THE BABYLONIANS

AN ESSAY ON THE NATURAL INEQUALITY OF MAN

EPISTLE

TO THE BABYLONIANS

AN ESSAY ON THE NATURAL
INEQUALITY OF MAN

Charles L. Fontenay

THE UNIVERSITY OF TENNESSEE PRESS
KNOXVILLE

LIBRARY OF CONGRESS CATALOG NUMBER 68–9778

STANDARD BOOK NUMBER 87049–088–3

DEDICATION

*Dionysos, der in allen meinen Kindern
wiedergeboren ist, gewidmet.*

THE FOLLOWING ESSAY, research for which has occupied a respectable percentage of my time during the past six years, springs from the question most often asked by man: "Who am I?" It does not answer that question, but it proposes a philosophical foundation from which the answer may be sought.

The personal circumstances which made that question of overriding importance to me after I had already lived quite pleasantly for forty-two years are not pertinent here. It suffices that they were such as to cause me to question, at the same time, the answer most commonly offered and accepted, which is: an individual's identity is so completely social that its meaning lies in his contribution to others of his kind. But if not that, then what is the answer, for a creature who is mortal? And why does the common answer not satisfy the requirements of truth?

The "why not" must be answered first, to validate any further inquiry. It is qualified by the obvious fact that part of the individual's identity and meaning does lie in his contribution to others, just as a part of his identity and meaning lies in the contributions of others to him. These reciprocating areas of human meaning, conforming to both the Golden Rule and the Social Contract, are so apparent that it is easy to be satisfied with them. But the intuition of something beyond them is confirmed if it is followed through.

The clue to this confirmation lies in taking the common answer to its logical extreme, and asking: "What would be the result if every individual human acted only for the purpose of contributing to others of his kind?" If the answer to this question is sought diligently and honestly, not through a single intellectual discipline but through each one that becomes applicable to the search, the findings are surprising. One does not find a utopia, but an animal herd, hardly advanced beyond the stage of man's ancestors of a million years ago.

This is what *I* have found, and upon this I take my stand:

Human altruism is legitimate and important, but it is not man's altruism that has led him from the jungle to civilization. The human trait responsible for man's most spectacular rise above the bestial level is not a "social" trait at all; it is the intangible conviction of the individual that he is born free, that he has the inherent right to converse one-to-one with the universe without paying undue tribute to the opinions of his society.

Conversely, I conclude that every attempt by man to deny his individual meaning in the interest of better social adjustment, however well intentioned, has not led to social perfection, but to regression.

This essay is an effort to document that finding by means of a brief look at human history and prehistory. This look is not solely historical, nor even primarily so. It draws upon such applicable fields as evolutionary biology, anthropology, psychology, and political philosophy, for only through such a synthesis can a new viewpoint be attained.

Yet even the term "synthesis" is somewhat misleading here, because it implies putting together (however creatively) findings of unquestioned conclusiveness, and such universally accepted findings are not always available. Each of these fields right now is racked with epistemological controversy, some of it as violent as that between Darwinian evolutionary theory and fundamentalist religion in the nineteenth century. To deal with these fields in any meaningful way necessitates, of course, taking some position in their controversies. This I have done, in the main, by utilizing accepted findings in one field as a measure for judging controversial issues in another field.

One of the fields so utilized, for example, is the recent subdivision of biology, ethology, or the study of comparative animal and human behavior. Although obviously related to comparative psychology, the two springing from the same roots in scientific research, ethology in its modern form is only about two decades old, and its definitive formulations could be said to extend no farther back than the work of J. von Uexküll in the 1920's. Further, the significant findings of ethology were almost unknown in this country until very recently, although Robert Ardrey had treated some aspects in highly literate fashion. There exists virtually no English translation of the extensive work of one of the two principal figures in this field, Adolf Portmann, professor of zoology at the University of Basel; and some of the really significant work of the other, Konrad Lorenz, director of the Max-Planck-Institut für Verhaltensphysiologie at Seewiesen, is just becoming available in English.

Thus, this essay must be viewed as fundamentally speculative and philosophical in its approach. It "proves" nothing but advances a rather complex theory. I think this is justifiable as more than a mere intellectual exercise. As Portmann remarks,[1] life demands from man more than the certainty offered by piecemeal investigation of facts; it demands the construction of some comprehensible whole. In the same sense, Köhler has commented[2] that in a period of scientific advance almost any hypothesis is better than "mere waiting."

Admittedly, however, there is not much point in conducting extensive research unless one answers *some* question, and the one I hope I answer here is: "*What* am I, if not an interchangeable cog in the great social mechanism of the human species?" This is, to some extent, the same question as: "What is my *social* meaning, *as an individual?*"

CHARLES L. FONTENAY
Nashville
August, 1968

[1] Adolf Portmann, *Biologische Fragmente zu einer Lehre vom Menschen* (2. Aufl.; Basel: Benno Schwabe & Co. Verlag, 1951), p. 129.
[2] Wolfgang Köhler, *Gestalt Psychology* (Mentor ed., New York: New American Library, 1959), p. 35.

APPRECIATION

IS EXPRESSED to the following for their permission to quote from the works cited:

Harper & Row, Publishers, Inc., 49 E. 33rd St., New York, N. Y. 10016: Gaston Viaud, *Intelligence: Its Evolution and Forms*, the translation by A. J. Pomerans of *L'Intelligence*.

The editors of *The Saturday Evening Post*, 666 Fifth Ave., New York, N. Y. 10019: *Adventures of the Mind from The Saturday Evening Post*, edited by Richard Thruelsen and John Kobler.

Alfred Kröner Verlag, Stuttgart: Friedrich Wilhelm Nietzsche, *Der Wille zur Macht* and *Also Sprach Zarathustra*.

Revista de Occidente, Barbara de Braganza, 12, Madrid: José Ortega y Gasset, *La Rebelión de las masas* and *España invertebrada*.

Robert C. Cook, president, Population Reference Bureau, Inc., 1507 M St., N. W., Washington, D. C. 20005: *Human Fertility: the Modern Dilemma*; also for his courtesy in supplying recent data on birth rates by educational level.

Random House, Inc., 457 Madison Ave., New York, N. Y. 10022: Thomas Robert Malthus, *On Population*.

The Ronald Press Co., 15 E. 26th St., New York, N. Y. 10022: Gregory A. Kimble and Norman Garmezy, *Principles of General Psychology*.

CONTENTS

FOREWORD *page* vii

APPRECIATION *page* x

1 THE PRIMAL IMPERATIVE *page* 3

2 THE TIE THAT BINDS *page* 12

3 THE ROPE OVER THE ABYSS *page* 24

4 SHAPES BEHIND THE FACADE *page* 34

5 THE CULTURAL MAINSPRING *page* 45

6 THE LEAVEN IN THE LOAF *page* 55

7 THE ADVENT OF REASON *page* 63

8 THE ACCESSION OF THE CROWD *page* 74

9 THE GRECO-CHRISTIAN GIFT *page* 87

10 IN EQUAL CHAINS *page* 97

11 THE PEOPLE: YES OR NO? *page* 106

12 CITIES OF THE PLAIN *page* 115

13 THE GENETICS OF DECLINE *page* 124

14 THE SPOILED SOCIETY *page* 137

15 WHERE IGNORANT ARMIES CLASH BY NIGHT *page* 147

16 MAN IN TRANSITION *page* 157

APPENDICES *page* 167

GLOSSARY *page* 180

BIBLIOGRAPHY *page* 185

INDEX *page* 203

EPISTLE TO THE BABYLONIANS

AN ESSAY ON THE NATURAL INEQUALITY OF MAN

A people, it appears, may be progressive for a certain length of time, and then stop: when does it stop? When it ceases to possess individuality.

—JOHN STUART MILL: *On Liberty*

CHAPTER ONE

THE PRIMAL IMPERATIVE

*"Are you not," a Rugby master had asked him in
discussing one of his essays, "a little out of
your depth here?" "Perhaps, Sir," was
the confident reply, "but I can swim."*

—F. A. IREMONGER: *William Temple*

IN THE FULLNESS OF HIS PRIDE, Belshazzar the King gave a
feast in Babylon. At its height, the fingers of a hand appeared and wrote upon the plaster of the wall: *Mene Mene
Tekel Uphärsin.*[1] And upon that night Belshazzar was slain
and his kingdom passed into the hands of Darius the Mede.

Babylon on the Euphrates, Babylon the Great, was the jewel
of the ancient world. Its marvelous hanging gardens delighted
the eye. Its ziggurats thrust arrogantly into the heavens. Alexander, the world at his feet, went there to die beside its waters.

Belshazzar's Feast is a fable, but it tells a longer truth than
the historical facts surrounding the death of the Babylonian
general, Belshazzar, in the sixth century B.C. For today the
ground upon which the mighty city stood is a series of mounds
dug by archeologists.

Today, cities mightier than Babylon dot the realm of man.
By the marvelous intricacies of their technology, common people enjoy greater luxury than Belshazzar could imagine. Their
skyscrapers tower to a height that dwarfs the Babylonian temples. Men commanding many times Alexander's power fly between them to pull the strings that make the whole world dance.

---

[1] Translated by Daniel as: *Mene*, "God has numbered the days of your
kingdom and brought it to an end"; *Tekel*, "you have been weighed in the
balance and found wanting"; *Peres* (*Uphärsin*), "your kingdom is divided
and given to the Medes and Persians."

Yet there is handwriting on the walls of today's cities, too. The words written in the smoke of riots and the blood of battlefields are obscure, but they are ominous. We, who sit now at Belshazzar's Feast, anxiously await a Daniel to tell us whether the lion and the lizard shall inherit the courts of our glory also.

Other civilizations than Babylon, civilizations as great as Babylon, have fallen. Should one rely only on statistics for a conclusion, the computer would produce a 100 per cent probability that this world too shall end, whether with a bang or with a whimper. Two of the twentieth century's most erudite (and most controversial) historians, Oswald Spengler and Arnold Toynbee, considered the evidence they gathered compelling for the view that civilizations follow a cyclical course of rise and fall.

The remembrance of things past is no sure augury for the future, of course. It is not merely the past, but the present too, which must cause us to wonder if our civilization will break precedent and rise above its troubles, or if it will follow its predecessors into the gloom of a Dark Age.

To play the Daniel is to risk being found a Chaldean astrologer, but I anticipate the latter. This anticipation is not founded upon the conviction of any organic inevitability inherent in a "culture," *à la* Spengler, nor yet upon the moralistic foreboding which emerges from Toynbee's tangled analysis. I am convinced simply that this civilization, like others in the past, has reached a point at which it is no longer compatible with the stubbornly ingrained nature of man; and when the demands of one of man's artificial creations clash with his nature, he will eventually destroy what he has wrought and start again.

The waning influence of religion as a primary motive force of society has robbed Western man of the rationale it offered (whether true or false) for his existence *as an individual*. Science has not replaced this vital human ingredient, and efforts to do so in terms compatible with the scientific approach to reality have resulted so far only in a gross atavism.

This atavism is the assignment of meaning to the individual's existence in positive ratio to his participation in, and contribution to, society. The only solutions that receive serious consideration in today's world are collective ones. Psychology proposes adjustment to a practical "norm." Politics, economics, and sociology would bring all minorities, international and intranational, into the same orbit of privilege and responsibility (and, consequently, of total orientation to society) as the majority. Periodic "resurgences" of religion represent nothing creative and fundamental, but accommodations of an outdated orthodoxy to the prevailing temper.

In positivistic terms, this temper is highly rational; a part cannot have greater meaning than the whole, but must have lesser meaning and therefore must adapt itself to the welfare of the whole. The other side of the coin, which is overlooked, is that the whole is composed *only* of its parts. Although a whole may acquire characteristics not possessed by any of its parts individually, if no part has any intrinsic meaning of its own, the whole also is devoid of meaning. $O \times n = O$.

The tyranny of dominant religion often suppressed the uncommon man, but primarily it disciplined the common man, *as a responsible individual.* The collapse of that tyranny, with its binding ideal of individual excellence, has not been succeeded by an adequate substitute for its discipline under the ægis of either science or government. The result has been what Ortega termed a "rebellion of the masses," which he saw accurately as a reversion to a primitive human orientation.[2]

It would be correct to say that this rebellion was accomplished, at least in its political and economic phases, in the name of general human happiness. Such is not an invalid motive, but history is currently busy demonstrating that seemingly reasonable academic theory often undergoes a sea-change in the process of translation into political and economic action. The process by which Skinner's behavioristic utopia, *Walden Two*, would almost inevitably slip into a tyrannical Orwellian *1984*

[2] José Ortega y Gasset, *La Rebelión de las masas* (Madrid: Espasa-Calpe, S. A., 1937).

5

rests upon a single omission: an evasion of the problem of human values.[3]

Values are extraordinarily difficult to deal with because they are essentially subjective. Happiness is subjective, but it is not a value. It is an epiphenomenon, a symptom of the status of striving toward some more primary goal. As Allport points out, it is too incidental and contingent to be a goal in itself and is a product of motivated activity rather than a motivation *per se*.[4]

"Primary goal," "motivated activity," and "value" are terms inextricably related to the concept of "purpose," which has involved psychologists today in a raging and extremely fractionized debate over questions that are both metaphysical and epistemological. Generally, American psychology, especially the behavioral school, follows the Lockean tradition of the brain as *tabula rasa*, upon which is written its subsequent nature by the impact of outer stimuli, whereas continental European psychology follows the Leibnitzian tradition of the person as the source of acts.[5]

The difference is obviously important in the practical context of human affairs. If the Lockeans are right, men can be conditioned to a satisfied acceptance of almost any kind of society; if the Leibnitzians are right, conditioning cannot trespass beyond certain limits without creating pathological distortions. To state this differently, in the first case it is possible to shape the individual to an ideal society; in the second case society must be shaped to the nature of its individuals.

Working from the common assumption of man's evolutionary ancestry as a form of animal life, the two orientations diverge less on the question of how extensive a portion of his mental processes man holds in common with other animals than on the

[3] B. F. Skinner, *Walden Two* (New York: Macmillan, 1948); George Orwell, *1984* (New York: Harcourt, Brace & Co., 1949).
[4] Gordon W. Allport, *Becoming* (New Haven: Yale University Press, 1955), p. 68.
[5] For a discussion of these diverging traditions in psychology, see Allport, *ibid.*, Chaps. 2 and 3. Cf. Robert Ardrey, *The Territorial Imperative* (New York: Atheneum, 1966), pp. 17–38.

nature of these commonly held processes, that is, whether they are shaped by inner goals or imposed by the chance impact of outer influences. It is a question of the validity of Aristotle's concept of entelechy.

Aristotelian entelechy (self-contained process) is not the teleology set forth by Aquinas and adopted by such later thinkers as Teilhard de Chardin,[6] which implies an inherent purpose directed toward some final end. Aristotelian entelechy means only that an object has a non-random function because it is a particular object and not something else.[7] Applied to man, this concept means that man has inherent human goals rather than, for example, chimpanzee goals, because he is man and not chimpanzee. It implies, too—*contra* the Lockean viewpoint— that no conceivable process of conditioning could alter a human's orientation to the extent that he would fit naturally into the living pattern normal for chimpanzees.

The Leibnitzian view of the nature of mental processes seems the more intelligent one, since all life has to maintain a continuing tension if it is not to dissolve naturally back into the inorganic state. It has been demonstrated theoretically that life could have arisen by the random action of solar energy upon matter under early terrestrial conditions, yet the chances of a single chromosome's being assembled at random are estimated at only one in $10^{2.4 \times 10^9}$, a figure of such astronomical proportions that it defies statement in common terms.[8] The continuance of life cannot depend, therefore, on the random impact of the

[6] Teilhard de Chardin placed an essentially theological interpretation upon evolutionary science. He makes such finalistic statements as "man is irreplaceable. . . .he must reach the goal": *The Phenomenon of Man* (Torchbook ed., New York: Harper & Bros., 1961), p. 276. Adolf Portmann, who is inclined to agree with Père Teilhard on the uniqueness of man in the context of neo-Darwinian evolutionary theory, nevertheless notes, in "Die Evolution des Menschen im Werk von Teilhard de Chardin," in Ernst Benz, *Der Übermensch* (Zürich: Rhein-Verlag, 1961), that he has stepped far beyond the borders of biology into the field of mysticism.

[7] Cf. Samuel Enoch Stumpf, *Socrates to Sartre* (New York: McGraw-Hill, 1966), pp. 98–99.

[8] I. S. Shklovskii and Carl Sagan, *Intelligent Life in the Universe* (San Francisco: Holden-Day, Inc., 1966), p. 196.

outer environment but must rest upon the organism's ability to serve as its own non-random agent; this conforms to the Leibnitzian view of the person (the organism) as the source of acts; and mental processes are, of course, a part of life.

The living organism is not only an open energy system. It organizes additional inorganic matter, too, in growth and reproduction, to assure the development and continuation of this open energy system. The living organism thus incorporates a structural goal: not mere passive reaction to energy, like a machine, but self-aggrandizement in the interest of its own continuation. Life not only *is*; it *becomes.*

Life's self-aggrandizing tendency justifies Nietzsche's concept of "the Will to Power": "every specific body accordingly strives to become master throughout all space and expand its strength (its Will to Power) and push back everything which strives against its expansion."[9] There exist semantic objections to the use of the phrase "the Will to Power" in such a sense, not the least of which is Adler's utilization of it to describe a psychological rebellion against inferiority feelings.[10] The phenomenon of life to which I refer here is what Schweitzer called "Will to Live"—life's "determination to live itself to the full."[11] This is reminiscent of Ortega's "all life is the struggle, the endeavor, to be itself."[12] If we add to these formulations life's expansive force, without which it would not have spread and evolved, we have the Nietzschean "Will to Power."

Any concise term for a unifying concept of universal living motivation, such as Goldstein's "self-actualization,"[13] is mis-

[9] Friedrich W. Nietzsche, *Der Wille zur Macht* (Stuttgart: Alfred Kröner Verlag, 1959), Aph. 636, p. 430.

[10] Heinz L. Ansbacher and Rowena R. Ansbacher, eds., *The Individual Psychology of Alfred Adler* (Torchbook ed., New York: Harper & Row, 1964), pp. 111–12. See Appendix I.

[11] Albert Schweitzer, *The Philosophy of Civilization* (New York: Macmillan, 1960), p. 282.

[12] Ortega y Gasset, *La Rebelión de las masas*, p. 91.

[13] Kurt Goldstein, *Human Nature in the Light of Psychopathology* (Cambridge: Harvard University Press, 1940). Cf. Roy R. Grinker, ed., *Toward a Unified Theory of Human Behavior* (New York: Basic Books, 1956), p. 129.

leading in one way or another by virtue of its accrued connotations. Allport's "propriate striving"[14] contains the necessary elements for the concept, but he specifically limits it to the higher manifestations of psychic life. Therefore, I shall advance a term for this universal living motivation, for use in this context and expressive of the above definition, which is really no better than any of the others except that it offers the advantage of fewer preconceived connotations. The term is "self-affirming imperative," and it is a trait that is an intrinsic characteristic of all life, which naturally includes man. There is some reason to believe that it is stronger in man than in any other form of life, because man is one of the most complex and successful forms of life. For example, man's history, his accomplishments, and his usual behavior show him to be one of life's most aggressive creatures, and aggressiveness is quite obviously one way of expressing a self-affirming imperative.

It is a shallow criticism to object that people do not constantly quarrel and contend. The blind force of the self-affirming imperative has been modified by evolution, as the force of a river is modified by the contour and nature of the terrain; and Lorenz has shown amply how behavioral mechanisms shape the expression of aggressiveness in social animals.[15] Yet a force need not be eliminated by being modified, as the Colorado River demonstrated by cutting the Grand Canyon. Living organisms—including man—still compete with each other, when necessary, to express what they are.

Behind the checkered scene of organic life—a scene of visible competition, of cooperation and symbiosis, of eat-and-be-eaten, of live-and-let-live—lurks the vast force of "invisible competition." This is competition at the genetic level, into which nat-

[14] Allport, *Becoming*, pp. 47–51.
[15] Konrad Lorenz, *Das sogenannte Böse* (Wien: Dr. G. Borotha-Schoeler Verlag, 1963), pp. 89–195; Konrad Lorenz, *Evolution and Modification of Behavior* (Chicago: University of Chicago Press, 1965), p. 20; Konrad Lorenz, *Er redete mit dem Vieh, den Vögeln und den Fischen* (München: Deutscher Taschenbuch Verlag GmbH & Co. KG, 1964), pp. 115–28.

ural selection thrusts the heavy hand of death, a competition of efficiency in utilizing the environment.

To the extent of our present knowledge, the major dynamic agent of this competition is a factor of chance, which is the genetic mutation that offers the basic variations upon which natural selection acts. Since the mutation is necessarily so atomistic in its effect, there are some prominent biologists who feel that macromutation (sudden large evolutionary jumps) may be necessary to explain some of the major evolutionary steps.[16] It is possible, however, that these objections may be met by better knowledge of such phenomena as pleiotropy (capacity of a gene to affect several characters), the influence of polygenes (joint control of a character by several genes), and epistatic interaction (interaction of non-allelic genes).[17]

Whatever the process—a process which lies beyond the control of any individual or any generation—superimposed upon it are those activities that are the concern of the individual and the generation. These include a vast network of sexual selection, social relations, family relations, and all of those matters of choice with reference to which one may debate the question of free will versus determinism. The individual and the generation are engaged in a repeated discourse of cause-and-effect with the broad stream of life from which they spring. They are not only consequences of the past; they are also causes of the future.

As such a translator of the past to the future, the human individual finds himself in fundamentally the same position of responsibility as the first tiny unit of life. He alone can create certain elements of the future; without his action, they will not be. Only he can accomplish his particular task, whatever it may be, because he is unique; he is a focus of the biological and historical process that exists nowhere else, has never existed before, and will never exist again. His accomplishment of this

[16] E. g., Adolf Portmann, *Das Tier als soziales Wesen* (Zürich: Rhein-Verlag, 1953), pp. 240–51.
[17] Cf. Ernst Mayr, *Animal Species and Evolution* (Cambridge: Harvard University Press, 1963), p. 269; George Gaylord Simpson, *The Meaning of Evolution* (New Haven: Yale University Press, 1949), pp. 160–85.

individual task represents the fullest possible expression of the self-affirming imperative, the fullest expression of what he is. What is "right" for and to a man depends on what that man individually is, and he has no guarantee that others who tell him he is wrong are not themselves wrong.

No nearer approach can be made to a "self-evident value" or an absolute morality.

That such a troublesome constant as a self-affirming imperative should be attached to the already troublesome variable of human personality is understandably unpalatable to socially oriented thinking. Ultimately, however, society must adapt itself to the nature of its individuals, either gracefully or catastrophically.

CHAPTER TWO

THE TIE THAT BINDS

*No man is an Iland, intire of itselfe; every man is a
peece of the Continent, a part of the maine; if a Clod
bee washed away by the Sea, Europe is the lesse, as well as
if a Promontorie were, as well as if a Mannor of thy friends or of
thine own were, any man's death diminishes me, because
I am involved in Mankinde; And therefore never send
to know for whom the bell tolls; it tolls for thee.*
—JOHN DONNE: *Devotions, XVII*

THE MODERN DILEMMA posed by the clash between man's
innate nature and his social aims would be less difficult of
solution if it offered a clear-cut choice between individualism
and sociality, but it does not. It demands a solution somewhere
between outright anarchy and absolute collectivism.

It demands such a solution precisely because of the self-
affirming imperative—and the fact that the human who acts
under its ægis is to a large degree a social animal.

To say that man is a social "animal" has implications that
would be absent if one said merely that man "lives socially."
If man was social before he became human, we may assume
that the non-rational, unconscious inclinations which tended
him toward sociality as a prehuman persist in the deeper layers
of his present-day psyche. It is also reasonable to assume that
these inclinations retain some of their ancient force, that they
have influenced historical processes in society, and that they
affect man's attitudes toward society today.

Portmann[1] has observed that all of the highest stages of animal life are reached as social forms, and individuals of these

[1] Adolf Portmann, *Das Tier als soziales Wesen* (Zürich: Rhein-Verlag,
1953), p. 299. On p. 94, Portmann comments on the similarity of human
social life to that of other higher animals.

species find their fullest expression only in the social context. Similarly, Köhler[2] notes that the behavior of the chimpanzee's comrades constitutes the only adequate incentive for the chimpanzee to express his nature to the full. So necessary is society to man and so much is sociality a part of his nature that the proposal has been advanced seriously that cooperation is a higher orientation of life that makes competitiveness unnecessary.[3]

On the contrary, cooperation enters into the life-scene at a very early evolutionary stage—with the multicellular organism. Weiss[4] has cited an instructive example of slime molds that consist of separate unicellular organisms living as discrete individuals—which, however, unite by tens of thousands to form a coherent multicellular organism, with organized division of labor, for purposes of reproduction. Here, as exemplified by the multicellular organism, we have an almost perfect picture of cooperation. From the viewpoint of the individual cells, it is virtually absolute collectivism. The composite organism then becomes "the individual" and inherits the self-affirming imperative at a higher level.

Such cooperation among individual cells, which once in the course of evolution were able to exist independently, obviously has not eliminated competition. Now the larger, multicellular organism of which they are a part competes with other multicellular organisms, and the success of its competition in turn determines the welfare of its own cells.

To see how this same principle carries over to the individual multicellular organism in a social context, it is necessary

---

[2] Wolfgang Köhler, *The Mentality of Apes*, 2nd rev. ed., trans. Ella Winter (Vintage ed., New York: Random House, 1959), p. 251.

[3] E. g., Bertrand Russell, "The Expanding Mental Universe," in *Adventures of the Mind from The Saturday Evening Post*, ed. Richard Thruelsen and John Kobler (Vintage ed., New York: Random House, 1960), p. 303, looks with favor on the prospect of a cozy "social organism" and considers competition outdated. M. F. Ashley-Montagu, *Man: His First Million Years* (Mentor ed., New York: New American Library, 1958), p. 89, expresses the view that competition is symptomatic of "disoperation."

[4] Paul A. Weiss, in Roy R. Grinker, ed., *Toward a Unified Theory of Human Behavior* (New York: Basic Books, 1956), pp. 120–21.

to consider the species-preserving aspects of sociality.[5] Fundamentally, by participation and cooperation within a group or society, the organism is better able to deal with the environment and the competition of other species than it could as an isolated individual. Just as the multicellular organism serves the common interest of its component cells, society enhances the welfare of its individual members. It follows, too, that the supra-individual group may require some sacrifice of individual welfare in the interest of the common goal; but no mysterious suspension of natural selection is involved. The fittest still survive, but in this case "the fittest" biologically are those individuals who can cooperate to improve the society and thus make conditions better for everyone. In such a situation, natural selection differentiates primarily on the basis of social environments, one of which is more advantageous to its individual members than another.

The social animal evolves under the force of natural selection because the social animal is more efficient than the individual animal in a given set of circumstances. The most important genetic competition of the social animal is not with the animal of a different species, for his social nature makes him a "group competitor" with these other species. His most important individual competition is the competition with the other members of his own species, to adapt himself better to that sociality which is advantageous to individual survival.

We may look upon competition and cooperation, not as forms of behavior, but as abstract relationships between two or more organisms with reference to the same goal. The abstract relationships lead to the forms of animal and human behavior which we call "competitive" and "cooperative." Competition and cooperation may interact very intricately as *secondary derivatives* of the primary function of goal-seeking—or "homeostasis" in Emerson's use of the term.[6]

[5] Cf. Portmann, *Das Tier als soziales Wesen*, pp. 252–65.
[6] Alfred E. Emerson, "Homeostasis and Comparison of Systems," in Grinker, *Toward a Unified Theory of Human Behavior*, p. 162.

It is my position that all goal-seeking springs from the fundamental function that I have called the self-affirming imperative, for one simple reason: all other motivations aside, the lack of this fundamental motivation in an organism would handicap it in competition with any other organism that possessed it.

This position is a biological statement of Nietzsche's "Will to Power" concept, and it extends to his qualification of that concept: the "conspiracy together for power."[7] Since "conspiracy," like "will," has connotations of conscious intent, we may rephrase the qualification here as a "coaction for affirmation": cooperation toward a goal that satisfies the self-affirming imperative to some degree for both or all of the cooperating individuals.

Competition and cooperation may exist as relationships among groups of organisms, as well as among individual organisms. Sexual union is a reproductive coaction for affirmation. Social living is a coaction for affirmation, implying cooperation among the individual members of the social group but joint competition with other groups.

Insofar as it has inherited the role of bearer of the self-affirming imperative, the social group becomes "the organism," analogous to the manner in which the multicellular organism has inherited that role from its unicellular components. As noted, the social individual may be required to sacrifice some of his own interest, or even himself, for the group interest.

To carry the analogy too far would be anthropomorphizing. But, as Weiss[8] notes, a society is "integrated" in that its component members are connected with the whole rather than

---

[7] Friedrich W. Nietzsche, *Der Wille zur Macht* (Stuttgart: Alfred Kröner Verlag, 1959): "Aber er stösst fortwährend auf gleiche Bestrebungen andrer Körper und endet, sich mit denen zu arrangieren ('vereinigen'), welche ihm verwandt genug sind: *—so konspirieren sie dann zusammen zur Macht.*" ["But it continually meets with the same striving of other bodies, and concludes by coming to terms ('allying itself') with those closely enough related to it: *—so then they conspire together for power.*"]

[8] Paul A. Weiss, in Grinker, *Toward a Unified Theory of Human Behavior*, p. 122.

constituting random parts; and Piaget,[9] in the same sense, emphasizes the validity of speaking of society as "a coherent whole," analogous to a *Gestalt* in a statistical system of relations. Therefore, for discursive purposes, let us here apply to the social group *as a unified organism* the German term *"Masse."* This term has the advantage of not possessing previous associations for an English-speaking reader and is broad enough to encompass both formal and informal collections of individuals, including such groups as nations, tribes, mobs, herds, clubs, and fraternal organizations.

A significant difference between the social organism and the individual multicellular organism is that the former is not held together by the same physical and chemical bonds as the latter. It is true that chemistry is often involved in social recognition—rats react to other rats on the basis of odor, and social insects use both taste and smell for social recognition[10]—but this is not an actual chemical bond. The cement that binds together the component individuals of the *Masse* is more abstract. Parsons has called a social system "a behavioral system,"[11] and we may follow him here to the extent of calling the social bond a complex of interacting behavior.

Human behavioral systems differ widely among themselves, but all of them differ in many generic respects from those of other animals. This is to be expected, since the human line separated from its most closely related evolutionary line more than a million years ago and followed a radical course of differentiation. There is no evidence for sociality in any of the early mammals which survived the Mesozoic era into the Cenozoic, and there is certain circumstantial evidence against it. Whether sociality began to develop in the human ancestral line at the le-

[9] Jean Piaget, *Psychology of Intelligence* (International Library ed., Paterson, N. J.: Littlefield, Adams, 1963), p. 156.

[10] Cf. S. A. Barnett, *Instinct and Intelligence* (Englewood Cliffs, N. J.: Prentice-Hall, Inc., 1967), p. 98.

[11] Talcott Parsons, "Boundary Relations Between Sociocultural and Personality Systems," in Grinker, *Toward a Unified Theory of Human Behavior*, p. 328.

muroid or tarsioid level, or later, has not been determined and is not of real importance. What is important is the evidence that sociality was present in the *australopithecine* stage and continued its development into the human stage.

Lorenz makes the suggestion, admittedly with some trepidation,[12] that the survival value of the anonymous *Schar*, or horde, may rest in the inability of individual predators to concentrate on a single victim when confronted by a swarm of similar forms simultaneously. Regardless of whether such a factor was involved in the congregating tendencies of the early ground-living primates, we may speculate that one of the most primitive aspects of sociality that has retained some influence in the human species was its usefulness for warning purposes.

An aggregation of early primates, hunting insects and berries on the forest floor, would be mobilized to instant attention by the shrill cry of an individual who sighted danger. Collective attention would be focused on him. In that instant, he would be the "leader" of the *Masse*. His actions in response to what he had seen or heard would elicit collective, conforming reactions, which would enable the *Masse* to eliminate or escape from the danger he sensed.

This "crisis" action-pattern can be observed in contemporary social primates (except the chimpanzee) and in a more sophisticated form in certain human social actions. It is apparent in the coalescence of a mob behind a temporary leader. It also enters into certain emotion-charged movements, which can alter the course of history radically in a short time. The key elements of the pattern are the focus of attention and intention upon something deemed hostile outside the *Masse*[13] and the collective dependence upon a leader or leaders thought to know the best response to this "something."

Early in the evolution of the primate stock, the exaggerated development of the brain began. Quite obviously, the larger

[12] Konrad Lorenz, *Das sogenannte Böse* (Wien: Dr. G. Borotha-Schoeler Verlag, 1963), p. 203.
[13] Cf. Adolf Hitler, *Mein Kampf* (New York: Reynal and Hitchcock, 1941), p. 152.

brain with its increased potential makes possible more complex and more sophisticated social behavior and resultant social systems. But it also increases both the necessity and the possibilities for sociality in a peculiarly roundabout way.

As the hominid brain enlarged toward the human size, approaching a ratio to body weight of 1:40 (compared to 1:250 for a large dog, 1:350 for a sheep, 1:157 for the male orangutan), there arose the increasing problem of the passage of the large skull at birth through the female pelvis.[14] This problem was solved in part by the sort of measurements which are cited in beauty contests, but this was not enough. The human brain is still too big. So the human baby is born with only about a quarter of his adult brain weight (the gorilla brain, by contrast, has almost completed growth at birth); and other human physical features, deferring to the necessity for heavy brain predominance, are also comparatively undeveloped at birth.

The human is thus born "younger" than most animals and has a longer way to go to become a self-sustaining adult. In addition, he is a long-lived animal, and maturity is delayed by that fact. The hominid young therefore must depend on their elders for care and protection for a much longer period than do the young of other animals. Thus, the same enlargement of the brain which provides the physiological basis for the improved learning process (which can be superior to instinct in survival value because it offers a more variable response to environmental factors) also requires conditions guaranteeing that the most basic portion of this learning process shall occur in a social environment.

Whether this long maturation period in the company of one's elders and the possibly correlated phenomenon of infant sexuality, which Freud emphasized, bear any causal relation to constant sexuality would be an interesting question to investigate. In any event, the adult higher primate exhibits a sexual interest that is virtually incessant in contrast to the estrus pe-

[14] Cf. Weston la Barre, *The Human Animal* (Chicago: University of Chicago Press, 1955), pp. 75ff.

riods of other animals. This constant sexuality is apparently fundamentally a matter of almost uninterrupted feminine receptiveness, which unceasingly attracts the male.[15] In any event, the constant sexuality would necessarily reinforce a group cohesion implied by the long maturation period, on the principle that any mechanism which integrates the sexual pair has superior survival value if it results in greater group homeostasis. Even where a continuing sexual pair is not involved in the monogamous sense, constant sexuality in many primates tends to keep the males integrated with the group in the interest of sexual satisfaction.

A subsidiary result of constant sexuality important to the development of the behavioral system of the *Masse* may be the presence in the group of young people representing a continuous age spectrum instead of the sharply discontinuous age groups typical of social animals characterized by seasonal periods of rut.[16] The young hominid learns not only from his precise peers and from adults, but from "near peers" as well, with a consequent richness of variability in viewpoint and experience.

The psychological mechanism of this learning process is apparently rather complex, but I wish to generalize it under the term "mimesis." The semantic implications of this term, as used here, require some explanation.

Piaget[17] comments on the importance and extent of imitation in infants. Lorenz,[18] on the other hand, emphasizes that imitation is not involved when the instinctive behavior of a social animal elicits the same behavior from another of its group. Unquestionably, a considerable amount of "imitation" is involved in the human learning process, but there can be very little con-

[15] Cf. Carleton S. Coon, *The Story of Man* (2nd ed., New York: Alfred A. Knopf, 1962), pp. 64ff.; Robert Ardrey, *African Genesis* (New York: Atheneum, 1961), pp. 125ff.; Portmann, *Das Tier als soziales Wesen*, p. 100.

[16] Cf. Ardrey, *African Genesis*, pp. 72–73.

[17] Piaget, *Psychology of Intelligence*, pp. 125–26; cf. John C. Lilly, *Man and Dolphin* (New York: Doubleday, 1961), pp. 288ff.

[18] Konrad Lorenz, *Über tierisches und menschliches Verhalten* (München: R. Piper & Co. Verlag, 1965), p. 242.

scious imitation at early stages of life. Piaget's term "intuitive" would apply more accurately. One of the most recent and important suggestions is that there is involved a certain amount of what Lorenz calls *Prägung*, or "imprinting"—a purely involuntary, quite swift, and irreversible acquisition of a behavior quantum at a particular early stage of development.[19]

Therefore, the term "mimesis" will be used here in Toynbee's sense of "social imitation 'without prejudice.'"[20] This will be particularly appropriate in that I wish to apply the term "mimesis" in the same general (rather than individual) social sense in which Toynbee uses it.

The learning process—whether by mimesis or conscious instruction—by which the young hominid adopts behavior of proven survival value is accomplished more efficiently for the individual in small groups. A number of observers have remarked that small groups seem most "natural" for human activity.[21] Berrill goes so far as to suggest that the monogamous family has existed throughout the period that the hominid was a hunting animal,[22] but this is unlikely; it probably would make the *australopithecine* a family man. Rather, on the basis of comparison with other hunting animal groups, we should expect the young prehuman to have learned such generalized social roles as existed, first, in that smallest of all group contexts, the mother-sibling relationship, and, second, in the context of a total hunting group which itself was not very large. When the primary orientation shifted from the mother and siblings to the total group, there are many indications that "fraternities" and "sororities" based on age group and sexual differentiation com-

[19] *Ibid.*, pp. 270–71.
[20] Arnold J. Toynbee, *A Study of History* (Galaxy ed., New York: Oxford University Press, 1962), I, 191. Cf. Köhler, *The Mentality of Apes,* pp. 196ff.; Robert Eisler, *Man into Wolf* (New York: Philosophical Library, 1952), pp. 40, 110–11.
[21] Cf. Portmann, *Das tier als soziales Wesen*, pp. 98–99; Talcott Parsons, *et al.*, "The Small Group and the Larger Social System," in Grinker, *Toward a Unified Theory of Human Behavior*, pp. 192–93.
[22] N. J. Berrill, *Man's Emerging Mind* (New York: Dodd, Mead, 1955), pp. 87–89.

peted strongly with the nuclear family as a shaper of social orientation.[23] Such fraternities and sororities still exist in many preliterate cultures, and their analogues persist in the clubs and ritual societies of civilized cultures.

The paleolithic hunting society was still a small *Masse*, after all, probably ranging from as few as fifty to one hundred up to as many as a thousand members.[24] Even in the larger ones, recognition of all other members—the importance of which for social cohesion is mentioned by a number of authorities[25]—was still possible, although personal acquaintance among all members of the *Masse* would have been of a more limited type.

Like other highly social animals, man recognizes those "of his own kind" by the fact that they belong to his own *Masse* rather than by their identification with his same species. In the small groups of human society's early stages, it was possible to predicate this type of recognition on the knowledge of others gained as a result of long association with them; in a sense, an extension of the close acquaintance one had with mother and siblings. This differs hardly at all from the perceptual recognition of packmates among rats, except that the sense utilized is sight instead of smell.

In the primal small society, the stranger, who was not recognized by sight as being "one of us," was an outsider and assumed to be hostile to the *Masse*. The fact that he was a member of the same species made him even more dangerous, because he was known to be cleverer and more aggressive than other animals. The ceremonies of hospitality and non-aggression in later human societies attest to the persistence of these basic attitudes.

---

[23] José Ortega y Gasset, *History as a System* (Norton Library ed., New York: W. W. Norton, 1962), pp. 24–40, draws interesting conclusions from this likelihood.

[24] Cf. Carleton S. Coon, *The Origin of Races* (New York: Alfred A. Knopf, 1962), pp. 99–102.

[25] Cf. Köhler, *The Mentality of Apes*, p. 257; Lorenz, *Das sogenannte Böse*, pp. 67, 195, and 349; Lorenz, *Über tierisches und menschliches Verhalten*, pp. 120–21.

The assumptions made about the individual stranger applied even more strongly to a plurality of strangers, another *Masse*. Whether a true territorial instinct was involved or not is a question which must be weighed against other possibilities. Perhaps man is naturally aggressive individually, and his aggressiveness is suspended only through the necessity of long association with mother and siblings and, by later extension, with his social colleagues⌊But the fact is that, whatever the fundamental source of social aggressiveness, it expresses itself territorially.⌋ Unless some formal agreement of coexistence and mutual peace were executed—a recourse that was possible long before such agreements were put on paper—resistance to the encroachment of strangers, either individually or in groups, with the same sort of social mobilization found effective in the hunting of dangerous game, was an automatic reaction. Territoriality of this type would possess survival value in that it would reduce the threat of competition by other *Massen* for the same limited food supply.

This sense of social solidarity, presenting a solid front to a hostile world beyond the *Masse*—rather than some anti-social motivation—offers a logical psychological foundation for warfare as an expression of one facet of the most primitive form of human sociality.

This sampling of some of the aspects of prehistoric sociality of the human and his ancestors has been outlined in the conviction that, as Coon has stated,[26] the human species is a biologically continuous phenomenon, its capacities geared to its long existence as a hunting species. Such a viewpoint is important to the theme to be developed.

In considering the human and his society in this manner, I also tentatively follow Coon in setting the age of *Homo sapiens*, the large-brained successor to *Homo erectus*, at 250,000 years. The majority of paleontologists do not accept Coon's placement of Steinheim and Swanscombe man in *H. sapiens*, and prefer 30,000 to 40,000 years ago as the "date of rank" of *H. sapiens*.

[26] Coon, *The Story of Man*, p. 8.

The principle of the point I wish to make is the same in either case, and I prefer to adopt Coon's viewpoint partly for purposes of theoretical symmetry (see Table 1, p. 32 below). Beyond that, however, the evolutionary likelihood is that *H. sapiens* did not appear suddenly, as a macromutation, in the midst of the ranks of *H. erectus*, either 250,000 or 40,000 years ago, but developed his genetic differences from his predecessor gradually.

On Coon's scale, then, the historical period represents no more than about 3 per cent of the biological lifespan to date of "modern," big-brained man as we know him (about 20 per cent if we go along with the majority of paleontologists in dating *H. sapiens*). This not only takes his basic psychological structure back rather far toward the pack sociality of the *australopithecinæ* and the nearer-to-human social forms of *H. erectus*, but it means that complex, highly organized, civilized social forms have had a comparatively insignificant time to influence whatever forms of sociality man had already developed for himself as a big-brained, fully human creature.

In the dimly discerned millennia of paleolithic time, man became what he is, basically, both biologically and socially. All historical forms of social living, preliterate and civilized, have been erected on this foundation and have had to take it into consideration.

CHAPTER THREE

THE ROPE OVER THE ABYSS

Und ihr wollt die Ebbe dieser grossen Flut
sein und lieber noch zum Tiere zurückgehn,
als den Menschen überwinden?[1]
—FRIEDRICH WILHELM NIETZSCHE: *Also Sprach Zarathustra*

To LOOK UPON MAN in this way, as a highly intelligent and adaptable social animal who acquires his social habits and his orientation to reality through association and mimesis, explains a phenomenon which is otherwise puzzling: that a *H. sapiens* whose fossil forms indicate much the same psychological potentialities as exist in him today should not develop civilization for so many millennia. Until the cycle of civilizations began its upward spiral in immediate prehistoric times, this highly intelligent *H. sapiens* lived almost interminably at a paleolithic stage of culture.

There is another aspect to the question, however. Recognition of the role of mimesis as a molder of social processes explains man's long paleolithic "night," but it still does nothing to explain why and how he emerged, in some parts of the world, into an increasingly bright cultural "day." In the final analysis, if man is the same now as he was 200,000 years ago, there is no reason he should not have seen the advantages of agriculture and domesticated animals, initiated grain economies, and achieved the inventions that would have led to civilization 200 millennia earlier.

This dilemma has given rise to a tacit theory, based largely on cultural anthropologists' observations of the way in which some members of contemporary preliterate cultures are able to

[1] *And ye would be the ebb of this great tide, and rather regress to the animal, than surpass the human?*

adapt to sophisticated civilization. The theory is that key discoveries necessary to civilized culture, such as the grain economy and irrigation, were made fortuitously, and the rise of civilization then occurred as a result of cultural accumulation and fortuitous cultural interaction. In other words, man 200,000 years ago or 50,000 years ago *could* have begun the climb to the complexity of culture that actually started much later, but he was just unlucky.

This theory of cultural cumulativeness is valid enough, within limitations. But, whereas there may be reason to assume significant cultural contacts between early civilizations in the Nile, Tigris-Euphrates, Indus, and Huang-ho valleys, the weight of the evidence is that these peoples had no contact with the Peruvian and Mayan civilizations. The latter two human civilizations emerged independently within a space of time covering no more than 2 per cent of the lifetime of *H. sapiens* as a species.

Since the immediate environmental conditions permitting the rise of civilization must have occurred repeatedly at various places during the lifetime of *H. sapiens*, it appears very much as though he was not capable of initiating civilization until the last few millennia. If we wish to take the simplest probability suggested by the trend of human evolution, a change in the biological nature of man himself is dictated as the theoretical cause of the neolithic revolution and its consequences.

At first glance, this proposal encounters a seemingly serious objection. Man is a single biological species. Yet if he, as a species, underwent a biological change that made him capable of civilization, why was this change not expressed in a general advance to civilization everywhere? We know that the neolithic revolution occurred in only a few areas, if not just one, and expanding Western civilization recently came into contact with cultures that were still paleolithic and pre-lithic.

This objection, however, is based on the biologically incredible assumption that *H. sapiens* evolved suddenly from the prehuman on a species-wide basis not very long before the neolithic revolution and has remained an absolutely stable species since that time, experiencing no major physiological or fundamental psychological changes.[2] Furthermore, it should be noted that such an objection appears to be motivated to a considerable degree by contemporary social concerns. Most theories of a biological basis for civilization either have stemmed from outright racist propaganda or have incorporated racist assumptions. Emphasis upon man's unity as a biological species is considered of paramount importance, socially and politically, as a counter to racism.

The answer to the objection is simply that a species does not evolve to a new level all at once. A change appears somewhere in the species, and if it is favored by natural selection it spreads. The old characteristics tend to persist in some variable ratio to the new ones for a very long time, and even newer ones constantly appear through mutation; so most species, including man, are genetically heterogeneous and never quite stable.

Man evolved to his present state (varied as it is) through the normal process of natural selection; in my judgment, this may be accepted as axiomatic. If evolution stopped for him at some point in his history or prehistory, then he somehow escaped the effects of natural selection at that particular time.

Natural selection is based on a birth-death differential, the theory being that those individuals least adapted to their environment perish whereas those best adapted survive to procreate their "pattern" within the species. If man were not subject to the dictates of natural selection, such a differential should not apply within the human species. But it has applied, historically, and it still applies.

The only way a species may remain stable while still under the aegis of natural selection is for its environment to remain stable. Some oceanic species, for instance, have existed in a relatively stable environment for a very long time. But not man. His environment has changed not only because of his own mi-

[2] E. g., Weston la Barre, *The Human Animal* (Chicago: University of Chicago Press, 1955), p. 89.

grations, but it has also changed in the same locale. There were two ice advances during the Würm glacial period extending back no more than 75,000 years ago, and the Riss glacial period also occurred during the lifespan of *H. sapiens.*

A major function of society is to shut out an intractable environment behind walls of cooperation and technology and to create a more hospitable environment within the society. The society itself then functions as the environment for the individual members of the *Masse,* exerting its own peculiar pressures of natural selection upon them. The advocates of the "stable species, cultural accumulation" theory might argue, then, that the outer environment no longer has any selective effect on the individual within society.

The answer to this argument is, in fact, that the society, once established, is not a permanently isolated cell within the environment; the outer environment still must be dealt with, and it is dynamic. The result is that the individual members of the *Masse* do continue to interact with the outer environment, but they do so collectively. The impact of natural selection from the outer environment is still felt—disease, disaster, and death still take their differential toll—but the consequences are modified by the more immediate effects of the social environment. Second, the social environment itself is stable only in preliterate cultures. Civilized society is a kaleidoscope of survival pressures and could not serve as a stabilizing agent for natural selection except in a general way.

We must assume, then, that man has continued to evolve, primarily under selective pressure of the outer environment in the long paleolithic phase, and primarily under selective pressure of the social environment during historical times. Obviously, there was a time in his evolutionary past when he was not capable of initiating civilizations, and obviously, there was a later time when he was. It is logical to assume that the actual beginnings of civilized society occurred rather near to the time when he acquired this particular capability, rather than some 200,000 years afterward.

It will help us here to go back briefly for a theoretical look at man's evolution from an earlier primate form, because man's rise from *H. erectus* to *H. sapiens* may not prove to be greater in degree and significance than the later change differentiating paleolithic man from modern man genetically and psychologically.

To ask what "causes" an evolutionary change is to ask an ambiguous question. The direct cause is a mutation occurring in one or more individuals of a species. These mutations are of no evolutionary consequence unless they offer a survival advantage (either immediate or delayed) adequate to assure their spread in the species at the expense of other genetically based traits. Since this spread is determined by natural selection, (environmental pressures could be cited as the most readily observable "cause" of evolutionary change.) The direct cause of man's evolution from *H. erectus* to *H. sapiens*, involving increased brain size and a number of related changes, was a mutation or a series of mutations.[3] Such mutations could not have

[3] Robert Eisler, *Man into Wolf* (New York: Philosophical Library, 1952), advances a theory that a major mutation responsible for the nature of civilized man was that which converted him from a fruit-eating primate into a carnivore. This is undoubtedly true, but Eisler's scheme is based on what appears to be a major error: assignment of this mutation to a time too late in the evolutionary history of the hominid.

Eisler developed his theory before Piltdown Man was invalidated and before the apparently carnivorous nature of the *Australopithecines* was known; therefore, he sees the change from herbivore to hunting carnivore as occurring not too long before the Würm glacial period. On the basis of such a time schedule, he can speak of the "mutant" hunters subjugating surviving frugivore food-gatherers in historical and immediate prehistoric times and of resultant cross-fertilization as being responsible for variability in human mental traits and even for class differences.

The mutation to carnivorous (or, rather, omnivorous) habits apparently did occur and was highly important to the nature of *H. sapiens*; but it seems to have occurred even before the emergence of *H. erectus*. Hunting and cattle-raising cultures did subjugate agricultural cultures and impose themselves as aristocracies upon the latter; and this was important historically, and probably genetically. In my view, this was a *secondary* phenomenon, however, after man had been, as a species, a hunting carnivore for hundreds of millennia and subsequently, as a species in the neolithic revolution, had substituted agriculture and cattle-raising as successor methods of existence to hunting and food-gathering.

resulted in the evolutionary change from one to the other, however, except by conferring a competitive survival advantage. Superior intelligence is an obvious survival advantage in competition for the same ecological niche, and *H. sapiens* may have been assisted in his replacement of *H. erectus* by some severe environmental changes, such as the Riss glaciation.

Throughout the *australopithecine* and *H. erectus* phases of man's ancestry, and throughout the paleolithic stage of *H. sapiens*, the genus, we may safely assume, existed most of the time in rather close balance with the environment. A hunting and food-gathering culture did not permit more than this. Despite the increase in man's intelligence, he was still in much the same position as he had been before: a highly intelligent animal whose use of weapons and shelter was not adequate to give him an individual advantage over more specialized animals, either those he hunted or those that hunted him.

In this context, it was neither man's intelligence nor his manual dexterity that permitted his survival and gradual rise to a dominant position among species. It was his sociality.

"Aha," we may say, "civilization follows naturally from this fact and is founded on it, for civilization is an advanced form of sociality." But, however popular and widespread this idea, it is not correct. Civilization cannot follow "naturally" from sociality; for primitive society persists largely on the basis of a conformist learning process and traditionalism which suppress the very "advancement" that is characteristic of civilization as a form of sociality. Civilization could not follow "naturally" from human sociality, nor did it. It did not follow at all for many millennia.

A further mutation was necessary if man was to initiate civilization. This mutation permitted the individual to break the age-old pattern of mimesis. It permitted him to introduce some variability into the uniform context of paleolithic psychology.

The mutation may have occurred again and again, over scores of millennia. The natural rebel would be born, who objected to the restrictions and frequent stupidities of rigid social custom.

He saw ways to do things, better than the traditional ways. He would be ostracized and overwhelmed by his social colleagues, discriminated against personally and reproductively, and in that environment, the attempt to live outside the social context meant quick death.

So the cycle of social mimesis repeated itself interminably, solidifying custom and tradition in the various human *Massen*, changing only very gradually through minor and accidental variations in the routine that every child learned. In such an environment, established ways of living and thinking might conceivably persist for tens of thousands of years, as they have persisted unchanged throughout historical times in some areas of the world.

In view of the correlation in time, it is probable that a major environmental upheaval was largely responsible for the final survival in significant strength of the mutation(s) we hypothesize. This upheaval was the Würm glacial period, which made large areas of the north uninhabitable and profoundly affected climate in areas of significant human cultural change. Climatic change caused geographical shifts of animal and plant species, and, consequently, of the various (probably scattered) human *Massen* that had built stable social structures during a 60,000-year period of interglacial mildness. Near the end of the Würm glacial period of change occurred the mesolithic age, the transitional phase to the neolithic and civilization.

During the advance and retreat of the ice sheets, a total human population of 1½ to 2 million,[4] broken up into *Massen* of 350 to 1,000 people each,[5] collided as they migrated with climatic changes. There was a great deal of genetic and cultural

[4] Estimated roughly after Deevey: Theodosius Dobzhansky, *Mankind Evolving* (New Haven: Yale University Press, 1962), p. 299.

[5] Jacquetta Hawkes, "Prehistory," in Part I, *History of Mankind* (New York: Harper & Row, 1963), p. 121, estimates Upper Paleolithic hunter tribes at up to 1,000 members. Carleton S. Coon, *The Origin of Races* (New York: Alfred A. Knopf, 1962), p. 101, thinks most fossil men lived in populations of 500 or 600 members or smaller. Robert Ardrey, *African Genesis* (New York: Atheneum, 1961), p. 163, suggests primitive man lived in societies averaging about 100 members.

interchange, and territorial encroachment and competition for food led in many cases to the extermination of some *Massen* by others. Myriad conclaves of comparative isolation, both genetic and cultural, were broken up, notably in southern European and Asiatic latitudes, where northerners driven by the ice would have been thrown upon indigenous southerners.

The disruption of dependable social patterns by climatic change and migration, the accelerated alteration of these patterns through increased cultural contacts, and the heightened competitiveness among human *Massen* in a dynamic environment established a force of natural selection favoring greater individual adaptability, independence, and ingenuity.

Although environmental pressures might sometimes have been severe to dispersed human *Massen* which had long been accustomed to a stable environment, efficient responses to the new pressures could have been established through tradition and custom. Whereas "deviates" and individualists suffered selective penalties, those conforming most to tradition and best able to learn established custom thoroughly through mimesis became dominant individuals in their *Massen*—chiefs and priests. They enjoyed significant reproductive preference through plurality of wives and possibly other privileges. Genetic qualities preserving and reinforcing human sociality thus would be maintained to the almost complete exclusion of any conflicting traits.

In the confused movements and changes of the Würm glacial period, the pattern of dominance within the typical *Masse* had to change. Strict mimesis of traditional responses was no longer adequate for meeting altered conditions and for competing with newly met *Massen*. Now it was the intelligent innovator, the creator, who could break the chains of custom and bring forth new solutions, who achieved dominance with its accompanying sexual (and reproductive) privileges. Those *Massen* that discriminated against the individualistic innovator now were likely to be destroyed, either directly or indirectly, by those *Massen* that accepted his dominance.

31

In this altered and altering environment, previously suppressed mutations in *H. sapiens* gained a foothold. The theory presented here is that these mutations were of an order of importance to man's evolutionary development comparable to those responsible for the change from *H. erectus* to *H. sapiens*. Their effect was to shatter the absolute primacy of sociality in man's psychological structure and dilute it with the capacity for non-conformist, creative individualism.

TABLE 1

PROPOSED MAJOR EVOLUTIONARY STAGES IN THE HUMAN LINE

Time before present	Species
±900,000 years – 500,000	Australopithecus
±700,000 – 100,000	Homo erectus
250,000 – 0	Homo sapiens
25,000 – 0	Homo individualis

The basic evolutionary chronology of this theory is set forth in Table 1. As is apparent from the table, there is no question (yet) of the mutant "species" having displaced and succeeded *H. sapiens*. Rather, the neolithic and historical periods are conceived as a time of overlap which, on the basis of overlaps in previous species of the genus, still has a considerable period to go.

The theory is that, to an increasing extent over the past 15,000 to 25,000 years, individuals of the *H. sapiens* species have represented a mixture of the old, "pure" social human traits and a psychic potential for individualism which did not exist in the species before that period. This mixture varies widely among individuals and consequently among *Massen*.

The best evidence for this theory is the change in pace of cultural progress during the neolithic and historical periods as compared with the previous 200,000 years of *H. sapiens'* existence. The appearance within the species of increasing numbers of creative individualists would, under this theory, account for the initiation of significant cultural advances. Their contributions to the rise of various cultures in the historical period would mark them as identical with Toynbee's "creative minorities."[6]

Rather than attempting to be taxonomically accurate in selecting a label for the mutant, we prefer to take note of Bergson's idea, followed by Viaud.[7] Man in the majority should actually be called *"Homo faber"*—man the fabricator or toolmaker—instead of *Homo sapiens*. Viaud suggests that the term *"Homo sapiens"* be reserved for the minority of creative and abstract-thinking individuals, which sounds suspiciously like our "mutant."

Without interfering with the traditional term, *"Homo sapiens,"* used to designate the big-brained species from its inception to the present, let us suggest the position of the mutant form historically and currently as that of an incipient semispecies. Then we shall differentiate it, in terms primarily descriptive, by applying the term *"Homo socialis"* to *H. sapiens* as he was in preglacial times (and as he still is in the majority) and the term *"Homo individualis"* to the mutant form.

---

[6] Arnold J. Toynbee, *A Study of History* (Galaxy ed., New York: Oxford University Press, 1962), III, 239.

[7] Henri Bergson, *Creative Evolution*, trans. Arthur Mitchell (Modern Library ed., New York: Random House, 1944), pp. 153–54; Gaston Viaud, *Intelligence: Its Evolution and Forms*, trans. A. J. Pomerans (Science Today ed., New York: Harper & Bros., 1960), p. 21. F. S. Hulse, *The Human Species* (New York: Random House, 1963), p. 208, also refers to *"Homo faber,"* under approximately the same definition, but limits him to pre-*sapiens* man.

CHAPTER FOUR

SHAPES BEHIND THE FACADE

For these are men betrayed by contradiction within themselves. . . . It is his own social self that trips up the adventurer, and strangles him.
—WILLIAM BOLITHO: *Twelve Against the Gods*

THE WORLD THAT SCIENCE MEASURES is not the world in which man lives. Man, rather, lives in a world without dimension, without time, a world in which there are no objects but only images—the world of thought and feeling.

There are those who call the objective world the "real" world and man's inner world only an interpretive reflection of it. This is hardly true, even objectively. No factor, however immaterial, can be denied reality if it alters the shape of the physical world. Man's thoughts, his desires, his opinions, even his fantasies, change the world outside him substantially.

The marble-cold statistics of matter determine man's fate far less than does the pulsing drama of shadow shapes which stride the stage of his own brain. These phantoms, the ghosts of his unique humanity, whisper to him whom he shall love and whom he shall hate, when he shall flee and when he shall fight, even who his children shall be and whether they will survive. Evolutionary biology, if it is to embrace man, has to incorporate a new dimension: human thought as an agent of natural selection.

One may choose to say that this new dimension emerged with *Australopithecus* or not until *H. sapiens*; in any event, it is a dimension that must be considered in any attempt to view the evolution of *H. socialis* and the development of *H. individualis* as a variant upon the same stem. Only by considering this dimension can one see clearly that the traits of *H. individualis* constitute the essence of a transitional evolutionary form, which has manifested itself in historical times. In fact, this is the reason human history emerged from the blank pages of prehistory.

Although this idea bears many correspondences to Seidenberg's brilliant theory of historical man as a transitional form,[1] my different view of man's nature leads me to disagree with him completely about the inevitable disappearance of individualism and man's total submergence in collectivism. I conceive man more in the spirit expressed by Lorenz, as the link between the animal and the genuinely human.[2]

The differentiation made between *H. socialis* and *H. individualis* calls for a working definition. We may say that *H. socialis* refers to an individual or individuals in whom the mixture of sociality and individualism is predominantly social. In a conflict between individualistic and social motivations, the inclination is to subordinate the individualistic motivation to the desire for social acceptance, social status, or pure altruism. *H. individualis*, by contrast, tips the mixture of sociality and individualism toward an individualistic orientation. In a similar conflict, he will subordinate social considerations to individual motivations or principles.

This difference, quite apparently, is a psychological one. It represents a difference in perception of and assessment of environmental factors (i. e., the social as contrasted to the nonsocial), and it is followed by a difference in response. One type of human (*H. socialis*) automatically groups his perceptions of reality around the primacy of social values, his responses to reality being oriented to the (often unstated and unrecognized) principle that collective thought and action ultimately produce a more efficient response to the environment than do individual thought and action. The other human type (*H. individualis*) either (*a*) is unable to discern the validity of social values, or

---

[1] Roderick Seidenberg, *Posthistoric Man* (Chapel Hill: University of North Carolina Press, 1950).

[2] Konrad Lorenz, *Das sogenannte Böse* (Wien: Dr. G. Borotha-Schoeler Verlag, 1963), p. 323.

(b) sees "through" or "behind" them to a superior structure of values. His responses to reality are predicated upon the principle that social values are secondary and subsidiary.

Whether *H. individualis* is of (a) or (b) type is important. If he is of type (a), *H. socialis* is justified in seeing failure to assign primacy to social values as a symptom of inferior intelligence or discrimination. If he is of type (b), the intelligence of *H. individualis* is superior to that of *H. socialis*, or at least different. The viewpoint adopted here is that *H. individualis* is of type (b), representing what Simpson[3] calls an improvement in perception of the environment and in flexibility of response.

This is a higher level of intelligence, but the acceptance of this view does not mean that the *H. individualis* psychological traits can be correlated directly or point by point with IQ rating. Although the intelligence components measured by IQ tests are an important psychological aspect of *H. individualis*, his definitive traits include a great deal more.

The necessity of these other traits to *H. individualis* is best exemplified by the contrast of the "high IQ" and "high creativity" populations studied by Getzels and Jackson.[4] The mean IQ of the total population (533 boys and girls) was itself exceptionally high: 132 points. The high creativity group had a mean of 127 points; the high IQ group, 150 points. Both groups showed accomplishment records equally above those of the school population as a whole. Those who scored in the top 20 per cent of each test were included in each group, except that those scoring in the top 20 per cent of both were excluded.[5] Other than giving evidence that the two intelligence com-

[3] George Gaylord Simpson, *The Meaning of Evolution* (New Haven: Yale University Press, 1949), p. 284.

[4] Jacob W. Getzels and Philip W. Jackson, *Creativity and Intelligence* (New York: John Wiley & Sons, 1962), pp. 13–24.

[5] This "overlap" group obviously could be quite important, as those who are in the top 20 per cent of both IQ and creativity could be nearer to *H. individualis* than top scorers in either group alone. On the basis of their figures, I estimated the overlap group at 63, or 11.8 per cent of the total. In answer to my inquiry about this, Dr. Getzels stated that the

ponents, IQ and creativity, are distinct, the results of the test support the research team's assumptions that conventional IQ functions tend toward intellectual acquisitiveness and conformity, whereas creativity is characterized more by inventiveness and innovation.

Since we say *H. individualis* is representative of a higher level of intelligence, let us say that we are not likely to have a specimen of *H. individualis* below an IQ level corresponding to the American median of 100. Very probably, the IQ would not be below 120. But an IQ of more than 120 does not guarantee that the individual is *H. individualis*. He may reach, say, 140 or 150 IQ without possessing the creativity level of *H. individualis*. High IQ level and creativity, indeed, may be only two of a number of factors required at a high level for *H. individualis*. Factors such as energy level and breadth of interest, which Getzels and Jackson did not study, may also be significant.

As may have become apparent by now, the difficulty in talking about "*H. individualis*" and "*H. socialis*" is that no "pure" type exists. It would be difficult even to theorize such a pure specimen, so true is it that everyone is to some extent social and yet also possesses some individualistic traits. The fact that the concept is thus "artificial" does not mean that it is either arbitrary or invalid. Most concepts are artificial in this sense. It is not the conceptual differentiation of the world, of humanity, or any other subject that leads to fanaticism and intellectual sterility, but it is the insistence on sharp, bright dividing lines between adjacent concepts—the demand for the "pure type specimen."

It will be helpful if we see *H. individualis* and *H. socialis* as theoretical extreme types and the human psyche as a spectrum between them, always containing elements of each. Although the traits of the individual psyche may place a person on the

---

number of the overlap group was not recorded in the report, since they were not interested in it. He referred me to a different study by E. Paul Torrence, to which reference is made in Chapter 13, below.

spectrum closer to *H. individualis*, for instance, than to *H. socialis*, he will still exhibit many of the characteristics of the latter. In addition, his position on the spectrum will vary with circumstances, being reflected in his behavior, which will be socially oriented at times and individualistically oriented at others. When we say that an individual is *H. individualis*, we simply mean that he exhibits more individualistic traits more of the time than do most other members of the species. An integral part of the "definition" is the recognition that the majority of thoughts and actions of the majority of individuals place them definitely on the *H. socialis* side of the spectrum. By extension, to call a population or a segment of a population *H. individualis* is to say that it is composed predominantly of *H. individualis* individuals.

The concept of *H. socialis–H. individualis* thus is a behavioral concept: differentiated behavior is its characterizing mark. Parsons' definition of a social system as a "behavioural system" contemplates that the system is structured as a pattern of roles. These roles, not individual persons, are the real components of the organized social system, and the individual is not important to the *Masse* except in the comparative efficiency with which he performs his role. Thus, from the standpoint of the *Masse*, important individual behavior is *role behavior*, which is generally acquired through the processes of mimesis, learning, and socialization.

Parsons points out[6] that a personality cannot interpenetrate with an interactional system of behavior unless the personality's organization is *congruent* with that of the system. This means simply that an individual cannot adjust to society unless the individual's psyche is organized in a way conforming to the social structure. This, Parsons states, points up the importance of Freud's superego concept, discovered independently by Durkheim. So the individual must adapt his personality to the

[6] Talcott Parsons, "Sociocultural and Personality Systems," in Roy R. Grinker, ed., *Toward a Unified Theory of Human Behavior* (New York: Basic Books, 1956), p. 333.

structure of the social system; from his standpoint, role behavior is adaptive behavior.

The general assumption of the behavioral school of psychology is that adaptive behavior is learned through stimulus and response of the human physiological structure, an assumption resting largely upon two premises: (*a*) Hebb's, that either innate or learned behavior can be defined only through the exclusion of the other; and (*b*) Lehrmann's, that one cannot exclude experimentally the possibility of learning within the egg or *in utero*. Lorenz[7] has answered these premises ably by pointing out that, in themselves, they require the assumption of a phylogenetically acquired programming of learning, or a prestabilized harmony between organism and environment. He notes that adaptedness to environment cannot be coincidental because the statistical probability of random adaptation through learning is the same as that through mutation, estimated by geneticists as approximately 10^{-8}. The behaviorist premise thus leads full circle back to the necessity of the innate.

The human obviously does not acquire this adaptive role behavior through physiological preprogramming (instinct) as the social insects apparently do. It is true that many general patterns of social behavior among higher social animals appear to pre-exist in the organism, as innate or inherent traits, but they are activated only through a developmental process of the individual.[8] If at a certain period of the individual's development, which may last only a few hours, an appropriate object or behavior pattern on the part of another individual enters his experience, he undergoes *Prägung*, or "imprinting." Thereafter, this object or this behavior pattern on the part of another continues to act as an *Auslöser* ("releaser" or "trigger") for the individual's own response.

This process is reminiscent of the periods in human infancy

[7] Konrad Lorenz, *Evolution and Modification of Behavior* (Chicago: University of Chicago Press, 1965), pp. 7–27.

[8] Konrad Lorenz, *Über tierisches und menschliches Verhalten* (München: R. Piper & Co. Verlag, 1965), pp. 268–74.

when certain activities, such as walking and talking, are learned "naturally." If the necessary social assistance is lacking during these periods, it is much more difficult for the child to acquire the behavior later. The pre-existing potential in the human is far more generalized than in any other animal, of course, and therefore can be shaped into a greater variety of specific behavior. It is my opinion that man, the learning animal *par excellence*, possesses a larger store of these potential general behavior structures, each of which can be evoked in response to the proper "releaser" at a different period of the individual's development. Further, I believe that this period of development—varying, of course, with the individual—may extend far into what we normally consider to be stabilized adult life. These processes, I believe, constitute the genetic basis of man's social behavior.

Both Portmann and Lorenz[9] have commented on the similarity of imprinting, and the *Gestalten* (forms or images) associated with it, to some of the theoretical constructions developed in human analytical psychology. Although Portmann emphasizes that firm evidence does not exist for applying the concept in the biological field, he does bring out the similarity of these *Gestalten* to the "archetypes" set forth in Jungian psychology. Jung explained the archetypes, the symbolic patterns of his collective unconscious, as resembling patterns of "instinctive behavior," which could be evoked in the psyche by the proper stimuli.[10] Anyone familiar with the maze of Jungian psychology will recognize how thoroughly his archetypes are involved with symbolism. Even more than patterns of instinctive behavior, they emerge as inherent patterns of non-verbal, symbolic comprehension of reality.

[9] Adolf Portmann, *Das Tier als soziales Wesen* (Zürich: Rhein-Verlag, 1953), pp. 234–37; Lorenz, *Über tierisches und menschliches Verhalten*, pp. 270–71.

[10] C. G. Jung, "The Concept of the Collective Unconscious," in *The Archetypes and the Collective Unconscious*, trans. R. F. C. Hull, Vol. IX, Part I, Bollingen Series XX (New York: Pantheon Books, 1959), pp. 42–53.

Language is a symbolic form of communication characteristic of man. According to Piaget, observation shows that the use of language rests on a more generalized "symbolic function" of the mind.[11] Whorf states that both language and behavior are "superficial embroidery" upon deeper, pattern-sensing functions of the mind.[12] The underlying structure implied by both Piaget and Whorf must have developed for a long time in the prehuman, as a means of comprehension and communication, before it reached the human stage of sophistication and complexity that permits language. The paleocortex, or "old cortex," of the brain apparently deals with experience non-verbally, making symbolic and emotional associations.[13] With reference to the concept of *H. individualis*, it is interesting to note that Spatz considers the human basal neocortex to possess the possibility of further evolutionary development.[14]

Now, we still possess the paleocortex, overlaid by the neocortex, and we still possess the generalized substructure upon which we formulate language. We express ourselves often in paleocortical ways, despite the presence of the neocortex.

I wish to advance the hypothesis that general patterns of behavior pre-exist in this substructure. Springing from genetically inherited features of the nervous and glandular systems, they are activated by proper stimuli at certain stages of ontogenetic development and given specific direction by the stimulus. Ardrey has called this "open programs of instinct."[15] In other words,

[11] Jean Piaget, *Psychology of Intelligence* (International Library ed., Paterson, N. J.: Littlefield, Adams, 1963), p. 124.

[12] Benjamin Lee Whorf, *Language, Thought, and Reality* (Cambridge: The Technology Press of Massachusetts Institute of Technology, 1956), pp. 55, 239, 257; cf. Susanne K. Langer, *Philosophy in a New Key* (Cambridge: Harvard University Press, 1942), *passim*; and Edward T. Hall, *The Silent Language* (New York: Doubleday, 1959), *passim*.

[13] John Pfeiffer, *The Human Brain* (Worlds of Science ed., New York: Pyramid, 1962), p. 61.

[14] Hugo Spatz, "Gedanken über die Zukunft des Menschenhirns und die Idee vom Übermenschen," in Ernst Benz, ed., *Der Übermensch* (Zürich: Rhein-Verlag, 1961), pp. 317–75.

[15] Robert Ardrey, *The Territorial Imperative* (New York: Atheneum, 1966), p. 24.

the individual human does not come into the world either as unshaped lumber or as a finished product. He is partly assembled; therefore, there is some choice in the form of the final assembly, but it is limited within a recognizable general pattern.

It is a major element of this hypothesis that many of these generally preprogrammed patterns, if not the vast majority, deal with man's adaptation to social life. This is based on the assumption that the social environment has been the individual's primary environment, because of sociality's superior survival value, since long before the appearance of *H. sapiens* and probably since *Australopithecus*. Through this preprogramming system, man is able to adapt naturally to role behavior, whether it is the complex and multiple role behavior of modern civilized society or the more generalized role behavior of the primitive society.

I wish to call the socially directed portion of this preprogramming system "the *collective ego*." Subjectively, it gives the individual a sense of union with other members of his own *Masse* (whatever the *Masse*'s size or nature) and a derivative sense of identity with the *Masse* itself. I call it the collective ego because, repeated in every individual member of the *Masse*, it constitutes the ego of the supraindividual *Masse* itself.

The term "collective ego" has classical Freudian overtones. Although a number of efforts have been made to decipher the human psyche and to reconcile such recent concepts as system theory, Cannon's homeostasis and its counterpart, heterostasis, Wiener's cybernetic theories and *Gestalt* theory, no satisfactory substitute for Freud's seminal sketch of the psyche has yet emerged. Instead, we get mere piecemeal focuses upon other aspects of the psyche than those which concerned him. His concept is still widely recognized as fundamental in analytic psychology, and it has a number of advantages, among them simplicity and a focus upon motivation. Therefore, one can hardly do better than Menninger[16] (without, however, agreeing

[16] Karl Menninger, *The Vital Balance* (New York: Viking, 1963), pp. 76–124.

42

with all of his conclusions) and attempt to fit applicable new findings into the ego-centered Freudian picture.

Freud's tripartite motivational system of the psyche consisted of the id, ego, and superego.[17] Simply stated, the id represents the residence of the instincts (fundamental motivations and desires), the ego attempts to serve as a mediator between the id and outer reality, and the superego is developed from the "ego ideal" as a social force, an internalization of authority which was originally that of the parents (or their surrogates).

Obviously, many aspects of the psyche are missing from this picture. The superego, particularly, emphasizes parental authority (especially, in Freud's own work, paternal authority) too much not to justify Ashley-Montagu's criticism that the theory was constructed on the basis of nineteenth-century European culture and does not consider adequately the differences of other cultures.[18]

It is partly for this reason that I put forth the collective ego as a separate concept. In the Freudian picture, it would include the superego, but it would extend well into the ego and might even be said to include some aspects of the id. And Jung's collective unconscious, however well it corresponds in some respects, is too broad to be considered synonymous with the collective ego; in Jungian terms, the collective ego should be seen as a portion of the collective unconscious.

In the sense that the Freudian ego is concerned with one's difference from and relation to the other (the reality beyond oneself), the collective ego is a non-ego function in assuming an identity with the other. Yet it is a movement toward the ego, in that this identity is limited. It is limited to the *Masse*, but not merely to the human (or prehuman) *Masse*, but to village, home, domestic articles, weapons, domestic animals, everything that is a part of the working *Masse*. To the collective ego, every-

[17] A diagram of Freud's concept is contained in his *New Introductory Lectures on Psycho-Analysis*, trans. W. J. H. Sprott (New York: Norton, 1933), p. 111.

[18] M. F. Ashley-Montagu, *Man in Process* (Mentor ed., New York: New American Library, 1962), pp. 252–78.

thing that is of the *Masse* is "I." Everything that is not of the *Masse* is "not-I."

The collective ego serves as a functional focus for social impulses and processes in the same way that the ego serves as such a focus for individual impulses and processes. It is analogous to the ego at the collective level in that it assesses reality on the basis of the social milieu instead of the individual milieu.

The prehuman was a psychologically unified animal; he was a social animal. The collective ego, through which he was one with his *Masse*, represented his psychological means of dealing with outer reality. With the increase of brain capacity corollary to his becoming *H. sapiens* and the concomitant development of the ego, he became a dual creature, part social and part individual.

The collective ego is shaped in the individual by the social activation of inherent, generalized behavior patterns. This is the segment of the psychic structure that dominates the behavior of *H. socialis*. It unconsciously orients his thought and action to the social environment (with its accompanying values) represented by his *Masse*. His logical processes are limited by that orientation.

Only insofar as he possesses, and is at times oriented to, the characteristics of *H. individualis* can he look at society objectively and be rational about its problems. Otherwise, he is a man under hypnosis, who compulsively obeys the hypnotist within himself, rationalizing any objections that may be raised by his individualistic ego.

CHAPTER FIVE

THE CULTURAL MAINSPRING

A system consists of truths, a history rests on facts.
—OSWALD SPENGLER: *The Decline of the West*

LET US NOW JUXTAPOSE the premises from which we propose to portray the individual as a biological influence upon history:

1. The individual is activated by the primal urge of the living creature, the *self-affirming imperative*. Society is also thus motivated, in the form of a *coaction for affirmation*, a collective motivation that can oppose and override the individual motivation.

2. Man in his pre-*sapiens* period was a completely social animal, in which a collective ego focused his perceptions in the service of the coaction for affirmation. In his *sapiens* period, man has developed an individualistic ego, which tempers and frequently opposes the collective ego.

3. These human psychological characteristics are biologically derived and are subject to genetic transmission under Mendelian laws of inheritance. The effect of culture on them, over many generations, has been to replace in large part the natural environment as an agent of natural selection. Natural selection, under these circumstances, determines how much man is controlled by the ego and how much by the collective ego, individually and collectively.

By implication, therefore, not only is the individual human a dual creature psychologically at this stage of his evolution, but the species collectively has been in evolutionary transition during its entire historical period and for quite a long time before. There is no reason to assume that it is not still in transition.

Man (and his ancestral line) has been a social species for at least a million years, but in the last few millennia the forms of his societies have undergone in some cases a radical alteration. Departing from the pattern of tradition-based, stable, low-technology society characteristic of the long paleolithic era, they have blossomed into a number of "civilized" societies marked to a greater or lesser degree by innovation, comparatively swift change, complex organization, and high technology.

It is reasonable to see a cause-and-effect connection between man's continuing evolution and this radical change in the form of his sociality. If we observed such a striking advance in social forms among the social insects, or even among the other primates, we would know at once that a genetic change was involved, and it seems completely logical to apply this cause-and-effect relationship to man.

Such a relationship between biological evolution and human social forms makes possible a far more satisfying explanation of a certain historical phenomenon than is offered by the theory of cultural accident. Whereas primitive, preliterate cultures may exist substantially unchanged for generation after generation, civilized cultures have exhibited a marked rise-and-decline pattern. When they first appear in history as civilized societies, they display remarkable advances, absorbing or displacing more primitive societies. Beyond a certain level, however, no further advances are made, and eventually the society falls at the hands of a more vigorous society.

The pattern has been repeated many times. It is particularly noticeable in the historical line lying directly behind modern Western civilization, as in the cases of Sumer, Babylonia, Persia, Greece, and Rome. It can be seen dimly in the Minoan and Mayan civilizations, and it will be recognized also in Chinese, Indian, and ancient Egyptian history if one observes that apparent rejuvenations of the same civilization in each case followed an infusion of vigor from outside, at least at the higher administrative levels. The pattern has been apparent enough to give rise to a number of cyclical theories of civilization, some of them rather far-fetched. The mysticism is removed, however, if we look upon the civilized level of social living as the reflection of a more advanced biological level of man—a level more advanced compared to the one indicated by primitive social living.

Distinguishing these two biological levels as *H. socialis* and *H. individualis*, we observe that populations may vary, collectively, in the proportion of individuals who are markedly at one level or the other. James Harvey Robinson[1] has stated that if a few thousand selected infants in the world were strangled at birth, civilization's progress would not only halt but decline, because the majority of human beings are at best able only to maintain the civilization in which they are reared. The context of his remark makes it clear that he is talking about an inherently determined minority of *H. individualis*. In the same vein is Hermann Weyl's[2] remark that if ten or twelve particular individuals were to die suddenly, the structure of present-day physics would collapse. Once more, the importance of an exceptionally able minority to a broad area of human endeavor is implied.

Let us say that the general biological level of the social animal, man, at the present stage of his evolution is such that, were he a uniform species, he would live at a paleolithic social level or perhaps a little higher. But he is a species in evolutionary transition and highly variable individually. The genetic components of his newest complex of biological traits, *H. individualis*, are spread thinly through the species. Nevertheless, as in the case of genius (which is closely related), the creative traits of *H. individualis* occasionally reach such concentrations in a single individual that a creative personality of considerable stature stands out above the human landscape. Further, the population characteristics that permit this genetic concentra-

[1] James Harvey Robinson, "Civilization," *The Encyclopædia Britannica*, 1953 ed., V, 739.
[2] Cited by José Ortega y Gasset, *La Rebelión de las masas* (Madrid: Espasa-Calpe, S. A., 1937), p. 62n.

tion in a single individual imply, statistically, a concentration of *H. individualis* genes in a population which raises considerably above normal the probability that a number of creative individuals will appear simultaneously in that population.

These creative personalities influence each other reciprocally. They compose a creative minority, which, though it may be rather small in relation to the total population, can initiate an advanced form of civilized thought and activity that is adopted and utilized by the general population through the normal social mechanism of mimesis. Such a proposal implies, correctly, that the general human majority is not capable of initiating civilization or maintaining it unaided but is capable of living at a civilized level if that level is initiated and maintained by a creative minority. Also, it follows that the subsequent decline of a civilization is the result of the dissipation of that genetic concentration of creative individualists. The creative minority dissolves, and the population relaxes to a social level more natural to the human social animal.

Civilization thus is a form of social living not characteristic of humanity in general or in the majority. On the contrary, it is reared by the creative minority, *H. individualis*, and the majority of the population constitutes the human material from which it is built.

Here is the essential test of the hypothesis: two types of human society would confirm it—(*a*) a civilized society in which a creative minority was present at least in its growing stage, and (*b*) a non-civilized society in which a creative minority was absent; two other types would falsify it—(*c*) a civilized society in which a creative minority was never present, and (*d*) a non-civilized society in which a creative minority was present.

On the basis of the information available, we can make such a test tentatively. For this purpose, we can utilize Toynbee's list of "civilizations," on the ground that it is no more subject to criticism than any other historical scheme.[3] We may say im-

---

[3] Arnold J. Toynbee, *A Study of History* (12 vols.; London: Oxford University Press, 1934–1962), I, 51–106.

mediately that three of his basic nineteen civilizations fit into category (a), the civilized society in which a creative minority is present: the contemporary Western and orthodox Christian civilizations, and the ancient Hellenic civilization (including Rome). It is from our comparatively complete historical knowledge of these societies that we derived the idea of the importance and influence of individualism in the first place. The difficulty lies in demonstrating that the coincidence of civilization and individualism is general and not merely a special case.

If we recognize that creative individualism is not necessarily either the economic individualism associated with American and Western European industrialism or the sentimental individualism typified by bohemianism and the Romantic movement in art and literature, we can immediately extend membership in category (a) to the Far Eastern, Hindu, Syriac, Arabic, and Iranic civilizations, on the basis of their cultural history.

Archeological and semi-historical evidence indicates that four others—the Babylonic, Sinic, Sumeric, and Egyptiac—should be assigned tentatively to category (a). For example, the genius of a single individual, Imhotep, is credited with giving Egyptian civilization a sudden upward boost about 3000 B.C.

Thus, twelve of the nineteen basic civilizations listed by Toynbee may be assigned to category (a) (fourteen of twenty-one, if one follows him in dividing the Far Eastern and Orthodox Christian each into two). This leaves seven—the Andean, Indic, Minoan, Mayan, Yucatec, and Mexic—all of which have long been extinct, and what records they may have left were to a large extent destroyed by conquest. I do not wish to qualify this hypothesis merely on the basis of the inadequacy of historical records. Therefore, I prefer to conclude that the available evidence does not justify their assignment to either category (a) or category (c), civilizations wherein the creative minority is missing, and they should be omitted as evidential factors.

When we turn to category (b), non-civilized societies lacking a creative minority, we can justify it only by a generalization: the frequently stated anthropological impression of the strength of traditional patterns of behavior in the hundreds of contemporary "primitive societies" (to use Toynbee's term). That is to say, persisting conformity in social conduct implies the absence of creative individualists. We cannot go beyond this generalization because these societies, being essentially preliterate, lack records, both of history and of the possible influence of creative individuals.

Some may argue, in support of the presence of a creative minority in some non-civilized societies—category (d)—that cultural patterns of the Dobuan and Kwakiutl societies, for example, emphasize extreme individualism, but I do not consider this a valid argument. Such individualism is not creative individualism, in the sense of finding non-traditional solutions to problems or of being in contact with a non-social context of reality; it is just another form of conformist social behavior.

That some creative individuals arise in primitive societies cannot be questioned. All societies have found some cultural and technological solutions to environmental problems, and it is probable that these are more than mere accidental and collective accretions from traditional social patterns. Many primitive societies tolerate the non-conformist, such as the shaman and the *berdache*, and these non-conformists may make creative contributions to the culture. But it is noteworthy that this tolerance usually implies a peculiar, marginal role in the society, preventing the non-conformist from making a normal contribution back into the gene pool.

The question at issue is not the occasional appearance of isolated creative individuals but the simultaneous presence of such individuals in adequate numbers to influence the society.

Our testing of the hypothesis has been only moderately successful. Not only does it omit Toynbee's "fossilized" and "abortive" civilizations—which possibly could be looked at—but it omits certain societies that can be called neither "civilizations" nor "primitive societies" in Toynbee's terminology, such as Dahomey, the Iroquois Confederation, the Seminoles, and the

Cherokees. The flaw in this approach is more basic than any number of sins of omission, however. The deficiency is found in the positivistic Philistinism of attempting to validate (or invalidate) a synthetic and abstractive hypothesis by methods reminiscent of doing simple sums on a slate. Some resort to such methods in a supportive role is unavoidable (e. g., the extrapolations in Chapter 13, below), but the results should not be considered conclusive. The human phenomenon is more complex than that, and civilization, as well as individualism, is a human phenomenon.

For example, Toynbee considers the Jews to be a "fossilized civilization," but such has not been their role in the West. They have constituted a vital and often progressive subculture, which has contributed considerably more than its share of the creative individualism that built Western civilization. The same may be said of the role in India of another of Toynbee's "fossils," the Parsees. Nor does a civilization ordinarily exist in isolation. The Gauls and Britons did not become civilized indigenously, by virtue of any creative minorities of their own, but adopted Roman civilization. Preliterate African societies today are having Western civilization imposed on them.

The previously attained, cumulative level of a society's technology (and, probably, less tangible cultural elements) sets limitations on the possible achievements of creative individualism at any particular time and place. The lack of effect of the scientific work of Leonardo da Vinci is a good example. Hero's invention of the steam engine or the Arabian invention of the battery, in the context in which they reappeared later, could have advanced the civilizing process in northern Europe and even America by several centuries; but at the time they were mere curiosities.

The restrictions of technological level also interact complexly and intimately with limitations of the natural environment. The social genius of the Iroquois could not overcome the forest without metal tools, and the achievements of the Maya are all the more remarkable for their lack of both the wheel and

51

metallurgy. Limitations of natural environment suppress civilization, of course, for man is still a biological species. His wide range of physiological adaptability does not imply necessarily a corresponding wide range of efficiency, either physiological or mental.

One of the most neglected major studies of this century is Ellsworth Huntington's extensive research into one natural factor, climate.[4] This study was shoved aside apparently because much of his subsidiary commentary was based on outdated and subsequently invalidated information. The criticism does not apply to his major theme, however, any more than Darwin's acceptance of Lamarckism invalidated his evolutionary theory. The correspondence between two of Huntington's world maps—one showing gradations from what he determined to be the optimum climate for human endeavor, the other showing contemporary levels of civilization as judged by a large number of authorities from different nations—is too striking to be entirely coincidental. He concluded that this optimum climate—involving a number of factors—was correlated with a high level of civilization. His research into such clues as tree rings and former lake levels led him also to the hypothesis that the optimal climatic zone in ancient times lay more southerly than now and may have been a factor in the high level of Hellenic, Indian, Egyptian, Minoan, and even the American civilizations.

If climate is such a major factor, as it logically should be, a climatic optimum would have to coincide with other natural advantages in order to permit creative individualism to increase genetically and contribute to the growth of civilization. Thus, it can be seen that the presence of creative individualists is not the *only* requisite to the growth and maintenance of civilization. Nevertheless, their presence is indispensable. Without them, all other contributing factors could be at their optima in vain.

[4] E. g., Ellsworth Huntington, *Civilization and Climate* (New Haven: Yale University Press, 1915).

This brings us to the questions raised by historical patterns: Why has the creative minority always dissipated and disappeared? And will the same thing happen again, even at the high level attained by Western civilization?

The answer lies in the fact that a genotype—specifically, the genotype of *H. individualis*—is manifested significantly only as a result of natural selection. If a genotype is present in significant numbers, it will disappear only as a result of natural selection. Natural selection is simply the survival impact of the environment upon the phenotype. If the phenotype survives effectively in its environment, it contributes to the genotypes of the succeeding generation; if not, it does not. There is, statistically, a direct ratio between survival effectiveness of a phenotype and its contribution to the genotype of the next generation.

The environment in which natural selection affects the survival of the human social animal is dual; it is both natural and social. These two facets of the environment influence each other reciprocally, so that their effects are difficult to isolate; but it is apparent that the ratio of their impact upon natural selection will vary with circumstances. The most important such circumstance is the form of social living in force, because the individual's direct dealings with the natural environment are determined by the character of the society in which he lives.

We have seen how the natural environment in prehistoric times may have dictated such a drastic change in social structure that a new type of human, *H. individualis*, emerged. We have referred to Huntington's evidence that natural factors retain a strong influence upon the form of social response, even today. Yet, paradoxically, we are going to find that the comparative importance of the social facet of the environment to the process of natural selection increased with the advent of *H. individualis*, rather than the other way around.

The reason for the paradox is that *H. individualis*, being less socially oriented than *H. socialis*, was better able to mitigate the pressures of the natural (non-social) environment. Mitigation of pressures of the natural environment resulted in a comparative increase in the importance of the social environment as a factor in natural selection.

I believe that the rise and fall of civilizations in the historical period represent the flow and ebb of man's effort to adapt his social forms to a biological change in his own nature.

CHAPTER SIX

THE LEAVEN IN THE LOAF

Statesmanship should quickly learn the lesson of biology
as stated by Conklin, that "Wooden legs are not
inherited, but wooden heads are."

—ALBERT EDWARD WIGGAM: *The New Decalogue of Science*

H SOCIETY PROGRESSES as a result of the influence of a creative minority composed of *H. individualis*; but *H. individualis* does not exert influence as a creative minority under all conditions.

The creative minority is a major factor of the progressive phase of civilization in Toynbee's historical theory. Toynbee, however, specifically disclaims any implication that there is a biological difference between the creative minority and the mimetic majority and protests his allegiance to "the uniformity of human nature."[1] One may be permitted, perhaps, to accept Toynbee's basic concept here but at the same time to reject his modifying disclaimer. If the creative minority is not fundamentally a biological phenomenon, the patterns Toynbee finds in the rise and decline of civilizations must be impossibly coincidental, or else represent historicism in Popper's sense of the word: laws of historical process that are essentially arbitrary.[2]

A creative minority is defined necessarily by mental traits that differentiate it from the majority of the population. The question, whether differences in mental capacities are inherent or environmentally caused, has been argued for two and a half centuries, since John Locke enunciated his "common-sense"

[1] Arnold J. Toynbee, *A Study of History* (12 vols.; London: Oxford University Press, 1934–1962), XII, 148–49, 305.
[2] Karl R. Popper, *The Open Society and Its Enemies* (Torchbook ed., New York: Harper & Row, 1963), I, 3ff.

dictum that the human mind is initially a blank sheet upon which traits are written by experience only. One may choose today among a range of opinions extending from that of Watson, a psychologist, that any normal child can be developed into any kind of adult by conditioning, regardless of his heredity, to that of Pendell, an economist, that "brains" are "solely hereditary." Both views are extreme, and the position adopted here is that of a biologist, Medawar, that at least half of the observed variation in intelligence is hereditary. As another biologist, Mayr, comments, it is immaterial in this context whether the hereditary component represents 25 per cent or 75 per cent of the total variation.

An example of the evidence for a biological foundation of mental differences is the correlation between IQ ratings of individuals of differing blood relationships (Table 2). The correlation of intelligence between identical twins raised apart (.77) has been shown to be higher than that for fraternal twins raised together (.63).[3] What is inherited in such cases, of course,

TABLE 2

BLOOD RELATIONSHIPS AND CORRELATIONS BETWEEN IQ'S

Degree of relationship	IQ correlation	Genetic correlation
Same individual (reliability coefficient)	.91	1.00
Identical twins	.90	1.00
Fraternal twins	.65	.50
Non-twin siblings	.50	.50
Parent and child	.50	.50
Parent and foster child	.25	.00
Grandparent and child	.15	.25
Unrelated individuals	.00	.00

Source: Based on Gregory A. Kimble and Norman Garmezy, *Principles of General Psychology*, 2nd ed., Copyright © 1963, The Ronald Press Co.

[3] Howard H. Kendler, *Basic Psychology* (New York: Meredith, 1963), p. 625.

56

is not some specific orientation or pattern of thinking, but the physiological capacity for learning. There is no reason to assume that inheritance of this capacity in man differs from that in other mammals. That inheritance of this capacity occurs on a differential basis among members of a mammalian species is evidenced by Tryon's controlled experiment in selective breeding of rats on the basis of ability in maze-solving; after seven generations, the progeny of "maze-bright" rats and those of "maze-dull" rats had separated into two distinct populations which hardly overlapped in their comparative ability at maze-solving.[4]

Admittedly, the correlation of IQ on the basis of blood relationships and the Tryon rat experiments deal with IQ-measurable components, and the "intelligence" measured in formal IQ tests represents only a partial qualification of the creative minority. A creative minority is more likely to conform to the "high creative" group studied by Getzels and Jackson[5] than to their "high IQ" group. In these studies of school children, they found the "high creative" group 23 IQ points below the "high IQ" group on the average, yet achievement scores of the two groups were equally superior to those of the school population as a whole. Significantly, members of the "high creative" group were found to be largely non-conformist and thus not often liked by their teachers. They were also more humorous and more violent than the "high IQ" group and more oriented to "growth"—the latter a rather direct expression of the self-affirming imperative. On the other hand, the "high IQ" group was oriented more to "safety"—certainly reminiscent of the conformist "safety in numbers" rationale of the collective ego.

The criteria on which IQ tests are constructed do not include the imagination and originality characteristic of creativeness. They are founded largely on memory, logical construction, and

[4] *Ibid.*, pp. 622–23.
[5] Jacob W. Getzels and Philip W. Jackson, *Creativity and Intelligence* (New York: John Wiley & Sons, 1962), *passim.*

prior information, qualities which serve a superior mimetic function well; and mimesis is a social trait of the non-creative majority. A creative minority could hardly be abnormally deficient in IQ-measurable traits, of course, but it would appear to require a high ratio of the creative characteristics delineated by Getzels and Jackson, too.

Should we assume that the creative characteristics are inherited to the same extent as IQ-measurable traits? There is no reason not to do so. Creativity is as much a function of intelligence as are those qualities probed in IQ tests. Furthermore, physiological factors are known medically to affect intelligence, emotional orientation, motivation, energy level, and other psychological characteristics. Williams has studied extensively some physiological differences which are primarily inherent, such as those in neuronic, glandular, and enzymatic structure; and he expresses the view that, logically, there should be the same correspondence between morphology and function in human differences as in differences between the human species and other primate species.[6] That is to say, we assume logically that humans think and act differently from monkeys and apes because their brains are physiologically different. Therefore, why not also assume that inherent physiological differences in brain structure among humans, although less extensive, would likewise cause different humans to think and act differently?

The creative minority is responsible for those inventions and discoveries that constitute the technological basis of civilization at any stage, but it would be an oversimplification to consider the creative minority as merely a technological elite. It deals primarily in ideas; poets, novelists, and religious leaders sometimes contribute more profoundly to the orientation of society than do inventors and scientists. Rarely are members of a creative minority engaged in direct enforcement of social regulations. Their influence is disseminated less through outright precept than through a psychological osmosis similar to

[6] Roger J. Williams, *Biochemical Individuality* (New York: John Wiley & Sons, 1956), pp. 44–45, 198–99.

that by which the child learns from its elders. The creative minority influences its society as a result of the non-creative majority's practice of mimesis.

Mimesis is, in fact, the supreme social achievement of *H. socialis.* The perfection of mimesis by the human animal made the highest form of mammalian sociality workable, by providing the psychological means for learning and acquiring culture. Mimesis is accurate imitation to the limit of the imitator's ability, without innovation. *H. socialis*, the imitator, is highly adaptable intellectually, but his adaptability lies primarily in his ability to shift his mimesis to a different model when the social barometer indicates that he should.

The value of mimesis is that it permits the individual to utilize the experience of others. As long as the environment is stable, the experience of previous generations in dealing with it remains effective, and a society can survive almost indefinitely upon an intellectual foundation of mimesis. Any marked instability of the environment, however, renders mimetic ability inadequate as a learning process. The conservatism of mimesis, its lack of initiative, prevents it from altering the social pattern of response to the environment.

Departures from mimesis, rare in *H. socialis*, are characteristic of *H. individualis*. *H. individualis* can serve as a bellwether for *H. socialis*, altering the orientation of his mimesis in ways which permit the *Masse* to deal effectively with an altered environment. When this happens, a creative minority can be responsible for the swift development of a culture of far greater magnitude than one would anticipate from the paucity of its initiators. The minority constantly finds better ways to meet the society's problems, and the *H. socialis* majority adopts them through mimesis.

The obvious problem here, in the name of civilization, is to get the *H. socialis* majority to switch allegiance from its established ways to the new ideas of *H. individualis*. This is not by any means an automatic reaction. The unoriginal person may learn by mimicry, but he also may exercise his choice as to whom he mimics. The collective ego has established itself successfully and has continued to be effective through a conservatism that leans toward the mimicry of socially established patterns of reaction rather than the ideas of some innovator.

The criteria of the collective ego are rooted in the primal structure of human society, a leader-follower structure which, except in its simplest forms, takes the form of a hierarchy containing generally recognized levels of status and authority. In a leader-follower structure, an individual decides primarily on the basis of authority whether he should practice mimesis. If the requisite authority is present, the social individual's collective ego initiates the accepted response to this authority.

In the long-stable *Masse*, both authority and response are normally established by tradition. When tradition fails or is challenged, however, or when the *Masse* is so large or so unstable that authority is uncertain, *H. socialis* must fall back on another criterion, reputation, founded in Carrington's "additive socialisation" ("safety in numbers") principle.[7] Reputation is based on the awareness that a significant percentage of the *Masse* accepts the claims of the concept or the individual in question. Thus, in a society like that of the United States, where established lines of authority are multiple and confused, advertising based on extensive sales or widespread use of a product is often more effective than a straightforward statement of the product's superiority.

When both traditional authority and reputation are uncertain, the collective ego must depend upon the primal criterion, individual assurance. Individual assurance in the human expresses itself in behavior markedly resembling that of dominant individuals in the hierarchies of some social animals. The individual exhibiting this trait may not actually have superior knowledge applying to a specific situation that the group must deal with, but he is followed as though he does. In a modern

[7] Richard Carrington, *A Million Years of Man* (Mentor ed., New York: New American Library, 1964), pp. 66–67.

context, the response to individual assurance can express itself in mass hypnosis and mass movements.

Visibly, none of these criteria—not even individual assurance—is necessarily a component of the psychological structure of *H. individualis*. Authority, reputation, and individual assurance are, rather, traits of the social leader, and this is a different thing altogether. Therefore, under normal social circumstances there is no guarantee that a creative *H. individualis* minority will contribute anything to the *Masse*'s culture. Indeed, there are factors which militate against it. A Hero may invent the steam engine without improving technology; a Greek intellectual aristocracy may prove that the world is a round planet revolving around the sun without gaining acceptance for the concept.

The successful society, primitive or civilized, is not one in which *H. individualis* is likely to receive a hearing, nor one in which he is likely to thrive. This is to be expected, since he is a departure from the social norm, and the success of the social norm makes him superfluous.

In order for the peculiar abilities of a creative minority to affect a *Masse*, those individuals bearing the traits of *H. individualis* must at the same time be numbered among those who are looked to as possessing authority, those who are accorded reputation, and those who are confident enough of their standing with others to feel individual assurance. Such a correspondence of the characteristics of social leadership with those of *H. individualis* occurs when a society is called upon to meet challenges for which traditional responses are no longer adequate. When this occurs, whether it results from a change in the natural environment or from development within the society itself, the usual conformist discrimination against *H. individualis* is eased and he can become an effective factor within the society.

A creative minority must attain some minimum size in a society in order to exert any major effect, because the creative process is to some extent a cumulative one. The traditional behavior of a society is that of an integrated structure, resistant in its entirety to disruption at any one point. The isolated creative act is unlikely to effect any major change in orientation of the society; it requires the support of other creative acts directed toward the solution of the same general problem. Even when a single potent figure in the *Masse*'s hierarchy is a strong example of *H. individualis*, his cultural influence, although spectacular, is likely to be temporary; Ikhnaton could change the religious orientation of Egypt only during his own lifetime. A further advantage accruing from a numerous creative minority is its better statistical chance of authoritative representation in the social hierarchy. Such representation increases its chances of activating the mimesis of the non-creative majority and achieving dissemination of its innovations as acceptable elements of the society's behavioral pattern.

A simplified definition of the conditions under which a *Masse* should be expected to exhibit a cultural burst, then, is when an alteration of the society's environment, outer or inner, makes traditional responses to it inadequate and thus renders the creative personality more valuable to the society than previously in comparison to the traditionalist. Under such conditions, natural selection confers a reproductive advantage upon *H. individualis* and fosters the build-up of a creative minority.

CHAPTER SEVEN

THE ADVENT OF REASON

I think, therefore I am.
—RENE DESCARTES: *Les Discours de la Methode*

MAN EXISTED FOR AN INCREDIBLY long time at a simple level of culture before developing his earliest civilizations, which in turn remained at a stable cultural level for many centuries. The thesis that *H. individualis* was responsible for this major step forward requires a delineation of the environmental change fostering his emergence.

It is necessary to establish the comparative time context of this development in order to emphasize its revolutionary nature. If we consider the period since Swanscombe Man a single 24-hour day, the neolithic revolution occurred but an hour ago, and the first cities appeared only about 30 minutes ago. Such a comparison indicates how basically man is *social*, rather than *civilized.* The primitive hunting and food-gathering culture was such a satisfactory environment for a fully human creature that he competed successfully with other species for hundreds of centuries without the benefit of cities or civilization. During these hundreds of centuries, *H. socialis* got along very well without the disturbing influence of *H. individualis*.

In the primal society that existed for most of man's metaphorical 24-hour day, the *Masse* was a matrix within which the individual expressed his existence. It was not the extension of himself as an individual but a greater unity with which he felt coextensive. *H. socialis* could breathe this environment as a fish breathes the sea in which it is immersed. There could be dominance and subservience here; there could be differentiation of components of a larger whole; but there could be no

63

Galileo redefining the divine order of the universe, no Prometheus defying Zeus. The *Masse*, not the individual, was the true representative of the species.

In a very real sense, the *Masse* itself was the environment to which *H. socialis* responded. The *Masse*, as a social "coaction for affirmation," is a collective response to the natural environment. The natural environment shapes the *Masse*, and the form thus imposed on the *Masse*, in turn, requires certain responses from the *Masse*'s individual members. The typical form of the human *Masse* in paleolithic times was an adequate response to the natural conditions that prevailed then, and its maintenance with very little change required the conformist, mimetic traits of *H. socialis*.

Some incompatibility obviously had to creep into this happy marriage between stable man and stable environment before that adulterer, *H. individualis*, could create a new union. A general statement, such as Simpson's observation that the trend of evolution has been toward greater individualization, reaching its peak in the human,[1] does not suffice as an explanation for the rise of *H. individualis*. Evolutionary trends depend upon mutations, and a constant rate of genetic mutations is the rule in any species; but a mutation must be favored—or, at least, not inhibited—by natural selection in order to persist and spread. When the environment tolerated repetition of the same social behavior, generation after generation, a *H. individualis* mutation was not favored. Clearly, one cannot just say a mutation created the incompatibility between man and his paleolithic environment, and let it go at that.

The fact that a *H. individualis* mutation (or mutations) could not persist and influence society as long as the environment remained favorable to *H. socialis* does not mean, however, that this mutation waited for the environment to change before appearing at all. Biological processes do not operate so fortuitously. We may speculate that at some point in the evolution

---

[1] George Gaylord Simpson, *The Meaning of Evolution* (New Haven: Yale University Press, 1949), pp. 284, 306.

64

of the new species, *H. sapiens*, from the ancestral species, *H. erectus*, the total human genetic complex reached a stage at which a single, not unlikely mutation would cause a major reorientation of the individual's inherent potential: the *H. individualis* mutation. To say "a single mutation" probably oversimplifies the matter; but a single gene affects the action of many other genes in the total complex through epistatic interaction, and a single mutation could bring about small but widespread changes in such significant areas as neuronic structure, endocrine secretion, and energy-bearing efficiency of enzymes in the blood. Very probably, the "*H. individualis* mutation" involved a number of different genes which, singly, did not affect the phenotype noticeably. Whenever too many of them combined in paleolithic times, the phenotype came too close to *H. individualis*, and the individual was eliminated selectively because of the superior survival value of the *H. socialis* phenotype.

A change in man's environment had to come about before innovation could become more important than tradition in solving social problems and *H. individualis* was permitted to come into his own. This fact points up a peculiar problem: not that there was such a change, but that the change began so long before the neolithic revolution that is the major evidence for the prehistoric emergence of *H. individualis*. The Würm glacial period represented a major change in the previously stable climatic conditions of the Riss-Würm interglacial; yet it was only at the close of the Würm, when climatic conditions began to improve, that the neolithic revolution occurred. *H. sapiens* was already here during the Würm; Buettner-Janusch assigns him an age of well over 100,000 years, and the Würm began 70,000 years ago.[2]

The theoretical solution to this problem which comes to mind at once is that it was not until the end of the Würm that the evolving human genetic complex reached the stage at which

[2] John Buettner-Janusch, *Origins of Man* (New York: John Wiley & Sons, 1966), p. 26.

a *H. individualis* mutation was possible. There is another solution, however, which seems more suitable: that it took the particular kind of environmental change that occurred at the end of the Würm, rather than that which initiated the Würm, to "break the cake of custom," as Bagehot puts it. Presumably, conditions similar to those which ended the Würm also ended the earlier Riss, but *H. sapiens* was 100,000 years younger then, and it is easier to speculate that he was incapable of a *H. individualis* variation. During the Würm itself, most of Europe was frigid; this was a radical change from the climate that permitted the savannah-and-steppe hunting existence of paleolithic man, and—although it may have brought about its own significant innovations, as we shall see—the environment was too severe for any such development as the neolithic revolution. In Africa and Asia, the effect of the Würm glaciations was presumably to push the savannah and steppe belts farther southward than they are today, and hunting man there could meet the change by moving with the climate, without changing his way of life.

The only ancient peoples we know to have been forced to adapt to a cold climate during the Würm were the Neanderthals, who were contemporaneous with its first half. Presumably, during the Riss-Würm interglacial, the ancestors of these people were one with the rest of the evolving human species, all living on European savannahs—a type of environment which encourages the hunting-pack culture at a low technological level, not dissimilar to that which the *australopithecinæ* may have had. As the ice descended over northern Europe during the outer Würm, the Neanderthals, unlike the peoples of Asia and Africa, were prevented from southerly migration by the Mediterranean Sea. The Neanderthals were forced into smaller social units[3]—perhaps family-size, or a little larger. This is a social context fostering greater individualism, and it is perhaps

[3] Jacquetta Hawkes, "Prehistory," in Part I, *History of Mankind* (New York: Harper & Row, 1963), p. 119.

significant that the Mousterian Neanderthals reached their cultural peak in this severe and changeable climate.

The Neanderthals—whether they are an extinct offshoot of the species, or whether they contributed genes to our own ancestry—were not the shambling brutes they have been pictured in many popular texts. On the criterion of brain size, they were as human as modern man. They stood erect and, although their brows were flattened, they were not flat-nosed but had extremely prominent noses. It is significant that Neanderthal remains indicate religious practices connected with burial customs, for religion and morality are inextricably intertwined, and both are closely involved with individualism. Neither religion nor morality is necessary when individualistic tendencies are absent, for then socially desired habits are instilled and followed unconsciously, through mimesis, when there is no glimmer of individualistic skepticism and rebellion.

The Göttweig interstadial period, which began about 40,000 years ago and lasted for about 11,000 years, was a comparatively mild period; and the Crô-Magnons who displaced the Neanderthals during this period, although fully modern in appearance, pursued a paleolithic hunting existence. If art is a symptom of individualistic leanings (and I think it is), the Crô-Magnons had them, as evidenced by their cave paintings; but they did not initiate the neolithic revolution.

The neolithic revolution awaited the end of the Würm. When the ice retreated slowly and the rain belts moved northward at the close of the last Würm glaciation, circumstances favorable to individualism occurred particularly in one area inhabited by humans. This was the region of the Caspian Sea, a body of water larger in glacial times than at present. As the ice melted, swamps and tree-covered hills replaced the steppes and cross-country movement became difficult. Large scale pack-type hunting became impossible, because the big game of the steppes was gone and small prey was not big enough to go around if run down by a pack. As in Neanderthal times, the traditional social response to the environment was no longer adequate; but now the environmental challenge was different— and perhaps, too, the genetic potential of the men who met it was different.

The terrain forced the inhabitants to settle in small communities. It was a small-group, sedentary existence which, in itself, favored individualism. Also, success attended the individual who could come up with more efficient ideas for killing or trapping the game, or who could find alternate sources of a stable food supply—such as those who thought of penning trapped animals for future needs instead of killing them at once and those who thought of planting seeds instead of just gathering fruits.

Division into small, essentially endogamous communities is especially significant from the standpoint of evolutionary biology. Each small population is affected by local selective factors, which tend to be normalized by gene flow in large, interbreeding populations. Hardin[4] shows how small populations, drifting away from each other genetically, are more subject to extinction than are large populations; on the other hand, they have a better chance of attaining higher evolutionary levels by traversing genetic paths closer to lethal environmental limits than normalizing selection permits in large populations.

This picture is particularly apropos to a social species like man. Environmental pressures, through competition among individuals, keep members of large interbreeding populations clustered closely around the adaptive peak. There are also social pressures tending to the same end. The populations of the steppe and savannah culture were, in this sense, a single large interbreeding population, because the different *Massen* were highly mobile. There was enough contact among them, whether friendly or hostile, for considerable genetic interchange. When the Neanderthals broke up into smaller populations at the beginning of the Würm, those who survived traveled an evolu-

[4] Garrett Hardin, *Nature and Man's Fate* (Mentor ed., New York: New American Library, 1961), pp. 252–54.

tionary path leading to increased adaptation to bitter cold; when a similar population breakup occurred at the end of the Würm, the surviving small populations initiated the neolithic revolution.

Post-Würm conditions intensified competition among *Massen*. This, rather than competition among individuals within a *Masse*, probably has always been an important factor in human evolution, because man is a social species. A *Masse* would develop its own norm, both cultural and biological, around which its population clustered. This *Masse* competed in survival terms, either directly or indirectly, with other *Massen* possessing different norms. The fact that there was genetic interchange among the populations of the paleolithic hunting culture did not eliminate such inter-*Masse* competition; the *Massen* were partly isolated from each other genetically, and the uniformity of the environment impelled the different *Massen* to compete toward attainment of the same norm of response.

The small communities of the Caspian region during the neolithic revolution were competing toward a new norm of social response to the environment, to replace the hunting pack response. The level of response eventually stabilized was dual. One aspect of it was agriculture; the other was cattle-raising. Although the two interacted and supplemented each other, emphasis on the latter led to the nomadic cultures of the great Asian steppes and emphasis on the former evolved into early urban civilization.

Competition toward the new level of response fostered individualistic response. In the autonomous or semi-autonomous small communities of the immediate post-Würm period, the ideas of creative individuals offered competitive advantage, both for the individuals and for their *Massen*. An evolutionary premium was placed on individual ingenuity. Those small communities fortunate enough to possess such ingenuity survived and thrived to contribute their characteristics to the future; those incapable of relinquishing the old pack-culture patterns succumbed.

The neolithic revolution lasted long enough for the combined process of inter-*Masse* competition and genetic exchange to establish the *H. individualis* mutation strongly in the gene pool of the peoples of the Caspian region. Of course, the neolithic revolution is not a sharply defined period, beginning suddenly on a certain date and ending just as suddenly on a later date, even in a single region. But it can be said with some justification to have lasted at least from the time of a proto-neolithic settlement at Jericho about 7800 B.C. until 5000 B.C., when farming had diffused through an area extending from the Caspian Sea to the Persian Gulf and the eastern Mediterranean Sea. This represents approximately one hundred generations, ample for a major modification of a genotype if a strong selective factor is operating.

During this period, the individualistic ego in the human psyche entrenched itself so strongly that it could not be dislodged by the collective ego in the competition for survival advantage. Through such inventions as agriculture, animal domestication, tool-grinding, and pottery, a new plateau of response to the environment had been created. Any human *Masse* at this level of response possessed an overwhelming survival advantage over any *Masse* below it. At this level of response, continued contributions of the individualistic ego were indispensable.

Although this hypothesis is expressed in terms of the conditions prevailing in the Caspian basin at that time, the same selective factors may have been present in the upper Nile, Indus, and Huang-Ho valleys, or similar cultural conditions may have arisen by cultural diffusion from the Caspian area later. These other areas today possess the same general climatic type (steppe) as a large portion of the Caspian area. In any event, once the step to a new level of response had been taken, cultural diffusion and competition among *Massen* would make its spread inevitable. *Massen* that did not adopt elements of the new approach by mimesis, thus altering their social structures to permit a genetic increase of individualistic traits, would be eliminated or subordinated wherever the two cultural levels came into contact.

The villages which began to cluster on the drying land of the upper Euphrates region some 10,000 years ago were not paleolithic villages, nor can we believe that their inhabitants exhibited a paleolithic psychology. There was community cooperation, but not the communism of the hunting and food-gathering culture. Planning for the future, based on the prospects of crops and herds, replaced day-to-day dependence on finding game and tubers. Since a sedentary existence made possible the accumulation of goods, a new kind of individual competition began to develop within the *Masse*, competition for the acquisition of private property, instead of for the hierarchical status insuring a good share of the hunt's immediate spoils. This fact modified the *Masse's* hierarchical system in several ways; although comparative wealth and hierarchical status often went together, the man who achieved some wealth could be independent of the hierarchy and pursue a relatively isolated life if he so chose.

When the neolithic villages spread down the rivers, the cultivation of wheat, barley, and rice in the deltas made possible much larger populations than were characteristic of the old hunting culture, and the first urban civilizations evolved. This raises the question: when response to the environment was stabilized at a new level, in a large population context, why was not *H. individualis* rendered unnecessary and *H. socialis* restored to supremacy? The answer is that this did occur to some extent, but not to the extent of reverting to the paleolithic stage of attitude and behavior.

The social success of the great grain economies minimized both the challenges of the natural environment and the effects of competition from other *Massen*. Further creative contributions by individuals became less necessary to the *Masse*. A resurgence of the collective ego occurred, and the small *Massen* of the neolithic period, seething with creative ferment, were converted into the notably collective civilizations of the ancient

71

East and Near East. These civilizations revived the rigid hier-archical structure of the primal herd-*Masse* and returned to tradition-directedness at a more sophisticated level.

At its best, the first stage of civilized individualism did not eliminate that pervasive sense of identity with the *Masse* char-acteristic of earlier cultures, but it was mitigated to some degree. There were gaps in it which allowed rather strong individualis-tic tendencies to be expressed sometimes. A larger priesthood and craftsmen's class might feel a satisfying sense of differen-tiation from the masses, but communal life was so close and so necessary that this was more a sense of hierarchical status than anything else. Even the Pharaoh considered himself the imper-sonation of the *Masse*, rather than an individual distinct from it.

Yet, there were solid advances in the conditions hospitable to individualism, which had been lacking even in the creatively adapting neolithic villages. Mumford[5] has cited two character-istics of urban life representative of these advances: (*a*) due to the comparative rarity of individuals of exceptional ability, the concentration of large numbers in a city offers a better statisti-cal chance for their cooperation, at the same time affording them more various challenges; and (*b*) the urban breakup of the tribe's primitive solidarity emancipated the autonomous in-dividual, even though at first he existed only at the very top of the civilized society.

The course of collective human existence moved smoothly, if at a low level, before the neolithic revolution. A cyclical pat-tern of social events cannot be isolated in paleolithic times. There may have been one, at an indiscernible plateau of mani-festation, for creative individualism was not entirely absent from paleolithic culture. Progress was made and techniques changed, even though slowly. But after the neolithic revolu-tion, creative individualism appeared as a constant disturbance in the even tenor of collective life, and a cyclical pattern began to impose itself on history.

[5] Lewis Mumford, *The City in History* (New York: Harcourt, Brace & World, 1961), p. 109.

Those *Massen* which achieved success on the basis of contributions by creative individualism tended to sink back to repetitive, tradition-oriented behavior. But the complexities of their own social structure and the threats of other *Massen* seeking to prey on their success raised new problems, which were solved by a resurgence of creative individualism or which dragged the societies to destruction.

CHAPTER EIGHT

THE ACCESSION OF THE CROWD

*This natural inequality of the two powers of population
and of production in the earth and that great law of
our nature which must constantly keep their
effects equal form the great difficulty that
to me appears insurmountable in the
way to the perfectibility of society.*

—THOMAS ROBERT MALTHUS: *On Population*

IN THE EARLY DECADES of this century, Ortega cried that "mass man" was flooding over Europe, creating such a "fullness" of people that everything—the houses, the hotels, the trains, the walks, the beaches—was crowded.[1] Twenty centuries earlier, Polybius complained that Greece was suffering from a scarcity of men, leaving the cities desolate and the land waste. These two men, 2,000 years apart, felt the same sense of impending doom, but for opposite reasons.

Ortega and Polybius were not concerned merely with population size, but with marked changes in population size, the one with increase, the other with decrease. The comparative effects of the large and the small populations on the incidence of *H. individualis*, genetically and behaviorally, have been sketched in simple terms. These effects, however, are predicated on relatively stable populations; unusual alteration of population size, up or down, has its own implications, which deserve examination.

Also, the phenomenon of excessive population density needs to be looked at, as one of the most important aspects of human congregation in its influence on both *H. individualis* and *H.*

[1] José Ortega y Gasset, *La Rebelión de las masas* (Madrid: Espasa-Calpe, S. A., 1937), p. 35.

74

socialis. A large population of a *Masse per se* need not be a dense population; it depends upon the extent of the territory occupied by the *Masse* and the population's distribution in that territory. At any rate, the "large population" of the paleolithic hunting society was very small in comparison to the populations of most civilized *Massen.* Neither a really large population nor a dense population represents that normal to humanity during its long prehistory.

Perhaps the best approach to these several elements of the social/individualistic relationship is to outline the great population changes that have affected the species as a whole, and then to speculate as to their causes and consequences.

The total population of the human species and its immediate ancestral species has increased from that of a probably rare and localized forest animal to more than 3 billion as of mid-1965. It remained relatively stable until the age of "modern man"—that is, essentially, historic man—dawned at the close of the Würm glaciation. Since then, the numbers of mankind have increased rather swiftly, but not always at the same rate. The differences in the rate of increase can be divided into some general periods.

On the basis of Deevey's estimates,[2] prehuman and human population rose from 125,000 to 3,340,000 during the first 97½ per cent of the million-year period from the *australopithecinæ* to the present, representing an increase of 2,672 per cent or less than 0.3 per cent per century. This rate of increase did not jump significantly in the next 15,000 years, extending to the neolithic revolution; the increase was only 60 per cent, or approximately 0.4 per cent per century. In the next 4,000 years, however, from 8000 to 4000 B.C., population surged forward 1,520 per cent or 38 per cent per century. Yet from 4000 B.C. to the beginning of the Christian era, human population almost reverted to paleo-

[2] E. S. Deevey, "The Human Population" in *Scientific American*, No. 203, cited by Theodosius Dobzhansky, *Mankind Evolving* (New Haven: Yale University Press, 1962), p. 299.

lithic stability, increasing only 1.3 per cent per century. From the time of Christ to A.D. 1700, the rate of increase averaged 24.1 per cent per century, and since 1700 it has been about 147 per cent per century.

Obviously, there must be a reason for such a variable curve of population increase; and it must be something other than a variation in human fertility, which presumably is constant. The simplest answer is the application of the Malthusian theory. This theory, enunciated by Thomas Robert Malthus late in the eighteenth century, was that a population of any species tends to increase unchecked until it reaches the limit of the food supply, at which point it is reduced again to manageable proportions by such natural checks as starvation, disease, and war. The elemental theory has been modified by a large number of observations of animal behavior in this century, which indicate that various practices are followed in many species which prevent a population's ever reaching the actual starvation stage. This is particularly true for a species like man, who is capable of voluntary population control. The historical facts associated with changes in the world-wide human curve of increase, however, signify that the unalloyed Malthusian theory applies in general terms.

The first break from the million-year period of near stability of human population, initiated in the 4,000 years from 8000 to 4000 B.C. when increase jumped to 38 per cent per century, is the time of the neolithic revolution. Agriculture and animal husbandry were adopted, greatly enlarging the stable food supply, and new techniques of tool-making were developed. The next 4,000 years, when population almost stabilized again, was the era of the ancient civilizations, which endured without any revolutionary change in technology or food-production methods. At first it is hard to understand the rise in the rate of increase to 24.1 per cent per century during the next 1,700 years, as this period includes the collapse of the Roman Empire and the technological descent into the Middle Ages. At the beginning of this period, however, the mold-board plow was invented, permitting the heavy soils of northern Europe to support much heavier settlements;[3] and during these 1,700 years, China rose to its peak of power and culture. The phenomenal population explosion of the last three centuries, of course, has come on the heels of the Industrial Revolution and the opening up of new lands to civilized colonization.

It can be said safely that the world-wide population growth has not been uniform at any time since the neolithic revolution, at least. While populations in some areas were waxing, those in other areas remained stable or declined. As an example, Ortega states that the population of Europe rose from 180 million to 460 million in about a century after 1800,[4] a 156 per cent increase compared to an increase of about 78 per cent for the world as a whole during the same period. By comparison, the Tasmanians became extinct during the nineteenth century and local populations were exterminated in many areas of Asia, Africa, and America.

Differential rates of population increase constitute a raw measure of comparative success in the competition among *Massen*, as twentieth century dictators have recognized. This is always true when biological populations compete in the same ecological niche. If the two populations are in the same species, as human populations are, the genes characteristic of the more fertile population augment their claim to represent the entire species and, unless changed circumstances halt the trend, may replace the less fertile population completely. Competition among human *Massen* is far less often military than economic and cultural; the *Masse* with the superior means of exploiting resources and the more efficient social organization thrives and grows, while its competitor languishes. If the thesis that the creative contributions of *H. individualis* are responsible for improvements in social and technological methods is correct, those

[3] E. M. Jope, "Agricultural Implements," in Charles Singer *et al.*, eds., *A History of Technology* (New York: Oxford University Press, 1956), II, 86–90.

[4] Ortega y Gasset, *La Rebelión de las masas*, p. 60.

Massen which possess an influential component of *H. indivi-dualis*—a creative minority—succeed in this form of competition. *Ergo*, the genes characteristic of *H. individualis* themselves participate in the general population increase of the *Masse* and are strengthened as species traits. Such natural selection among *Massen* augments the natural selection affecting individuals and may be more important than the latter in the historical spread of *H. individualis* as a species variant.

Migration is the major activity through which the competitive force of the expanding population operates. In other animal species, various social mechanisms operate to trigger migration in response to overpopulation in relation to food supply.[5] This animal process invites obvious comparison to migrations of human peoples,[6] but in the case of man more subtle factors than dietetic motivations may also be involved. Population pressure on the food supply clearly was responsible for the great Irish emigrations of the nineteenth century and may have had a part in the ancient Greek colonization of the Mediterranean area; but it was less apparent in the extensive migrations of the British peoples, which have increased genes of that stock 50-fold since 1600, compared to a world population increase of only 6-fold.[7] There have been very few habitable areas in the world which were not already occupied at some level of population density during historical times; therefore, migration results in either replacement of one population by another or mixture of two populations—in either case, a considerable change in the genetic composition of the invaded area. This change, even when the invaders are absorbed, is *toward* the invaders' general genotype insofar as it differs from that of the aborigines, because some genes of the invader genotype did not exist at all in the area previously. When the population increase that leads to migra-

[5] V. C. Wynne-Edwards, *Animal Dispersion in Relation to Social Behavior* (New York: Hafner, 1962), *passim*.

[6] Hudson Hoagland, "Cybernetics of Population Control," in *Human Ecology*, ed. Jack B. Bresler (Reading, Mass.: Addison-Wesley, 1966), p. 357.

[7] F. S. Hulse, cited by Dobzhansky, *Mankind Evolving*, p. 284.

tion is the result of creative contributions to technology or culture, rather than some natural enhancement of the food supply, the effect of the migration is to disseminate the genes of *H. individualis.*

The picture is rarely that simple, of course, in a highly variable species such as man. After all, "*H. individualis*" and "*H. socialis*" are terms chosen discursively to represent variant elements—heterogeneous within themselves—of the same human species. The *H. socialis* component of a *Masse*, as well as its *H. individualis* component, derives fertility benefits from the contributions of *H. individualis*; further, the neighbors of a *Masse*, without a creative minority of their own, may adopt elements of its technology and culture by mimesis, experience a fertility rise of their own, and be drawn to immigration into or conquest of the cultural "heartland" by the prospect of sharing in its comparative wealth. Barbaric forms of social living typical of steppe and savannah areas in historic times foster some traits of the *H. individualis* personality and, as will be examined subsequently, the great movements of Semites, Aryans, and Mongols in the distant past represented in part an influx of these characteristics into civilized regions; but they also represented to some degree a resurgence of characteristics of the old *H. socialis* hunting pack into *Massen* leavened and uplifted by a *H. individualis* component.

Changes in population character, whether toward or away from a higher ratio of *H. individualis*, can occur through the same migration process *within* a *Masse*. Kulischer states that after the mid-nineteenth century there was a heavy migration of former serfs from eastern Germany into western Germany to fill industrial jobs.[8] The fertility rate had fallen off in western Germany, and he estimates that by the early years of this century 40 per cent of the population of the west German industrial centers was of east German extraction. Kulischer sees the westerly migration of people whose ancestors had been agri-

[8] Eugene M. Kulischer, *Europe on the Move* (New York: Columbia University Press, 1948), pp. 163–66.

cultural serfs under Junker overlords for centuries as responsible for a "change in quality" of the German people, the rise of the Prussian mentality, the submergence of the intellectual atmosphere typified by Goethe and Schiller, the progressive "barbarization" of Germany, and much of Germany's part of the blame for the two world wars. This sort of migration within a *Masse*, altering the *Masse*'s dominant character in the direction of that of the migrating element, is closely related to similar changes as a result of differential fertility among population elements living in the same area, which will be examined in detail later.

A brief survey of the effects of variations in population size and fertility rate on the social influence of *H. individualis*, at different collective levels, leads us to consideration of the ultimate determining factor: the effect of natural selection on individuals in different demographic conditions. No environment, natural or social, affects a total population with equal force. Aside from the fact that an environment is rarely homogeneous and individual members of the population are born into different portions of it, no two individuals are equipped exactly alike genetically for dealing with the environment. The population range thus normally includes those who are best adapted to the environment, those whose adaptation to the environment is so poor that they die without issue, and all grades of adaptation in between, from those almost at the peak of health and success to those constantly at death's door and interminably beset by ill luck.[9] In a stable environment and in the absence of modifying factors, the successful reproductive rate tends to vary in positive ratio to adaptability (by "successful" reproductive rate is meant the number of progeny who not only survive but also produce progeny themselves); and those characteristics of the better-adapted individuals which are genetically determined tend to increase in representation and influence in the population.

A given environment does not exert a single, unidirectional

[9] Cf. Ernst Mayr, *Animal Species and Evolution* (Cambridge: Harvard University Press, 1963), pp. 186–87.

selective force, however, but a complex of interacting selective pressures of varying importance. When the environment changes, the relative weight of selective pressures is apt to change, too. In extreme cases, an individual trait that was deadly before the environmental change may become advantageous, whereas a previously adaptive trait may lose its advantage. An oft-cited example is the European peppered moth, *Biston betularia*. Under natural forest conditions, the light-colored moths of this species blend in hue with the background of lichen-covered tree trunks, whereas dark mutants are more visible to predatory birds and are usually eliminated; but in industrial areas where smoke from chimneys darkens the tree trunks, the selective advantage is reversed and dark populations have replaced light ones completely in some regions. The analogy to a theoretical change in the relative survival value of pack cooperation versus individual initiative in early man is apparent.

Relative population size, relative population increase (or decrease), and relative population density not only reflect relative collective success in adapting to the selective complex of the environment, but they also are themselves important variables in the environmental complex exerting selective pressure upon individuals. Of the three variables, relative population density probably exerts the most force.

Some of the effects of population density are purely Malthusian; population density usually is the end result of a population increase that presses the number of people ever more closely against resource limitations. For example, in an area of northern India cited by Huntington,[10] the population rose from 30 or 40 million to about 180 million in the years between 1600 and 1900. A laborer's daily wage bought twice as much food in 1600 as in 1900 and it was more nourishing food, including more meat and butter in the diet. One change in absolute selective pressure during this 300-year period is easily seen; an in-

[10] Ellsworth Huntington, *Mainsprings of Civilization* (Mentor ed., New York: New American Library, 1959), pp. 450–51.

dividual who was unable to find any profession but that of a laborer had less chance of surviving and reproducing at the end of the period than at its beginning. It would be difficult to say, however, what psychological traits are most favored or obstructed by natural selection as a result of a dense population relative to resources; and psychological traits are at issue in differentiating *H. individualis* from *H. socialis*.

Some modern experiments and observations, on the other hand, notably those of Calhoun with rats, show biological and psychological effects with strong selective implications as a consequence of population density alone, where food and other resources were completely adequate. When Norway rats were crowded at a density twice that determined to be normal, their usual patterns of social behavior were disrupted by such phenomena as abortion and infant mortality, failure of care for the young, sexual aberration, hyperactivity, and withdrawal from social interaction.[11] The distribution of these behavioral phenomena represents the response of individually differentiated genetic equipment to severe environmental pressure, and their reproductive consequences represent a selective process operating upon that genetic equipment. Coon cites an experiment in which mutation in a single gene location resulted in a fruitfly able to live in populations three times as dense as previously.[12]

Rat behavior is not a guide to human behavior, and neither is fruitfly behavior. But some evidence has been accumulated that a meaningful parallel exists in the area of response to population density. The work of Christian and others showed that at least some of the phenomena associated with crowding in mammals resulted from acute physiological stress, which affects glandular processes violently. Many concentration camp deaths are thought to have been caused by stress. Further, the be-

[11] John B. Calhoun, "Population Density and Social Pathology," *Scientific American*, Feb., 1962; briefed by Garrett Hardin, *Population, Evolution, & Birth Control* (San Francisco: W. H. Freeman & Co., 1964), pp. 80–85; summarized by Hoagland in *Human Ecology*, pp. 353–56.

[12] Carleton S. Coon, *The Origin of Races* (New York: Alfred A. Knopf, 1962), p. 110n.

havioral symptoms exhibited by overcrowded rats are highly reminiscent of some problem behavior of humans in crowded urban areas, especially in slums, manifested in delinquency, hypertension or apathy, and increased incidence of such ailments as schizophrenia and cardiovascular diseases. Coon believes that selection by neuroendocrinological competition is a new, non-Malthusian evolutionary concept.[13]

Of particular interest in relation to the evolutionary history of the human creative personality are the dislocations of hierarchical behavior observed by Calhoun among overcrowded rats. The normal settlement of males into a status structure was replaced by two extreme social forms, differentiated on the basis of the four interconnecting pens, which were arranged in sequence. In each of the end pens, a single dominant male ruled over a harem of females, as well as a group of extremely subordinate males who never engaged in sexual activity; reproduction by females, nesting, and care of young were normal and healthy in those pens. Most of the males crowded themselves into the center pens (whereas females were about equally divided among the pens) and engaged in frequent fighting, with now one and now another male assuming the dominant position. In these pens there was such disruption of reproductive behavior that in one experiment 99 per cent of the young died before weaning. In addition to the constantly fighting dominant, or "alpha," group of males in the center pens, three other kinds of males were identified there: homosexual males, extremely passive males, and hyperactive males that were also hypersexual and sometimes cannibalistic. Carrighar has observed that overcrowding in some animal species leads to prostasia, a hierarchical social order based on aggressive dominance.[14]

Although no exact analogy can be drawn, we can see in the densely populated portions of our own society interesting parallels to the intense status struggles of Calhoun's "alpha"

[13] *Ibid.*, p. 111.
[14] Sally Carrighar, *Wild Heritage* (Boston: Houghton Mifflin, 1965), pp. 175–77.

rats of the inner pens, to the homosexuals, to those which have withdrawn pathologically from society, and to the hypersexual and hyperactive "probers," as Calhoun called them (no contemporary instances of cannibalism come to mind). As for the prostasia mentioned by Carrighar, its most recent notable manifestations were in the German Nazi and Italian Fascist states, and it is also evidenced in modified form in most Communist political structures.

Prostasia represents an extreme form of a hierarchical social order present in most historical human societies, both preliterate and civilized. One may assume with little danger of error that, if inherited behavior patterns exist in the human species as in other mammalian species, the tendency to arrange social relationships in a hierarchical order is one such "instinct" possessed by man. Such a human "instinct" conforms both to the necessity that children learn from their elders for a long period and to the practice of mimesis which has been set forth as a trait of *H. socialis*. It is not difficult to discern that prostasia is positively related to Popper's "closed society"—the magical, tribal, or collectivist society—and negatively related to his "open society"—the society in which individuals are confronted by personal decisions.[15] The creative individualist—who, by definition, is more at home in the open society—obviously suffers restrictions in a rigid hierarchy.

The paleolithic hunting culture was not as much of an open society as might be assumed on the basis of its small populations (in relation to later civilized populations) and its direct contact with a demanding natural environment. Its technological level was so low that close, organized cooperation in the hunt and the orderly distribution of spoils presumably required strict, if informal, lines and levels of authority and privilege. The neolithic revolution probably marked man's first tentative step toward an open society. It brought technological advances raising the level of man's ability to cope with the environment; it broke

[15] Karl R. Popper, *The Open Society and Its Enemies* (Torchbook ed., New York: Harper & Row, 1963), I, 173.

up typical pack activities; and, most important, its conditions required some freedom of individualistic creativity as the price of survival.

Post-neolithic man divided into two broad social forms in Asia and northern Africa, the agricultural-civilized and the pastoral-nomadic. Both forms possessed characteristics favoring *H. individualis*, and both possessed characteristics hostile to him. Huntington has noted how the nomadic life constitutes a social environment permissive of individualistic traits; that is, it embraces an essentially democratic way of life, mobility, and the necessity that individuals be resourceful, dependent on initiative, and self-reliant.[16] On the other hand, close organization and obedience to authority are needed in raids and migrations, and the sparse, loose social structure bars the accumulation of a cultural background providing the soil for advanced innovation. In the growing cities of the deltas and river valleys, manifold cultural contacts and a frequent surplus of resources provided the incentives for creativity, and a variety of social niches offered the individualist more opportunity to find a hospitable role than did the uniform economy of the steppes. But as population density increased in the sedentary areas, the need grew for closer communal control of more complex social relationships, and authoritarian governments and organized military establishments were required increasingly for defense against the nomads. The nomad culture maintained its hospitality to individualism at a low but significant level; the urban cultures were more permissive of individualism at first but gradually developed an ever more rigid prostasia.

The foregoing résumé of the impact of the post-neolithic social environment upon the mutant, *H. individualis*, who was responsible for it, highlights one very important point: the cultural process which *H. individualis* initiates may develop to a stage at which it reacts against him. This reaction comes about when the centers of culture and control of those *Massen* that he has influenced achieve such social success that their popula-

[16] Huntington, *Mainsprings of Civilization*, pp. 180ff.

tion reaches the numbers and density requiring advanced and increasingly rigid hierarchical structures in order to keep the machinery of society moving. A strict hierarchy demands a conformity to regulation that makes the individualist dangerous to the welfare of the state, and the freedom of thought necessary to creativity is looked upon with suspicion. Absolute population density may appear in areas of the *Masse*, bringing with it tensions and pathological behavior that not only constitute a peril to the survival and normal reproduction of individuals living within those areas but also create a social atmosphere in which individual independence and creativity are impossible.

In the long run, the factors that react against *H. individualis* undermine the success of the *Masse*, and it declines. *H. individualis* suffers a selective disadvantage—a fertility disadvantage—because *H. socialis* is naturally able to adapt better to the mimesis and conformity to regulation demanded by increasing hierarchical rigidity. The statistical consequence is to make the densely populated *Masse* more "social" collectively, due to the percentage increase of *H. socialis* in the population and the accompanying percentage loss of its "leaders"—leaders in the sense of those capable of creative innovation, rather than in the sense of those who exercise social dominance.

There was justification, then, for the foreboding of both Ortega and Polybius, but on different grounds. Polybius viewed a society already in the stage of decline, a dwindling population in a Greece that had attained the peak of creative success and, through the social mechanisms set in motion by that very success, had destroyed or driven away its creative minority. Ortega, with a true instinct, saw the gradual reversion to primitive psychology in a modern context, with the surge in population growth which precedes decline and brings it about by requiring ever stricter authoritarianism and social regulation and by creating pockets of pathological density in the cultural centers of civilization.

86

CHAPTER NINE

THE GRECO-CHRISTIAN GIFT

*Liberty of spirit, that is to say, potency of intellect, is
measured by the capacity to dissociate ideas
traditionally inseparable.*

—José Ortega y Gasset: *La Rebelión de las masas*

MAN MAY BE THE MOST swiftly evolving animal in the
world right now, and not one in whom evolution has
ceased, as some anthropologists believe. Their belief is based
on the lack of evidence for such gross physiological changes as
testify to evolutionary processes in other species, including
man's own ancestors. Man is so fundamentally a thinking animal, however, and the nature of the environment he has created
for himself is so unique, that human evolution, logically and
primarily, should proceed in the tremendously complex network of his cerebral cells, where its effects would not be visible
directly but be manifested only in the results of man's thinking activity.

The results of man's thinking activity are apparent in history, and I submit that it is more reasonable to look upon them
as evidence of continued evolution of the cerebral area than
as the opportune unfolding of a potential already present in
prehistoric times. I do not believe, for example, that a Crô-
Magnon infant could adapt himself to the modern metropolitan
environment as easily as a contemporary infant who is heir to
forty generations of Western civilization.

The neolithic revolution has been depicted as an isolable
highlight of man's cerebral evolution. It should be possible
theoretically to isolate other events illustrative of this evolution.
One, which I should like to label conveniently an "individ-

ualistic revolution," reached its climax around the middle of the first millennium B.C. and set the basic pattern for Eurasian civilizations of the post-Christian era.

The sixth century B.C. saw the birth of Zoroaster in Persia, the Buddha and Mahavira in India, Confucius and Lao-Tse in China, and Pythagoras in Samos. It was the century of such men as Thales, Anaximander, and Heraclitus in Ionia, of Solon in Athens, and the last of the major prophets in Israel. In China, iron was introduced and the "hundred schools" of philosophers arose. The pivotal importance of the sixth century to modern civilization of both East and West is not difficult to discern. The Hebrew prophets and, to a lesser extent, Zoroaster laid the ethical and metaphysical foundations of Judaism, Christianity, and Islam; Buddha, Confucius, Mahavira, and Lao-Tse did the same for the great Oriental religions. At the same time, the Ionian thinkers were working out the basic concepts on which modern Western science is founded. The Athenian political institutions established by Solon stand in direct ancestral line to those of modern America and Europe.

For each recorded name and progressive step during such a period, we must assume the existence of an extensive stratum of contributing individuals and contributory innovations, many of them ignored by recorded history and missed by subsequent research. Assuming that creative individualism is genetically based, the existence of such a stratum signifies more than a purely cultural phenomenon. The outstanding individualist represents a rare concentration of typical *H. individualis* genes, and such a concentration is more likely statistically when the incidence of these genes is high in the population. A high incidence would also imply a supporting stratum of individualists of lesser stature.

Other circumstances of that time bear out the supposition of a widespread social ferment. Ionia and Attica were moving out of the period which has been called the Greek Middle Ages, and Ionian ships explored as far west as Britain. As iron appeared in China, steel appeared in the Middle East. Cyrus the Great

conquered Babylon and founded the Persian Empire, the culture of which was to impress Alexander the Great so profoundly two centuries later. Republican and democratic states
existed all over India, and the "classical" period of culture was
dawning in China. Only Egypt remained essentially static,
despite a minor cultural revival under Psametik.

The sixth-century "individualistic revolution" could not have
been a rootless phenomenon, especially if genetically based. To
speculate on its origins, we must glance back a thousand years
or more before it, when the two major streams of post-neolithic
culture—the urban-agricultural and the nomad-pastoral—began to collide and merge for the first time on an extensive scale.
At that time, the two oldest civilizations, Sumeria and Egypt,
already were more than 2,000 years old. They had had ample
time to undergo the genetic process described in the last chapter: the effective dissipation of a creative minority through
discrimination against *H. individualis* by means of rigid social
regulation and the demand for conformity. The Indus Valley,
Minoan, and Chinese civilizations were much younger, but they
had progressed far enough toward urbanization to offer a rich
cultural potential for spectacular development under the impact of creative forces either from within or from without.

Upon this complex of civilizations there descended the
charioteers from the grasslands like a flood throughout the middle of the second millennium B.C. These invading nomads and
semi-nomads—Indo-European speaking peoples, Mongols, and
Semites—lacked the environmental and cultural background
making civilized innovations possible, but all of them came
from a natural and cultural environment that demanded a
democratic sort of individual freedom and self-reliance. They
possessed and treasured the very traits which urbanization and
the practice of stabilized agriculture had tended to breed out
of the civilized peoples, including an impatience with strict and
repetitive routine and the inclination to interpret reality directly from nature instead of from social tradition.

As an example, we may take the Indo-Europeans, who are

most important to the subsequent course of our own Western civilization. Thought to have originated in the Caucasus region, they were mobile, cattle-raising folk who had the dog and the horse. Linton[1] pictures the typical "Aryan" society as three-leveled: the nobility and the commoners, both Aryan, and the serfs or conquered population. There were no kings as such, but families producing leaders over several generations formed an aristocracy. Differences between nobles and commoners depended primarily on wealth and prestige. High value was attached to individual independence and initiative, and sons of the patrilineal families were on their own when they came of age.

Although what started the grasslands peoples on their migrations is not known certainly, the cause might have been climatic changes. The Thermal Maximum of 5000 to 3500 B.C., during which the climate was generally warmer and more moist than now, was followed by a long drying period, climaxing about 2200 B.C. Huntington set forth the theory, accepted provisionally by Toynbee, that the great nomadic invasions from the Eurasian steppes were set in motion by periods of aridity in the nomads' homelands, reducing pasturage for their cattle and creating temporary overpopulation in the steppes.

At any rate, the Indo-Europeans conquered India some time between 1700 and 1550 B.C. Other Indo-Europeans, the Kassites, attacked Babylon as early as 1746 B.C., and still others, the Hittites, burned the city in 1595 B.C. The Indo-European Achaeans began moving down on the mainland holdings of the Minoan civilization in Attica about 1400 B.C., and the Hittites had long been putting pressure on the other side of Ionia. Long before, Semitic nomads from the Arabian steppes had moved into the Tigris-Euphrates region to worry the Sumerians and had founded Babylon. The Hyksos, very probably Semites, invaded Egypt some time after 1700 B.C. but were ejected after two centuries of rule. Chinese tradition has it that the Shang dynasty was founded about 1520 B.C. by invaders, probably

[1] Ralph Linton, *The Tree of Culture* (New York: Alfred A. Knopf, 1955), pp. 261ff.

Mongols; Fairservis sees even an Indo-European influence upon the Shang.[2]

The grasslands charioteers were barbarian destroyers; but when they shattered the structures of the civilizations, they made possible their rebuilding along somewhat different and perhaps more progressive lines. I suggest, too, that, moving in as conquerors and remaining as a ruling class, the nomads brought both a cultural outlook and an infusion of genes which turned the accumulated riches of the old cities to new and more vigorous account. I think the genetic and cultural mixture of prairie independence and urban sophistication brought about eventually the "individualistic revolution."

During the millennium preceding 500 B.C., almost all of the established civilizations were overthrown and revivified in different form by the invaders from the steppes. The Indus Valley civilization was succeeded by the later Indian culture; the semi-legendary Hsia kingdom of China, by the Shang dynasty; the Minoan civilization, by the Hellenic; Sumeria, Elam, and Hatti, by Babylonia and Assyria and finally by the Persian Empire. Only Egypt endured, and the nearest approach it made to rejuvenation in the same terms as the others was the brief monotheistic rebellion of the Pharaoh Ikhnaton (Amenhotep IV) in the fourteenth century B.C. against the priestly theological system. Although Ikhnaton failed to accomplish anything permanent in Egypt, if Freud's theory that his monotheism influenced that of Moses and the Jews[3] is correct it brought consequences of major and lasting import to Western history.

Of these ancient civilizations revivified in the "individualistic revolution," the one generally considered to be "apparented" (to use Toynbee's term) to our own Western civilization is the Hellenic. Such apparentation, quite obviously, was not the direct development of one civilization into another. The magnifi-

---

[2] Walter A. Fairservis, Jr., *The Origins of Oriental Civilization* (New York: New American Library, 1959), pp. 130–32.

[3] Sigmund Freud, *Moses and Monotheism*, trans. Katherine Jones (Vintage ed., New York: Vintage Books, 1959), pp. 21ff.

cent social structure of the Roman Empire, the final phase of the Hellenic civilization, all but crushed individualistic enterprise as it reverted to the faceless collectivism of the earlier empires. It took a new infusion of freedom, vigor, and individualism from beyond the northern marches to clear away the deadwood of the Roman state and make room for the new growth of European civilization. The cattle-raising people swept over the decaying Roman Empire as they had swept over other empires time after time in the past.

More clearly than in other historical lines, we see here an ebb and flow of individualistic creativity: the neolithic revolution breaks the shell of primitive collectivism and then sinks back into the collectivism of the first empires; the "individualistic revolution" shatters the ancient imperial collectivism but in turn devolves into the collectivism of Rome; then the northern barbarians destroy Roman collectivism. This, of course, raises a pertinent question for man today. If the cycle is being repeated and the trend is once more approaching the collectivism of the distant past, it is essentially world-wide. There are no great reservoirs of grassland barbarians left. Our barbarians will have to come from somewhere else.

The swing back toward collectivism was already well under way during that period of ancient Greek history most familiar to us. The much-admired Greek Classical period which ensued from the social ferment of the sixth century actually was a period of ripeness and beginning intellectual decline. The greatest creative thinkers of the Hellenic civilization were one to two centuries earlier than Plato and Aristotle, whose thought exhibits an autumnal finality. Miletos, not Athens, might have come to us as the focal point of Hellenic brilliance if its creative works had been as well preserved.

The logical processes of the ancient Hellenic thinkers have a more familiar flavor for us than those of any of their predecessors or contemporaries; they are like a sneak preview of the modern Western mind. Indeed, they are our intellectual ancestors, as the Jews are our moral ancestors. For this reason, it is important to examine briefly how each of the two orientations, Hellenic and Jewish, contributed to the ethical background against which Western views of the relation of the individual to his society have developed.

To find the wellsprings of the Hellenic upsurge of individualism—keeping in mind Ortega's equation of "liberty of spirit" and "power of intellect"[4]—we need only be familiar with the cogitations of the great Greek thinkers. Here are men who are concerned with the question of justice, not merely in its social sense but in its cosmic sense. The question of justice in its social sense is essentially pragmatic: "How much of his natural right should an individual be required to sacrifice for the sake of efficient social interaction?" The question of justice in its cosmic sense is essentially idealistic: "Why should any individual be required to sacrifice any of his natural right if he has not intentionally sinned against the universe?" The latter question is, *per se*, a criticism of society; it recognizes that society cannot fulfil a portion of its *raison d'être*, for man assembles socially as much for spiritual self-expression as for material benefit, and the one increases only at the expense of the other in the social context.

Here we touch upon the ultimate measure of individualism, as it is the ultimate measure of any genuine science and art: the broader reference point of the universe, instead of the intrinsically narrow reference point of human relations and the social context in which they occur. The concept of justice in the cosmic sense does not arise from a sense of social identity and social welfare, but from a sense of individualism—the differentiation and comparative rights of *individuals.*

At least by the time our eyes are drawn to the stage of Greek history, however, the Hellenic concept of cosmic justice was a matter of academic and philosophical rather than pragmatic concern. It contributed intellectually to Western individualism, but before the theoretical concept could instigate widespread

[4] José Ortega y Gasset, *La Rebelión de las masas* (Madrid: Espasa-Calpe, S. A., 1937), p. 55n.

action it had to be impregnated with moral urgency. This necessary moral element was supplied by a provincial and intransigent little people who believed fiercely in the righteousness of a God who noted every sparrow's fall: the Jews.

The Jews, too, were originally grasslands people. The Roman historian Josephus identified the Israelites with the Hyksos, those invaders of Egypt from the Arabian grasslands, whereas the Greeks and Romans sprang from Indo-European peoples who originated in the Asiatic grasslands. The semi-nomadic backgrounds are similar, but the development of ethical thought proceeded along different lines.

The Jews were more social (more race-conscious, *Masse*-conscious, nationalistic) than the Greeks. On the other hand, the Jewish people and the elite of ancient Greece had one characteristic in common which is not generally recognized; both placed God above society. The Jews did so in an emotional, deeply religious way; the Greek intellectuals did so by subordinating belief in the arbitrary action of orthodox (originally tribal) gods to a belief in the existence of universal, rational laws. Both orientations recognized a cosmic reality superior to social laws.

Under the Jewish concept of monotheistic divinity, a justice superior to social justice could not only nullify social justice, if God so desired—as witness the case of Job—but could visit reward or punishment upon the *Masse* itself. The Greeks sought to comprehend social justice, the Jews, divine justice; and, though different, they are the same in their devastating effect upon pragmatic morality.

Indications are that a tremendous force of individualism existed *in potentia* among the Jews—a potential not fully realized because the individualistic force was suppressed by an extraordinary social solidarity, forced upon the Jews by their exposure to powerful enemies. Then, the turbulent forces in the Jewish *Masse* brought on the revolt against the Romans, the destruction of Jerusalem in A.D. 70, and the eventual dispersion of the Jews. This dispersion itself contributed greatly to the advancement of individualism in the Western world but not so much as the appearance and teachings of Jesus.

In retrospect, Jesus appears to have exemplified in his person and thought the sum of the individualistic rebellion within the Jewish *Masse*. Even though one of the major, and probably unforeseen, effects of his teachings was the establishment of an orthodox church, which reacted against individualism, another and much more important effect was a system of morality oriented to the equal value of individuals in the eyes of God, no matter what their earthly lot. The latter influence of Jesus was to profoundly affect the biological direction of the human psyche. Serious abstract thought was to turn increasingly to the implications of such a cosmic concept of justice, and the social environment thereby became more hospitable to individualism.

Greek rationalism and Jewish monotheism bestowed upon the individual the philosophical authority to criticize society, through their concepts of a law superior to the social law. Christianity went further; its theology developed the concept of a heavenly social law, an ideal law of interhuman relations applying universally to individuals uniformly imperfect in comparison to God, uniformly tainted with the original sin of Adam. This was a step forward. It measured sociality by a stricter yardstick, representing an effort to combine social law and cosmic law ideally in the philosophical milieu of a hoped-for heaven. In such measurement, social law, even the law of the church itself, often was found wanting.

In addition, the Christian ideology of justice and morality contained its own abstract contradictions. Since a precondition of this ideology was that it represented divine perfection, some of the best minds of the Western world devoted themselves to analyzing and rationalizing this perfection. It may be said that the roots of self-satisfied Victorianism lay in the soul-searching of the Middle Ages. Modern individual consciousness springs in part from the philosophical conflicts inherent in the attempt

95

to translate Jesus' teachings into terms for which they were not spoken—a practical social structure. In other words, the attempt was made to give unto Cæsar that which belonged to God.

In this development of individualistic consciousness, rather than in its more social ideologies, lies Christianity's greatest contribution to human progress. By creating the motivation for the individual to question *cosmic* reality acutely and consciously, it fostered a genetic increase of *H. individualis*, not just a transient cultural adaptation. It is possible that in his words, "I have not come to bring peace, but a sword," Jesus exhibited awareness of the ultimate effect of his pitting the value of individual rectitude and justice against that social orientation which subjugates the judgment and conscience of the individual to communal interest. However legendary or however historically accurate it may be, the part played by Pontius Pilate in the drama of Christ exemplifies social orientation and dependence upon social justification, in counterpoint to the magnificent and solitary figure of Jesus, the victim of social injustice.

CHAPTER TEN

IN EQUAL CHAINS

All men are, by nature, unequal—
this is the censored truth of our century.

—GARRETT HARDIN: *Nature and Man's Fate*

IT IS PERHAPS SIGNIFICANT that Thomas Jefferson described men as born "equal and independent" in his draft of the Declaration of Independence. As it was finally adopted, the document omitted the word "independent."

Despite this prophetic omission, the original orientation of American social philosophy was more libertarian than egalitarian. In one sense, the real American Revolution was not in 1776, nor yet (as Jefferson proclaimed) when the Republicans ousted the Federalists in 1800, but in 1828 when Andrew Jackson was elected. The libertarian basis of the American system was replaced by an egalitarian one at that time. Marx considered the individual inconsequential as an historical factor. The Russian Communists at least have not made the modern American mistake of equating theoretical human equality with human freedom. The French in 1789 did consider *liberté, egalité, fraternité* simultaneously realizable, but by the revolution of 1848 they were more concerned with the opposition of social classes and less so with individual liberty.

In fact, the various American, French, and Russian revolutions of the last two centuries all fit into a consistent pattern that shows the philosophy of Western society developing toward increasing egalitarianism. In view of the essential cultural unity of the West, it is not surprising that the Russian Revolution was egalitarian rather than libertarian, reflecting the long way Western society had traveled on the road toward egalitarianism since 1776.

97

The origins and development of the now-dominant egalitarian orientation in Western civilization can be traced, in general terms. As previously noted, Western individualistic philosophy is founded on the Greco-Christian concept of justice as being the equality of all in the sight of God. This concept is a direct continuation of the traditional Jewish differentiation of the divine from the mundane. Under this concept originally, equality of spiritual right did not extend to equality of an earthly lot, which the truly religious must consider essentially inconsequential. For a long time, egalitarianism had no expression beyond this. As a fundamental philosophy, however, it had gained its foothold. It was present, ready to be activated in a more practical realm when conditions were right.

Dobzhansky[1] observes that the idea of biological equality arises from its confusion with ethical and legal equality, but that it is entirely different. An attempt to resolve such confusion leads to two questions: (*a*) Is the idea of biological equality valid? (*b*) If it is not, how can ethical and legal equality be justified?

As for biological equality, let us take two individuals differentiated by only a few of those physiological variations listed by Williams.[2] Individual A has twice as many heart beats per minute as Individual B, half again as many blood cells per cubic millimeter, nearly twice as much phosphate concentration in the blood and three times as much protein-bound iodine, fifteen times as much Vitamin A concentrated in the blood, thyroid glands six times heavier and gonads four times heavier, and eleven times as much androgens concentrated in the urine; Individual A requires eight times as much alcohol concentration in the blood to become intoxicated, has nearly half again as much oxygen in the blood at 44,000 feet elevation, needs four

[1] Theodosius Dobzhansky, *Mankind Evolving* (New Haven: Yale University Press, 1962), pp. 52–53.

[2] Roger J. Williams, *Biochemical Individuality* (New York: John Wiley & Sons, 1956), pp. 28, 33, 50, 53, 56, 81, 87–88, 108, 125, 137, 152.

times as much calcium and Vitamin B1, and, although both A and B have 20-20 vision, A perceives movement forty-two times more easily in peripheral vision.

Each of these variations has been found, by these factors or more, to occur in "normal" individuals. They represent individual differences which have at least a partial genetic basis, although how much has not been fully determined. They are differences that would affect the psychological characteristics of the two individuals. Individual A could be expected to be more energetic and alert than Individual B, and more strongly sexed. He would be a better aviator and a better mountainclimber, would handle himself more intelligently at a drinking party, and would be less likely to be killed by a stalking wild animal or a speeding automobile.

Biological egalitarianism is a fiction. It is, furthermore, so convenient to certain sociological and political theories that it is difficult not to believe that it is a deliberate fiction.

Such physiological differences as those depicted above could affect the principle of ethical and legal equality. Individual A, for example, should not be convicted of driving while drunk on the basis of the same test as Individual B. To assign to him the same responsibility for control of his actions at the same level of sexual provocation would be questionable. He would require a richer diet in some respects in order to remain in good health, and this fact could lead to wide legal and ethical ramifications.

On this basis, the validity of legal and ethical egalitarianism also would appear to be a fiction. Indeed, in order for it to be valid, certain complexities, such as individual differences in susceptibility to intoxication, should be taken into consideration. But the logical extreme to which this carries us is the principle of preferential treatment on the basis of inherent superiority; and the example of many societies characterized by class distinction shows that such a principle is just as suppressive of individualism as is fanatic egalitarianism.

Resolution of the difficulty lies in the recognition that both the principle of preferential treatment and the principle of egalitarianism are *social* principles. Both represent efforts to deal with the phenomenon of individualism in social terms, whereas individualism is a phenomenon of a different philosophical order from sociality and cannot be resolved completely in social terms.

The principle of preferential treatment and the egalitarian ethic are opposed to each other only in the philosophical context of sociality. From the individualistic standpoint, they are phenomena of a similar nature, and one usually merges into the other, e. g., historical developments in both the United States and modern Russia. In opposition to both, individualism puts forward the libertarian ethic. Legal and ethical egalitarianism is valid in its effort to reconcile natural inequality with justice. Its imperfections are unavoidable, but they are lessened when the libertarian ethic is given its proper due.

The egalitarian and libertarian ethics are commonly confused in modern thought because of the opposition of both, at different levels, to the principle of preferential treatment. This confusion is of very ancient vintage, and its appearance now may be a symptom of regression in social thinking.

Sociality is a "coaction for affirmation." Its justification originally, as a substitute for free individualism, lay in the necessity for it to deal with the environment, if *individuals* were to survive. Within the context of sociality, individual competition expressed itself in a struggle for preferential treatment. The outcome of this struggle was the hierarchical structure of the primitive *Masse*. The criterion of survival applied to the *Masse* as a whole. If the *Masse* failed, its individual members were lost. Thus, preferential treatment (status within the hierarchy) had to be correlated rather well with individual ability and responsibility, for the sake of efficiency in *Masse* organization.

Yet, the *Masse* had to guarantee a minimum level of existence to all of its members, for the *Masse* could not operate without those at its lower hierarchical levels, as well as those at its higher levels. At the minimum level of existence, the egalitarianism of necessity presented its constant demands, a submerged counterbalance to the principle of preferential treatment. The prehistoric breakup of primitive social solidarity strengthened this submerged egalitarianism and gradually made it a social factor.

The creative individualist, in ratio to his individualistic tendencies, shuns high status within the hierarchy, for that, too, has its own conformist requirements. Rather, he aims at freedom *apart from* the hierarchy. In this aim, he sometimes has found in egalitarianism—the right of *all* individuals to certain social minima—an ally against the principle of preferential treatment, which would have made his freedom contingent upon achievement of hierarchical status (and this, as often as not, proves to be no freedom at all).

Both the basic freedom of action and the creative activity sought by individualism require a subsistence (economic) level higher than that prevailing at any but the higher hierarchical levels in most past societies. The individualist, then, rejecting the hierarchical status conferring the leisure and freedom he desired and at the same time retaining his desire for leisure and freedom, adopted the view that freedom and leisure should not be confined to high hierarchical status.

The individualist actually sought a libertarian ethic divorcing him from the economic limitations of society, so he could live and prosper without having to conform to the demands of others. He could not know this, usually, because the collective ego remained such an ingrained (indeed, instinctive) element of the human psyche. Even had he known it, society would have denied him its realization, for society's role as a coaction for affirmation implies control of the total economic structure affecting its members. Thus, economic egalitarianism, for many centuries, remained only a theoretical and utopian context in which the imaginative individualist felt that his kind could find freedom from the poverty of low hierarchical status under the principle of preferential treatment.

Only exceptional circumstances, such as those in parts of Western civilization today, have ever made it remotely possible to translate such utopian theory into practice. The contemporary circumstances are local and probably temporary, a reversal of the classic Malthusian formula, made possible because subsistence has increased faster than population.

Colonization of the Western Hemisphere, sparsely populated by peoples of a neolithic culture, is partly responsible for this reversal, but not as much so as technological developments. For instance, other lands have been opened up to humanity in the past without similar reversal, but at these earlier levels of technology the population could catch up to the new subsistence level before egalitarian theory could approach practical realization. (The great European-American technological revolution —comparable in impact to the neolithic revolution and based analogously upon widespread individualistic innovation—has brought economic egalitarianism nearer to practicality than ever before in history. The effects of its earlier stages were remarkable enough, but its real impact was not felt until well into the twentieth century.

Heilbroner[3] has pointed out that as late as the boom year 1929 a completely egalitarian distribution of the disposable income of the United States would have given each household only $2,300 annually. Even this was not too bad at that time, especially in comparison to the situation in poorer nations. But by 1958, he states, an egalitarian standard would have meant no worse than a uniform existence at a lower middle class level, which is not very uncomfortable in the United States. The same general trend is evident in Europe despite the population increase of the last century and a half, although its effects there are more spotty because of different national levels of technology and resources.

The economic status of the United States in 1929 would demonstrate, if such demonstration were necessary, that an extreme

[3] Robert L. Heilbroner, *The Future as History* (Evergreen ed., New York: Grove Press, 1961), p. 121.

egalitarian economic structure in any part of the Western world before this century would have meant a population subjected uniformly to poverty. The fact that minority groups in these Western countries enjoyed not only comfort but luxury meant that other groups lived at the bottom of the economic pyramid, at a level lower than that of free animals.

The fact is that inequality, with a severely depressed economic standard for a portion of the population, was the inevitable price paid for erecting civilization upon a base of resource development not far above the neolithic level.

Before the development of the great grain cultures of Asia and Egypt, an egalitarian level of village-and-garden culture would not have differed much from the living conditions of the present-day African kraal and Pacific islands. Status structures exist in such societies, but the resource surplus produced by their methods does not permit any great difference in living standards between the higher and lower "classes."

With the advent of the grain cultures the average, or egalitarian, subsistence level rose briefly, but it sparked population rises comparably greater than the resource increase. The result was not a more comfortable living standard on an egalitarian basis, but a less egalitarian economic structure. Some elements lived better than previously and others worse. Administrators, traders, and other non-productive elements of the population theoretically lived on the surplus of the productive workers. But the growth of administrative and trading classes sometimes demanded more than mere surplus and reduced the subsistence level of the producing many to pre-neolithic levels.

At the modern American technological level, which may continue for some time and even increase considerably, there is no question that a completely egalitarian economic distribution would be adequate to provide the surplus and leisure for creative effort. To those of egalitarian persuasion, this means that we can have our cake of civilization now and eat it, too, in fine egalitarian style.

In the first place, however, such an idea depends upon the

assumption that population will not increase faster than the resources made available by technology. Present population trends do not bear out that assumption.

Second, the elimination of the *economic* necessity for inequality—inequality for the purpose of maintaining an adequate surplus of material that goes for administrative and other non-productive tasks—does not guarantee that the *administrative* necessity for inequality has been eliminated. This is an important consideration, in that economic and political egalitarianism have always gone hand-in-hand. Where one appears, the other is sure to materialize eventually.

As in the case of the primitive *Masse*, the civilized *Masse* must lose its efficiency in dealing with the environment and eventually succumb unless its administrative structure is such that high status is correlated with ability and responsibility. The presence or absence of preferential economic treatment is not a determining factor in this correlation. The requirement is fulfilled only by dependence upon biological inequality.

Unfortunately, egalitarianism of any kind always falls back ultimately on the fiction of biological egalitarianism as its rationale. Buttressed by this fiction, egalitarianism inevitably exerts general conformist pressures which cannot be escaped by individual flight to some other areas of the social structure as is possible in a non-egalitarian society. These conformist pressures suppress individualism and social differentiation alike.

Human motivations and their expression are demonstrably so various that a completely egalitarian social structure could be established—and, once established, maintained—only by the severest kind of restriction upon individual freedom. This means, of course, that such a structure would not be truly egalitarian in the ethical sense; those who favor equality would be imposing their dominance upon those who do not.

The natural egalitarian retort, that human freedom was virtually non-existent at the lower levels in aristocratic societies, has substance. But the fact remains that some measure of freedom existed *somewhere* in those societies, else a creative minority could not have performed its task of guiding them to a higher level, and some outstanding individualists either were born into or achieved those freer levels of society.

There is a difference, blurred in today's thinking, between the egalitarian ethic and the libertarian ethic. They are not the same; and they are incompatible.

CHAPTER ELEVEN

THE PEOPLE: YES OR NO?

*Despotism, therefore, appears to me peculiarly
to be dreaded in democratic times. I should have
loved freedom, I believe, at all times, but in the time
in which we live, I am ready to worship it.*

—ALEXIS DE TOCQUEVILLE: *Democracy in America*

POLITICAL EGALITARIANISM IS, of course, democracy. To question the principle of democracy in the United States today is as perilous as it was to question the truth of revealed religion a century ago. It invites severe social sanctions. Nevertheless, the very existence of such sanctions, in view of democracy's claim to be the guardian of free thought and discussion, justifies the inquiry.

The egalitarian's political principle is that, unless the majority rules, it will be subjected to minority rule, which is a valid statement. His unquestioned assumption, however, is that majority rule is superior to minority rule, and this is not automatically true. In contrast, the libertarian resists *any* rule over his legitimate individual actions, by a majority no less than by a minority.

The egalitarian theory of majority rule reduces, ultimately and practically, to the principle of assuring the greatest benefit for the greatest number. This is its *raison d'être* in opposition to minority rule, which tends practically to concentrate benefits in the ruling minority. To those concerned about the evils of minority rule, the libertarian ethic seems of secondary importance. The egalitarian makes common cause with the libertarian when both are oppressed under minority rule. He may, indeed, *think* that he is concerned primarily with the libertarian ethic. But, once he has attained the benefits he sought, he is willing, even eager, to suppress freedom as harshly as did the minority he overthrew, in order to keep those benefits secure.

In contrast to such material benefits, freedom is an intangible thing. To the libertarian it needs no defense, for its value lies in itself. Its worth in relation to material benefits is more difficult to justify but just as real in the human equation.)

The criterion of the greatest good for the greatest number— which majority rule proposes to fulfil better than minority rule—is a reasonable one. It is compatible with society's excuse for being. In pursuing this criterion, however, a reasonable aim is to seek more than temporary preservation of these benefits; they must not only be obtained, but maintained, to possess maximum value.

The only reason for any "rule" at all in society, by either minority or majority, is the need for coordination. Society is a means of dealing with the environment collectively. Its rationale is that the environment can be dealt with more effectively in this way than by disparate individual approaches. Thus, the criterion for measuring majority rule and minority rule against each other reduces itself to determination of an effective course of social action to deal with the environment—including other *Massen.*) Omission of this requirement must erode the social body and make inconsequential any of its internal benefits.

Minority rule may vary in its methodology. The dominant minority, in the interest of preserving preferential treatment for itself, may assume a rigid "qualitative" distinction from the majority. If the dominant class was originally able and responsible, genetic and cultural transmission of these traits may guarantee an effective course of social action for quite a long time. But any ability which may reside or develop in subordinate classes is largely lost to the *Masse.* On the other hand, the society directed by minority rule may possess some form of vertical mobility. Although the majority is denied direct participation in determining social action, qualified members of the majority may be admitted to the ranks of the dominant minority and contribute to social direction.

The Chinese civilization was an example of such "open minority rule" for a long time. The privileged and hereditary aristocracy might be overthrown by invaders, but social action was still determined primarily by civil servants who might rise from any social class through proficiency at the examinations. The parliamentary division of the British government also combined the political themes of direction by a qualified minority and contributions by qualified members of the majority.

Majority rule, on the other hand, obviously carries the advantage of vertical mobility to its logical extreme. Since there are, theoretically, no class restrictions to participation in direction of social action, the abilities of the best qualified members of the entire *Masse* are utilized, once again theoretically.

Although it is not so apparent, majority rule also possesses the major disadvantage of "closed minority rule." Those members of society who are not of the dominant class are debarred from participation in determining the course of social action. The "dominant class" in this case is the majority. Those who are debarred are members of a minority, in that they do not agree with the majority; yet they may be highly qualified for determining the proper course of action.

Majority rule is not rule by "everybody." Like minority rule, it is rule by only one element of the population. The only qualification this element must possess in order to rule is numerical. Majority rule is rule by statistics. This being true, the effectiveness of collective action under majority rule rests heavily upon the egalitarian principle: the equal value of individual opinions. Some latitude may be permitted in establishing a range of "equality" in this respect. But if, for any reason, the opinions of a numerical minority of the population are substantially and consistently superior to those of a numerical majority in the field of social action, the democratic principle of majority rule is subject to question.

Pursuing this point to a logical extreme, majority rule in a home for the congenitally feeble-minded (IQ 50–69) would be disastrous. Survival of such a population would depend absolutely on its guidance by a minority of superior ability and intelligence—the home's staff. The same principle, however, must be conceded to have general application, because graduated differences in intelligence appear in any population, and every level of intelligence—not just feeble-mindedness—is congenital in part. The principle may be stated in unqualified form as follows: (government under majority rule is efficient in positive ratio to the population's median intelligence level./

The principle cannot be reduced to a mathematical rule. One cannot say, "When the median intelligence level of a population is below this particular point, majority rule will prove inadequate as a form of government." Efficient response to the environment, and therefore the "particular point" of adequate median intelligence level, depends necessarily on what that environment is. One can say only that, if the median intelligence level is below a particular point in relation to the particular environment, democracy cannot be considered an effective form of government for that population, and its only recourse is rule by a qualified minority.

Derivatively, it is possible that a *Masse* with a minority-dominant political structure may maintain an effective course of social action with a lower norm of general intelligence in its total population than a *Masse* with a democratic form of government. One cannot say that this will definitely be the case, of course, because the ablest minority may not be the dominant minority.

In terms of long-range effectiveness, government by the majority faces the most severe test of any political form. The biological challenge to all governmental forms springs from the fact that the social structure of a *Masse* largely determines selective pressures governing the types of individuals who will thrive and contribute to the inherent abilities of succeeding generations. Thus, each political form *must meet the critical test of maintaining a social structure which preserves an adequate qualitative level within its guiding human element.* In simpler but more general terms, effective democracy requires an intelligent electorate (not just an informed electorate); and the broader base of political control characterizing the democracy requires a correspondingly broader foundation of native intelligence.

When we say "intelligent" and "able" here, the meaning is, to an important extent, "creative" and "individualistic." No environment with which a *Masse* must deal, within itself or without, is completely stable. The environment constantly presents new challenges which must elicit an adequate response if the *Masse* is to continue to exist effectively. A creative response to many of these challenges is required, because nothing in tradition or the *Masse's* previous experience serves as a guide in meeting them. The individualism which is normal to the creative personality is necessary for making a break with previous practice and for proposing the solution.

The ancient Hellenic civilization experimented with both minority and majority rule. The early Hellenic political forms were not at all in the tradition of the old Egyptian and Mesopotamian societies around them but were derived from the old Indo-European king-council government characterized by free discussion. Like the Hittites, the Medes, and the Persians to the east, the early Greek system seems to have been one of autonomous communities dominated by aristocracies. Aristocrats were rather widely interrelated and formed an upper stratum of communication and association, sometimes friendly and sometimes hostile.

By 700 B.C., power (in Athens, at least) was concentrated in the hands of a strictly hereditary aristocracy.[1] Huntington emphasizes an increase in the stormy climate of Greece from 600 to 400 B.C. The storminess began to decline about the time of the Periclean period, 461–431 B.C., when democracy was developing to full flower. We may admit the significance of these climatic factors and yet sympathize with Heraclitus and Pindar

[1] Ellsworth Huntington, *Mainsprings of Civilization* (Mentor ed., New York: New American Library, 1959), pp. 593–95.

in their foreboding at the passing of the aristocracy which colored the social climate of the same period.

The Athenian citizenry must have been exceptionally able. It was not only capable of democracy but demanded it. Thucydides noted that "in ancient times . . . the leading men of Hellas, when driven out of their own country by war or revolution, sought asylum at Athens; and from the very earliest times (were) admitted to citizenship." Democracy in Athens came with a rush; Pericles was succeeded, in order, by a hemp dealer, a sheep dealer, a leather dealer, and a sausage dealer. Mumford[2] observes that the Athenian town council form of government reduced the ability of the propertied class to take undue advantage of public power but at the same time was "a conspiracy against the aristocracy of talent" by leaving to pure chance the possibility of getting and keeping able men in office. ⌊ It was a conspiracy against intellect as well as against talent in public administration.⌉ By the close of the fourth century B.C., Greek philosophers held essentially modern views about the shape of the earth and its relation to the solar system, for example; yet by this time Anaxagoras had been banished and Socrates put to death.

Complaints that state welfare practices were pauperizing the Athenian community have a modern ring. Mass hysteria in international relations under Athenian democracy affected the nation's activities in war and peace more than public opinion has thus far influenced the foreign policies of our own country. These symptoms of unease, we may say, represented a social reaction against the Greek adventure of individualism, the backlash of the powerful collective ego against the fears that freedom engenders in it.

From the beginning of Periclean democracy to the birth of Alexander of Macedon is only a century and five years. Thus effective democracy in Athens was short-lived in terms of chart-

[2] Lewis Mumford, *The City in History* (New York: Harcourt, Brace, & World, 1961), p. 155.

111

ing a collective course of action which dealt effectively with the environment, including other contemporary *Massen*. American democracy has already lasted longer than that of Athens.

Athens was but one scene in the drama of Hellenic civilization, however, just as the United States covers but a portion of the stage of Western civilization. The last act of Hellenic civilization was played in a Roman setting. Although the Romans never did establish democracy in the sense that it arose in Athens and the United States, popular political rebellions in Rome forced changes in the membership and policies of the dominant minority, with the result that the Roman "welfare state" at last became more notorious than the Athenian. The emperors were forced to keep the populace pacified, and the legions ultimately held the only power that could balance that of the masses.

Athens, then, remains the only example of outright majority rule in the Hellenic civilization. It follows that, despite its importance in the history of civilization and the development of the human mind, the Hellenic civilization cannot be cited as evidence of the superiority of democracy. Its greatest intellectual contribution preceded its democratic period; the democratic period was short; and the democratic center was relegated subsequently to a subordinate position.

The origins of American society were such that the guiding human element was of exceptionally strong quality. The selective factors which Huntington[3] cites as dictating outstanding intelligence and ability among the Puritans extended also to a large degree to other pioneer settlers.

The "radical" Thomas Jefferson believed in government *of* and *for* all the people *by* a well-qualified minority as naturally as did Alexander Hamilton. The 1787 Constitutional Convention expressed fear of government by "democratick babblers."[4] These opinions casting doubt on majority rule at its American

[3] Huntington, *Mainsprings of Civilization*, pp. 131ff.
[4] Thomas A. Bailey, *The American Pageant* (Boston: D. C. Heath and Co., 1956), p. 142.

beginnings are perhaps less significant than the dictum of Aristotle,[5] at the end of a democratic period, that democracy is the perversion of constitutional government, as tyranny is that of monarchy and oligarchy that of aristocracy.

Without passing judgment on the success of democracy at this point, we can say that the Athenian experience does not invalidate majority rule *per se*, even though it obviously does not validate it. It is not the abstract form of government which failed in Athens and is on trial in the United States; it is the form of government combined with the population which utilizes it. A population characterized by a majority above a certain level of intelligence and ability is not only capable of democracy but is justified in demanding it. This level need not be very high to maintain a paleolithic culture, but there seems to be scant recognition that it must be much higher to maintain a complex civilized culture.

A democracy assuredly is the form of government most natural and appealing to *H. individualis*. Democracy is a dual concept; it is and must be egalitarian in the legal and ethical sense, but it is philosophically libertarian. This is the natural atmosphere in which the creative individualist thrives; it is the only atmosphere which will not eventually drive him to rebellion against society itself.

By the same token, however, the libertarian philosophy creates the atmosphere that *H. socialis* abhors, that he fears instinctively, that he will strive incessantly to change into that womb which once protected him against the dark jungle: a closed society. In this aim, *H. socialis* has an advantage, for politics is by definition a social activity. Only "society" makes him feel secure. The nearer the *Masse* approaches the traditional, hierarchical structure of well-defined status, duties, and responsibilities, the less he has to face personal decisions and the more secure he feels.

Therefore, if *H. individualis* refuses either to submit to a

[5] Aristotle, *Politics*, Book III.

dominant minority or to serve as one, *H. socialis* will bend his efforts toward re-establishing one.

And *H. individualis* makes the task easier when he abdicates his natural capacity for clarification of such useful and attractive concepts as "equality." To *H. socialis*, this concept is a political tool which he can utilize to get what he wants; and to *H. socialis*, equality of everyone under the jurisdiction of a single, all-powerful leader is quite as comprehensible as equality without one, and much more secure.[6]

In the name of egalitarianism, *H. individualis* abolishes tyranny, but in the name of egalitarianism *H. socialis* reinstates tyranny.

Those who defend democracy intelligently do so for the sake of its libertarian principles. But they blind themselves to its shadow side, egalitarianism, which eventually translates free equality into enforced conformity and ends by stamping out liberty itself. *H. individualis* created both civilization and democracy as social environments more hospitable to the free individual. Always in the past, *H. socialis* has been able to seize control of these new environments, which are unnatural to him, and ultimately destroy them.

[6] Cf. Sigmund Freud, [*Group Psychology and the Analysis of the Ego*], trans. James Strachey (New York: Bantam Books, 1960), pp. 33–36, and Alexis de Tocqueville, *Democracy in America* (Mentor ed., New York: New American Library, 1956), pp. 306–308.

CHAPTER TWELVE

CITIES OF THE PLAIN

The stone Colossus, "Cosmopolis," stands at the end
of the life-course of every great Culture.
—Oswald Spengler: *The Decline of the West*

THE CITY, FLOWER AND SYMBOL of civilization, is also the
chalice of its decay. The rise of city towers in the midst of
fields and vineyards proclaims the growth of a civilization; the
lonely stones of a ruined city are a civilization's bones. Cities and
civilization are inextricably related, in actuality as well as se-
mantically; and when we seek that turning point at which the
creative minority, *H. individualis*, loses the influence necessary
to maintain his society's viability, we should seek it in the
changing role of the city as a human environment.

The fact that there is such a turning point necessitates a
conceptual division of the city's course of development, in this
context, into two major phases. The first phase is the establishment and growth of the city as the focus of a civilized environment offering advantages to *H. individualis*. The second phase
is the failure of the city, and the simultaneous decline of its
associated civilization, because it has become hostile to *H. individualis*.

This chapter will deal with the historical process whereby
the first phase is gradually converted into the second phase.
Causal factors and processes of the second phase will be examined in the next chapter.

In making the creative contributions that permit cities to
grow as foci of civilization, *H. individualis* performs a typically
human activity: alteration of his environment to make it more
hospitable to his living goals. But the creative contributions of
H. individualis are implemented in association with *H. socialis*

115

and with his help, and *H. socialis* inevitably modifies them to some degree to conform to his own needs rather than those of *H. individualis*.

The developing city in its early stages offers advantages to both *H. individualis* and *H. socialis*. For *H. individualis*, the urban concentration of resources, both material and human, provides a broader reservoir of information and tools on which to base his essentially synthetic creative activity. For *H. socialis*, population concentration increases both the possibilities for consociation and the security against outside threats which are important to his equanimity; and the gradation of social class confers a sense of hierarchical organization comforting in its reminiscence of the ancient herd structure. For both, the greater efficiency of resource utilization offers material benefits.

Abstractly, the process whereby these advantages eventually come to be outweighed by disadvantages is related to a general biological fact: that a non-social animal is oriented primarily to dealing with the natural environment and only occasionally to relationships with his species fellows; a social animal, by contrast, is oriented primarily to relationships with his species fellows, and the collective strength of the *Masse* serves as the individual's representative in dealing with the natural environment, protecting him from it like an invisible shield. Man primally is a social animal, but the variation, *H. individualis*, is to a great extent a non-social animal.

The city is a complex entity. The aspect of it most important to *H. individualis* is its service as a focus of elements of the natural environment, both material and immaterial, making them better available as subjects of creative activity. Its aspect most important to *H. socialis*, on the other hand, is its increased efficiency as a shield against the natural environment, permitting greater concentration upon the social activity of relations with his fellows.

As such a shield, however, the city, in both its human and material aspects, takes the place of simpler social groups as the individual's representative in dealing with the natural environment. The requirements for dealing with the natural environment change in time, primarily as a result of the city's population growth (which calls for greater demands on the natural environment) but sometimes because of changes in the natural environment itself, which are brought on by the impact of the city upon it. The material aspects of the city cannot change of themselves to meet these altered requirements; they must be changed by the human element of the city. Only that portion of the human element oriented primarily to the natural environment can make such changes realistically. This portion is the creative minority, *H. individualis*, and any process which reduces the influence of this minority contributes to the decline of the city.

The city thus cannot be considered independently of its natural environment. From the urban standpoint, the "natural environment" is a complex ranging all the way from such unalterable factors as climate and major terrain features to agriculture, mining, and other human activities in the areas surrounding or communicating with the city. The city must remain in balance with its environment in order to survive, in a way no different in principle from the adaptation of the non-social individual or the non-urban social group; and the requirements for maintenance of this balance are far more complex for the city.

The city serves as a focus of the human resources of its associated civilization, as well as its material resources. This fact is largely responsible for the early rise of the city—and, as we shall see, for its eventual decline.

In the early stages of city development, *H. individualis* is as often repelled by the city's congestion and restrictions upon individual action as he is attracted by its cultural and educational opportunities. The abhorrence of the city by American pioneer settlers is an example. Until the city has grown to the point that its cultural advantages far outstrip those of smaller towns, the tendency of *H. individualis* is to choose the freedom of the countryside or town unless he can live in the city on terms offering individual freedom beyond that available to the average city dweller.

In the early stages of the city's growth as an element of the civilized environment, then, a large proportion of the society's supply of predominantly *H. individualis* citizens remains in the country and the towns, usually as freeholders of various economic levels. That element which has migrated to the city either belongs to or is associated with an urban aristocracy, either formal or informal, and serves as the city's creative minority. This may account for the fact that literature, art, and music—all expressions of the creative mind—traditionally deal sympathetically with the aristocracy and the free peasant, but rarely so with the bourgeoisie, the representative of the conformist and materialistic side of urban life.

The rural environment is destroyed as a haven for *H. individualis* when the landed aristocracy is succeeded by large (often absentee) landowners oriented to the soil primarily as a source of wealth in urban, monetary terms, and when the general rural freedom at lower economic levels vanishes. This process occurs when the increasing demands of city population and city economy make speculative exploitation of land a profitable occupation. When it does occur, the rural element of *H. individualis* is frozen out and must seek what freedom it can find in the growing city. Such of this element as cannot find some connection with the urban aristocracy experiences either intellectual starvation amid the bourgeoisie or economic starvation amid the urban proletariat.

Let us now cite some historical examples of this process.

The early Hellenic cities grew out of communities of small farmers, and seventh-century Athens was ruled by a hereditary aristocracy of landowners. Introduction of a money economy and displacement of peasant farmers by imported slaves altered the relationship of the population to the land in Attica.[1] Solon's

---

[1] Cf. C. E. Robinson, *Hellas* (Beacon paperback ed., Boston: Beacon Press, 1955), pp. 45–48; Ritchie Calder, *After the Seventh Day* (New York: Simon and Schuster, 1961), pp. 240–43.

reforms early in the sixth century, which focused on the development of trade and industrialization, were less a first cause of subsequent events in Athens than a necessary response to an existing situation. The reforms led directly to the Athenian population boom, which, in turn, underlay the turn to Periclean democracy.

Before the Punic Wars, the Roman state, like early Athens, was dominated by a patrician class of landowners. The Punic Wars altered the agricultural balance in Italy. Italian agriculture benefited in productivity by the introduction of new crops, techniques, and farm implements, but Hannibal's devastation of Italy and the loss of peasant soldiery in the wars opened up great stretches of land to private exploitation, and the many prisoners of war made a great pool of slave labor available for the latifundia, or large estates. The free peasant could not compete with the slave as a farm laborer, nor could the small landowners compete with the latifundia. Tiberius Gracchus earlier had revived the Roman law limiting land holdings to 330 acres in an effort to reverse the trend toward elimination of small farmsteads, but to no avail.

One of the consequences of depopulation of the countryside, says Toynbee, was dependence upon a money economy, which collapsed in the third century A.D., carrying the social body down with it.[2] This process paralleled the introduction of money and the increase of slavery in Attica earlier, with similar consequences.

Economic and political events like those in Rome after the Punic Wars also followed devastating wars in China. China was unified in 221 B.C., ending the 260-year period of the Chan Kuo, or Warring States. During the two centuries of the first Han Dynasty which ensued (after the eleven-year reign of the only Ch'in emperor, Ch'in Shih Huang Ti), the influence of the old land-holding aristocracy was broken, free peasants were driven from their land and replaced by slaves on huge planta-

[2] Arnold J. Toynbee, *A Study of History* (Galaxy ed., New York: Oxford University Press, 1962), III, 170–71.

tions, and a national money economy was established. Just as the spread of the Italian latifundia drove the peasants into Rome to swell the city proletariat, so the Chinese peasants were driven into the cities by the economic developments under the Han. Hsiangyang, the capital, and Ch'angan both expanded to more than half a million population, and in 179 B.C. the emperor Wen authorized some of the nobles to go back to rural estates because he feared the capital might collapse as a result of congestion.[3]

Centuries later, a displacement of the small farmer in England similar to that associated with the Roman latifundia and the Chinese unification under the Han is outlined by Marx. In sixteenth-century England, the earlier rural aristocracy was succeeded by an increasingly urban timocracy.[4] There and throughout Europe, such developments were accompanied by the emergence of a money economy.

An English act of 1533 limited holdings of sheep to 2,000 head, but with no more success than the land reforms of Gracchus in preventing the disappearance of small farmsteads. By 1750, the English yeomanry had disappeared. Marx quotes a contemporary observer as stating that elimination of small farmers in England and their enrolment as workers on larger estates resulted in more efficient labor and greater production.[5] This also was the initial result of the Roman latifundia system. It is easy to see why an urban-centered society, feeling the pressures of rising population and increasing prices, would encourage this alteration in its agricultural environment.

In all four of these societies, we find the same factors associated: destruction of the influence of the landed aristocracy, the

[3] Marcel Granet, *Chinese Civilization* (New York: Meridian Books, 1958), p. 406.
[4] Karl Marx, *Capital*, trans. Samuel Moore and Edward Aveling (Modern Library ed., New York: Charles H. Kerr & Co., 1906), pp. 788–805; cf. H. G. Wells, *The Outline of History* (New York: Doubleday, 1949), II, 862–64; and Ritchie Calder, *After the Seventh Day*, pp. 281–82.
[5] Marx, *Capital*, p. 799; cf. Wells, *Outline of History*, II, 862–64; and Ritchie Calder, *After the Seventh Day*, pp. 281–82.

trend to a money economy, elimination of free peasants, and urbanization. In three of them—Athens, Rome, and China—they were processes which culminated in collapse of the societies: the outbreak of the Peloponnesian War in 431 B.C. began a chain of events which ended, in effect, with Philip's conquest of Greece in 338; Toynbee sets the end of the Roman "universal state" at A.D. 378, when the Goths destroyed the legions under Valens; and the Han Dynasty broke up into the San Kuo (Three Kingdoms) in A.D. 220 under the strain of palace revolutions and agrarian revolts.[6]

In terms of the present discourse, it is important to note that the factors listed as common to all four societies foster a plantation type of rural exploitation. That is to say, when political and economic control of the society is shifted to its urban centers, the rural areas are reduced to provincial status and assigned only the role of contributing to the welfare of the cities. Status, as well as economic and cultural opportunities, is downgraded for the rural population. The cities' now-superior opportunities and deterioration of the rural environment tend to draw the more energetic and creative elements of the rural population into the urban centers.

With this development, the city's role changes. Formerly, it was the cultural and commercial center of a predominantly rural landscape, a landscape rich in itself and for itself and fortified with many smaller towns. Now the city dominates; the towns ape it and depend upon it and the agricultural countryside is reduced to the status of its granary. Now, to really live in this civilization, to exert any social influence in this civilization, one must be a city dweller; and, as has been noted, the population density and social regulation of the city environment are intrinsically hostile to *H. individualis*.

In the first phase of civilized development, when urban cen-

[6] Although considerable time elapses here between possible "causes" and eventual effects, it should be noted that Toynbee considers "universal states"—as he calls both the Roman Empire and the Han Empire—last rallies temporarily staving off disintegration of a civilization.

ters are small, individualism may be largely submerged—that is, not markedly manifest socially—outside the city foci. In the rural areas, low population density prevents *H. socialis* from picking up creative contributions quickly through mimesis. Those creative individualists who live in the rural and small-town environment channel their creative contributions to the society through the city centers.

The population shift to the cities throws large numbers of the "submerged individualists" of rural areas into more direct contact with the cultural accumulation of the cities. This fact is adequate to explain the burst of intellectual and cultural activity that normally accompanies the transition from an agrarian to a metropolitan civilization. But the persistence of this phenomenon in later stages of urban civilization is an afterglow. The fully developed metropolitan environment neither permits the emergence of such "submerged individualism" as remains in the rural areas nor is it frankly hospitable to the intellectual creativity developed in earlier urban centers.

One is tempted to ask with Toynbee whether the real catastrophe is the disintegration and collapse of a civilization or its birth in the first place.[7] Actually, however, that is the wrong question. Reason tells us that the civilized environment offers more advantages, in almost every respect, than the savage environment, both to the creative individual and his non-creative brother. The real question is whether the environment offering those advantages can be created without incorporating in it the factors which lead to its own eventual destruction.

I am not sure that this question can be answered; but it may be possible to isolate a stage in the course of civilization which, as temporary as it has been historically, is most satisfactory for man as he is, composed of a variable mixture of *H. socialis* and *H. individualis* traits. This stage is neither, on the one hand, the rural or pastoral society without cities, which cannot be other than primitive, nor, on the other hand, the highly civilized, metropolis-centered society characteristic of the Roman Empire

[7] Arnold J. Toynbee, *A Study of History* (Galaxy ed.), IV, 585–88.

and the modern West. Theoretically, it should possess a loose unity but be composed of small, autonomous or semi-autonomous elements; historically, perhaps it was best represented by the city-states of early Ionia and Hellas and Italy and Germany of the late Middle Ages.

Such societies are not as efficient as the centralized society, either in their treatment of people or in their utilization of resources. They are not as comfortable for *H. socialis*, either, for they are characterized by a certain amount of social jostling and confusion and often by aggravating little wars. Historians are apt to treat them as "interim periods" of confusion and disorganization. But these societies have the advantage of cultural variety, leading to creative exchange. One element of such a society may offer *H. individualis* refuge from the conformist pressures of another, and the prophet without honor in his own country can turn to another.

Absorption of loosely unified, autonomous or semi-autonomous social groupings into a larger, more centralized social context occurs for reasons that have little to do with creative individualism but are typically social, in the sense of natural objectives of *H. socialis*: primarily, a more efficient organization of commerce, administrative power, and social regulation to make some particular social structure more secure. The success of this socially more efficient organization gives added impetus to the growth of cities as centers of commerce and administrative power, and their expansion to the limits of the contemporary technological potential thereafter is a self-sustaining process.

It remains for us to examine how this process works to eliminate the creative minority, *H. individualis*, as a guiding influence of civilization, environmentally and genetically.

CHAPTER THIRTEEN

THE GENETICS OF DECLINE

The age of great men is going; the epoch
of the ant-hill, of life in multiplicity, is beginning.
—HENRI FREDERIC AMIEL: *Journal Intime*

IN CENTRAL AFRICA, up to one-fifth of the population carries at least one gene which affects the blood's oxygen-carrying capacity and thus weakens the constitution severely. When a child gets a double dose of the genes responsible for this disease, he usually dies of anemia before adolescence. But those who have the milder form of the disease (only one defective gene) actually have a survival advantage over "healthy" people who don't have it at all—and all because man improved his environment in that area.

This paradoxical situation is perhaps the most frequently cited example of human genetic adaptation. The gene involved changes the hemoglobin structure of the blood, and the child who acquires this gene from both parents will die of sickle-cell anemia. But the slash-and-burn technique which permitted primitive agriculture created stagnant pools where the *Anopheles gambiæ* mosquito could breed, and the population density made possible by the agriculture established a reservoir of infection for the malaria carried by that mosquito. Even though they are not as healthy in other ways as those without the gene, those who inherit it from only one parent are more resistant to this malaria, and their reproductive advantage is sometimes as high as 20 per cent.

The primitive hunter of Pleistocene Africa presumably was fairly well adapted to his environment physiologically, but his way of life did not permit him to become very numerous. He found a way of life that would support a heavier population;

but a different, less healthy type of individual is better suited to the new environment he created.

Man's change from a rural to an urban environment during the course of civilization is more radical than the African's conversion from hunter to farmer. The genetic shift such a change fosters is more subtle and difficult to detect, but theory dictates it should occur. I think it is expressed in a selective disadvantage for *H. individualis*, the evidence for which, obviously, should be a relative decrease of the *H. individualis* element in the urban environment.

As has been brought out, the greatest creative period of the ancient Hellenic culture occurred in the Ionian cities in the sixth century B.C., before the rise of Athens as a leading population center. Extensive developments in mathematics, astronomy, and technology in Sumeria, unmatched for many centuries, long preceded Babylon's appearance about the twenty-seventh century B.C. and its growth into the major metropolis of the ancient world.[1] The great cultural flowering of ancient China—the time of the "hundred schools" of philosophers and many technological advances—occurred during the Warring States period, before the unification and urbanization processes described in the last chapter.[2] Western civilization has not yet run its course, but outstanding creative periods have preceded political unification or heavy urbanization in different countries, such as the Renaissance period in northern Italy, and the seventeenth and eighteenth centuries in France, Germany, and England.

The objection may be raised that Western civilization has been primarily metropolitan since the Middle Ages, but this is not true. No city in the Western world reached the probable population of ancient Rome, Carthage, and Babylon (one million) before the beginning of the nineteenth century, when London attained it. In 1800, Vienna, Europe's cultural darling,

[1] George Sarton, *A History of Science* (Cambridge: Harvard University Press, 1952), I, 68–82.

[2] Joseph Needham, *Science and Civilisation in China* (Cambridge: Cambridge University Press, 1954), I, 95–96.

had only 231,949 people; Paris had 547,756; and Berlin had 172,846. Except for London and Paris, European cities at that time were smaller than Hsiangyang and Ch'angan in the early Han Dynasty. The United States, France, and Germany changed from predominantly rural populations to predominantly urban populations about the beginning of the twentieth century; England and Wales accomplished the change by the mid-nineteenth century.[3]

Why should urbanization result eventually in the decrease of a society's *H. individualis* component? Because the strongly urban environment is unnatural for man in general, and especially so for *H. individualis*. The big city, which has always been the end result of civilization, is the extreme form of an artificial environment.

The human is still an animal who eats, drinks, and breathes, but his urban habitation shuts him away from the sunshine and the breezes, separates his feet from the moist earth, may even foul the air and water constantly. Eventually, as in a modern urban culture, man may live in artificial light, breathing conditioned air, drinking treated water, and eating only food which has been picked green for shipment and adulterated with preservatives.

This is a closed environment with a vengeance. Man lives in a crazily distorted caricature of the reality to which he was born. A neon-lit display of television sets behind glass looks more "natural" to him than a bluebird beside a woodland path or a treeful of ripe pawpaws in autumn. The artificial environment which he has created to protect him from hostile aspects of the natural environment contains elements more concentratedly poisonous to him than he could find in any natural environment.[4]

More subtle consequences are involved. No longer is the

[3] Warren S. Thompson, *Population Problems* (New York: McGraw-Hill, 1953), p. 106.
[4] See Appendix 5.

human a whole man, either within himself or as an active participant in the coordinated activity of a familiar group. Many of life's necessities come from distant sources with which he has no converse, and he is rarely acquainted with the results of his own labors, except indirectly and fractionally. Isolated, he is subjected to a dehumanizing influence, converted into a mere cog in an impersonal machine whose total form is beyond his grasp.

The extreme form of such a feeling of individual worthlessness is a prison psychology, for the metropolitan dweller is, in many respects, a prisoner in a cage of stone and wire and glass. The inmate of a prison may be well fed, well clothed, well doctored, protected; yet the fulfilment of his emotional needs is so bleak that often he will risk death to escape to an outer freedom where everything is against him. Failing this, he may develop a wide range of neurotic or psychotic ailments; and there is some evidence of a higher incidence of schizophrenia and similar troubles, as well as certain types of physical ills, in congested urban areas.[5]

In larger cities, man experiences some of the effects of simple population density that have been noted in certain animal species. To work surrounded closely by other people, to drive or ride to and from work in the midst of a jostling throng, to eat lunch with a stranger's elbow in your soup, to hear a variety of noises constantly beyond thin walls when attempting to relax or sleep—all of this inevitably has a psychological and physiological (and, therefore, selective) effect.

The various mental and physical effects of population density in animal populations add up ultimately to one result: severe attrition of the population until its density is reduced again to a point which may be far from ideal, but is bearable. The classic example of this sort of thing is the lemming, which reacts to

[5] Hudson Hoagland, "Cybernetics of Population Control," in *Human Ecology*, ed. Jack B. Bresler (Reading, Mass.: Addison-Wesley, 1966), p. 356. Also, see Appendix 5.

overpopulation by migration and mass suicide in the sea; but research with snowshoe rabbits and mice has shown endocrinological attrition on a widespread individual basis, resulting in collapse and death, apparently simply from stress. Some of Calhoun's Norway rats stabilized their population at 150 adults in a quarter acre, finally, when abundance of food and water had led to an expectation of 5,000; high infant mortality resulted from disrupted maternal behavior.

In the human, population density—or something in the congested urban environment, at least—tends to reduce population through a lowered birth rate. Historically, large cities have failed to maintain their populations by natural increase but have depended on in-migration from rural areas for their continued growth. As Emerson said, "The city is recruited from the country."

Reports of population declines in ancient times followed periods of extreme urbanization. In the first century B.C., Polybius complained that all Greece was afflicted with a failure of offspring, desolating the cities and leaving the land waste, although there had been no wars or epidemics. In both Sparta and Rome, unsuccessful efforts were made at different times to maintain the birth rate by legislation, tax exemption, and bonuses. Adoption was resorted to in Rome to counterbalance childlessness, but adoption does not affect a declining birth rate.

Thompson estimates a 2 per cent annual net attrition of London's population between 1700 and 1750, which was more than replaced by in-migration.[6] This picture has changed to some degree as a result of improvements in medicine and technology, but in a 1940 study of women who had already passed the childbearing age, only 2.7 children had been born to all of these women in the urban United States, compared to 3.3 children born to rural non-farm women and 4.2 to farm women.[7] Thompson cites a study showing that, among eight large American

[6] Thompson, *Population Problems*, p. 77.
[7] *Ibid.*, p. 177.

cities, only one, Pittsburgh, had more than 41 per cent of white women living in tracts where the ratio of children was high enough to replace the existing population (2.2 children per woman); in Chicago, only 10.9 per cent of white women lived in such tracts.[8] Children's Bureau statistics for 1947 showed that only 5 million of the nation's 30 million families were supporting more than half of the nation's 46 million children, and most of the supporting families were rural.[9]

Theories, such as those advanced by Sadler and Corrado Gini, that a biological change in human fecundity accompanies increasing population density and social complexity have little evidential foundation; but there may very well be some suppression of the actual birth rate as a result of psychological and endocrinological factors as well as from cultural choices. A study by Kiser of a group of childless women under fifty and married ten years or more in New York City showed that of 291 women who had never been pregnant, 77.8 per cent had never practiced contraception and 57.3 per cent had sought medical correction of their childlessness without success.[10] Figures cited by the Hoover Report from the 1930 census showed only 18 per cent of farm families childless, compared to 49 per cent in metropoles.[11]

Since the population of the United States was 72 per cent urban in 1960, the implication of an urban suppression of birth rate is an eventual population decline, as in ancient Greece and Rome. This is a rather bold implication, in view of a recent expert projection of a 318 million U.S. population by the year 2000.[12] Experts are sometimes wrong, however; Thompson, in 1933, *under*estimated the 1950 population by nearly eight mil-

[8] *Ibid.*, p. 181.
[9] Robert C. Cook, *Human Fertility: The Modern Dilemma* (New York: William Sloane Associates, 1951), p. 251.
[10] Thompson, *Population Problems*, p. 213.
[11] William F. Ogburn, "The Family and its Functions," *Recent Social Trends in the United States* (New York: Whittlesey House, 1934), p. 684.
[12] Herman Kahn and Anthony J. Wiener, *The Year 2000* (New York: Macmillan, 1967), p. 173.

lion because the rate of increase during the decade of the 1930's was temporarily more than halved.[13] It is worth noting, too, that the extreme declines in population in ancient Greece and Rome lagged a considerable time behind their heaviest trends to urbanization.

In any event, an urban population decline presumably affects both *H. individualis* and *H. socialis*. The theory here is that it affects *H. individualis* first, and its major effects on *H. socialis* occur only after the dissipation of the *H. individualis* component has resulted in a gradual breakdown of social mechanisms. The earlier decline of *H. individualis*, hypothetically, occurs because he is affected more adversely than *H. socialis* by urban pressures of overcrowding, social regulation, and the like, for reasons which have been stated. If this hypothesis is correct, we should expect to see a relative decline in the reproduction of *H. individualis* as urbanization increases.

There is some tentative evidence for this hypothesis to be found during the period in ancient Rome cited in the last chapter. After 264 B.C., when the first Punic War began, the form of Roman aristocratic rule remained much the same until the empire was established, but the composition of the aristocracy changed. A large plebeian and immigrant element mingled with the old aristocracy, and, as patrician families died out, the aristocracy assumed an increasingly plebeian character. By the time Julius Cæsar established the empire, there were only fifteen or sixteen such patrician lines surviving, to one of which Cæsar himself belonged. If we assume that the creative minority responsible for Rome's cultural rise was centered in its original aristocracy, this trend constitutes an example of a decline of *H. individualis*.

When we attempt to assess the contemporary situation, the question arises: how does one identify *H. individualis* statistically? Individually, one may say with some assurance that Emerson, or Einstein, or Hemingway, or perhaps the man next

[13] Thompson, *Population Problems*, p. 367.

door, is *H. individualis.* But the nearest approach we can find to an objective criterion for *H. individualis* broad enough to be utilized statistically is IQ level.

Since the definition of *H. individualis* rests heavily upon innate creative ability, and Getzels and Jackson have emphasized that this is an element of intelligence distinct from that measured by formal IQ tests, statistical identification of *H. individualis* on the basis of IQ level may seem questionable. However, Torrance suggests that, above 120 IQ, creative abilities are more important than IQ level,[14] the implication being that the two are more or less correlated below that "cut-off point." If we can assume that the *H. individualis* minority exists at the very top of the creative scale, we may define *H. individualis* as being *included in* that part of the population (8.9 per cent) of 120 IQ and above.

We must go yet further afield, because there exist no indisputable statistics, either, for a differential birth rate based on IQ performance. Of the records of differential birth rates that do exist, I prefer those based on educational level rather than on such factors as economic status. This is not to suggest that one's IQ level (and correlated creativity level) could be determined individually merely by ascertaining his educational level. But I believe that the correlation of IQ level with educational level is valid statistically; that is, if any random 1,000 individuals with some college education are tested, we may reasonably expect that they will be more likely to average 120 IQ or above than a random 1,000 individuals having no more than an elementary school education.

There is some indirect evidence in support of this general correlation. The long-range studies by Terman and his associates of California school children in the gifted IQ range showed that nearly 90 per cent of the selected group (1,500, with an average IQ of 150) attended college and 70 per cent graduated,

[14] E. Paul Torrance, *Guiding Creative Talent* (Englewood Cliffs, N. J.: Prentice-Hall, 1962), pp. 62–63.

percentages far above the general population average.[15] Medawar cites a number of studies showing "a clear *negative correlation*" (his italics) between family size and IQ performance;[16] and a negative correlation between educational level and family size will be shown below (Table 3). These two correlations support the assumption of a *positive* correlation between IQ performance and educational level.

For our immediate purpose, we may therefore define *H. individualis* statistically in the present American society as an element included among the most educated 10 per cent of the population. I would like to narrow the definition further, because there are so many highly educated conformists and dogmatists extant, and I suspect that the true *H. individualis* represents a minority of not more than 1 or 2 per cent, rather than 10 per cent. This is as close as we can come on the basis of the necessary correlations which have been made, however, because the correlation between creativity and IQ breaks down above 120 IQ.

What is happening reproductively to the most educated 10 per cent of the nation is illustrated by figures from the 1960 U. S. Census Report (Table 3). Those who have completed four years of college represent about 6½ per cent; those who have had one or more years of college, about 15 per cent. It will be noted that the entire group with some college education averages fewer children than the population replacement index of 2.2 children per woman; thus, as a group, it is declining.[17]

On the other hand, the groups that are above the replacement index—that is, increasing in population—are those that have had no high school education, representing about 33 per cent

[15] L. M. Terman, ed., *Genetic Studies of Genius* (Stanford, Cal.: Stanford University Press, 1925), I.

[16] P. B. Medawar, *The Future of Man* (Mentor ed., New York: New American Library, 1961), p. 72.

[17] I use the conservative population replacement figure of Robert C. Cook (*Human Fertility*, p. 233). Warren S. Thompson (*Population Problems*, p. 168) places it at 2.52 per fecund woman.

of the population. On the basis of the Wechsler distribution,[18] this group of increasing population constitutes those of 93 IQ and below.

TABLE 3

AVERAGE NUMBER OF CHILDREN BORN TO NATIVE WHITE WOMEN
OF VARIOUS EDUCATIONAL LEVELS: 1960

Schooling completed	Number of women, aged 45–49 years	Children born
None	39,928	3.1
1–4 years, elementary	131,888	3.5
5–7 years, elementary	560,852	2.9
8 years, elementary	905,174	2.5
1–3 years, high school	1,110,821	2.2
4 years, high school	1,440,386	1.9
1–3 years, college	484,370	1.8
4 years, college	212,883	1.7
5 years or more, college	107,124	1.2

Source: Courtesy Population Reference Bureau: U. S. Bureau of the Census, Women by Number of Children Ever Born, PC(2)–3A.

When such a reproductive differential between groups continues for any length of time, it will result in sharp changes in ratios of genetic traits. For example, of 29 founders of the living Ramah Navajo Indians, 14 produced 84.48 per cent of the descendants and another 14 only 13.56 per cent.[19] This means that some genetic traits which once were equally represented in the population became predominant by a 6-to-1 ratio.

By a simple mathematical projection, we can discover what happens to the different groups in the 1960 census if the reproductive differential continues unchanged for four generations.

[18] Thus, the lower one-sixth of "average intelligence" and below. See Das Fischer Lexikon: Psychologie, ed. Peter R. Hofstätter (Frankfurt am Main: Fischer Bücherei, 1957), p. 289.

[19] Ernst Mayr, Animal Species and Evolution (Cambridge: Harvard University Press, 1963), p. 657.

In Table 4, the groups are listed by IQ level, correlated to the educational level of Table 3 via the Wechsler distribution, and the assumptions are made that intelligence is inherited and that the women in each generation mate at approximately their own IQ level. The reasons for assuming the inheritance of intelligence to a significant extent have been stated (see above, Chapter 6). As for the second assumption, a graph of Outhit's study of 51 American pairs shows close assortative mating on the basis of IQ level.[20]

TABLE 4

EXTRAPOLATION OF DIFFERENTIAL FERTILITY RATE[*]

IQ level	Generations			
	1st	2nd	3rd	4th
Below 58	79,856	123,777	191,853	297,371
58–72	263,776	461,608	807,814	1,413,675
73–83	1,121,704	1,626,471	2,358,382	3,419,654
84–93	1,810,348	2,262,935	2,828,670	3,535,838
94–102	2,221,642	2,443,806	2,688,187	2,957,005
103–116	2,880,772	2,736,733	2,599,897	2,469,903
117–124	968,740	871,866	784,679	706,212
125–130	425,766	361,901	307,616	261,474
Above 130	214,248	128,549	77,128	46,277
Totals	9,986,852	11,057,646	12,680,224	15,107,409

[*] The first-generation population is doubled for projection purposes, assuming one father for each mother. It is assumed that the new population in each generation is equally divided between the sexes, and the fertility rate thus is multiplied by half the total of each generation.

The projection of Table 4 shows a 52 per cent increase in the total population in four generations, but an analysis of the fourth-generation population shows the average IQ level to have declined from 100 points to about 91 points. The percentage of population below 80 IQ (light debility, borderline intelligence, and feeble-mindedness) has increased from 8.9

[20] Das Fischer Lexikon: Anthropologie (Frankfurt am Main: Fischer Bücherei, 1959), p. 306.

per cent to 22.3 per cent. The upper 15 per cent of the original population, which contains the *H. individualis* element, has declined to 6.8 per cent; in actual numbers, it has decreased by about one-third. This altered ratio of high and low extremes of IQ range would apply roughly to the generation coming of age about the middle of the twenty-first century. A comparison of Table 3 with figures from the 1940 census (see Table 6, Appendix 4) indicates very strongly that the reproductive differential did continue essentially unchanged over the twenty-year period between the births recorded in the two censuses, and that, as a result, the median IQ level of the population declined a point or two during those two decades.

The conclusion that the average intelligence level of Western populations is declining, accepted by Robert C. Cook and others,[21] has become highly controversial. An effort to check it by direct methods was made by the Scottish Council for Research in Education, which gave intelligence tests to all eleven-year-old children in Scotland who could be reached in 1932, and again in 1947. The somewhat surprising results were a slight increase in average IQ level between the tests.

None of the efforts I have seen to explain away these results seems sound, but one objection which I have not seen anywhere does seem to be a telling one. This is that the second measurement was not of the IQ of a succeeding generation. That is, the tests of the 1947 group did not measure the IQ level of *the children of the 1932 group,* but of children only a half-generation later—therefore of a different population, most of whom were not even children of the same parents as the first group. Thus, it was not a genuine empirical test of the theory and possesses evidential value certainly no greater than the evidence for the theory of decline itself.

---

[21] Cf. Medawar, *The Future of Man,* pp. 79, 83; Julian S. Huxley, *Evolution in Action* (Mentor ed., New York: New American Library, 1957), p. 133; Mayr, *Animal Species and Evolution,* pp. 659–62; Theodosius Dobzhansky, *Mankind Evolving* (New Haven: Yale University Press, 1962), pp. 315–18.

It is best to adopt the cautious attitude expressed by both Dobzhansky and Medawar: that the case has not been proved, but it remains so far from being disproved that it still should be a matter of concern. I think that the direct, unqualified projection of Table 3, as in Table 4, is too radical; but I believe that it is valid as one item of evidence favoring the hypothesis that Western civilization has entered a stage in which a selective factor operates against the survival and increase of the creative minority, *H. individualis*.

Urbanization is only one element of such a process, it is true; it is as much a symptom as a cause, as much a setting for the process as a part of the process itself. Theoretically, the process could occur without the presence of big cities, perhaps, but actually it does not, above the level of the primitive society. In an abstract sense, condensation of the paramount portion of a society's population in metropoles represents the return full circle to the environment of the savage *Masse*, despite its differences in size, technology, and social organization.

Ortega relates the story that one of the cultured provincials, Lucan or Seneca, upon arriving in Rome during the early empire and beholding the massive imperial buildings, felt that Rome was eternal and nothing new could ever happen again.[22] Similarly, most of us are so impressed with the achievements of Western technological civilization that we feel that, barring an atomic war, the human world can never become primitive again. Like Shelley's Ozymandias, we say to history, "Look on my works, ye Mighty, and despair!"

But imperial Rome was even then crumbling within, before the very eyes of those who revered her. Do we, too, offer our sacrifices at the altar of a dying culture?

---

[22] José Ortega y Gasset, *La Rebelión de las masas* (Madrid: Espasa-Calpe, S. A., 1937), p. 50.

CHAPTER FOURTEEN

THE SPOILED SOCIETY

*The ultimate result of shielding man from the effects
of folly, is to fill the world with fools.*
—HERBERT SPENCER: *Essays*

HEN THE FRENCH REVOLUTIONARIES asserted the social right of everyone to either employment or direct assistance, they were setting a pattern for the modern Western world, but they were less original than they thought. "Bread is due to the people by right in a well-regulated state," said Saint-Just; but Juvenal, speaking from experience, said seventeen centuries earlier, "The people that once bestowed commands now longs eagerly for just two things, bread and circuses."

At the time Juvenal wrote, the burden of the state was eating increasingly into the Roman Empire's capital wealth because of three major factors: (*a*) tremendous military expenditures, (*b*) the expanding government bureaucracy, and (*c*) extensive public works and public welfare.[1] There were already 320,000 recipients of the grain dole in Julius Cæsar's time.[2] Nor was the idea of public assistance new even then. Greek writers charged that Pericles introduced the people of Athens to public land grants, spectacles, and payment for public services, making them extravagant and licentious.[3] He provided free meals for the poor and employed them on public works.[4]

[1] Arthur E. R. Boak, *A History of Rome to 565 A.D.* (New York: Macmillan, 1955), p. 365.
[2] *Ibid.*, p. 236.
[3] Plutarch, *Selected Lives and Essays* (Roslyn, N. Y.: Walter J. Black, 1951), p. 137.
[4] C. E. Robinson, *Hellas* (Beacon paperback ed., Boston: Beacon Press, 1955), p. 82.

EPISTLE TO THE BABYLONIANS

The orientation to the welfare state as enunciated by T. H. Green ("The State exists to secure a 'good life' for its members") is the orientation to the state as the producer of security, from which Ortega says "mass-man" is born.[5] It fosters "mass-man"—the primitive, "pure" *H. socialis*—because in its philosophy it is a reversion to the communistic, protectivist primal *Masse*. The mystical idea of "the people" in the French Revolution[6] is no more than a psychological resurgence of the "group consciousness" of the prehuman herd.[7]

The primal *Masse* is the original human closed society. It antedates Popper's tribal closed society,[8] which is already more sophisticated and differentiated. The primal *Masse* is essentially an animal herd, the social behavior of its members determined by unconscious considerations. The herd is the biological and psychological unit, not the individual. When the able-bodied element of the herd brought down the big game of the Pleistocene savannah, the herd as a whole fell on the kill to consume it, and when an individual was hurt or in danger, the herd as a whole protected him. No individual contribution or responsibility was required in return for nourishment or protection; necessarily, in the human context, it was dispensed to pregnant females, mothers and young, and, by extension, to the aged, the crippled, the ill, and even the irresponsible and incompetent. Older men and cripples were being fed in Neanderthal society 45,000 to 70,000 years ago, and possibly in Sinanthropus times 360,000 years ago.[9]

Sexual selection for individual responsibility and ability, contributing to the further increase in brain size, could occur only

[5] José Ortega y Gasset, *La Rebelión de las masas* (Madrid: Espasa-Calpe, S. A., 1937), p. 106.
[6] J. L. Talmon, *The Origins of Totalitarian Democracy* (New York: Praeger, 1960), p. 102.
[7] Cf. Erich Neumann, *Ursprungsgeschichte des Bewusstseins* (Zürich: Rascher Verlag, 1949), p. 124.
[8] Karl R. Popper, *The Open Society and Its Enemies* (Torchbook ed., New York: Harper & Row, 1963), I, 57.
[9] Carleton S. Coon, *The Origin of Races* (New York: Alfred A. Knopf, 1962), p. 103.

after the development of speech, formal custom, and the idea of the nuclear family. The manner in which such selection operates can be seen in one of the most primitive of contemporary societies, the Tiwi of Melville and Bathurst Islands. There, the number of wives one obtains depends on one's ability to provide and to cooperate socially, and at the time of a recent study (1960), 13 per cent of the men had 58 per cent of the children in the society.[10] Paleolithic societies of this kind were still closed societies, in that they were tradition-bound and basically collectivist. However, differentiated sexual selection during that period built the human gene pool to the point that an exceptional environmental change—such as that in some areas at the end of the Würm glacial period—could permit the emergence of the *H. individualis* type.

The monogamous marriage pattern characteristic of Western countries, insofar as it is effective, has changed the thrust of selection but has not eliminated it. It shifts the emphasis from the number of fertile wives a man may have to the number of children one wife (or a sequence of monogamous wives) may have. Also, it places additional emphasis on the comparative survival of children to reproductive age, because lazy or incompetent men who would remain bachelors in a Tiwi-type society usually are able to find mates (legal or otherwise) in a monogamous society.

The orientation that the collective body of society, rather than the individual himself, is responsible for the individual's primary maintenance reverses the order of the selective forces which built the human species up to the inherent potential for civilization. The cause-and-effect sequence is simple; the state necessarily acquires the resources it dispenses from those who produce them, directly or indirectly, through taxation; these people are made unable thereby to rear as many children as they would otherwise, or, alternatively, to give them as good a material environment; the state's dispensation of welfare is, by

[10] *Ibid.*, pp. 97–98.

definition, made to non-producers of resources; they are made able thereby to sire or give birth to children, who usually must also be supported by welfare programs.[11] The cause-and-effect sequence is clouded by the fact that some individuals who pay the heaviest taxes are non-producers of actual resources, but, as a practical matter, the real producer bears at least his share of the increased governmental cost of welfare; this cost proves to be not merely a redistribution of surplus wealth, but a demand upon productive capital.

The theoretical contribution of extensive and continued social assistance programs to the sort of fertility differential depicted in Table 3 is obvious. Spengler assigns two centuries or more to the interval between the first uprising of the megalopolitan mob ("Napoleonism") and the collapse of a culture into formlessness ("Cæsarism").[12] Two centuries represent about eight human generations. The effects of directed selection for differential intelligence (which such a fertility differential is, to the extent discussed in the last chapter) over a comparable number of generations are indicated in Tryon's experiments with selective breeding of rats. After seven generations, those bred for "maze-dull" traits reached a statistical peak of 114 to 134 errors in negotiating a maze, compared to a peak of 64 to 74 errors in the original unselected population. (Those selected

[11] Cf. Robert C. Cook, *Human Fertility: The Modern Dilemma* (New York: William Sloane Associates, 1951), p. 314; Thomas Robert Malthus, *An Essay on the Principle of Population* (Modern Library ed., New York: Random House, 1960), pp. 355ff.

[12] Oswald Spengler, *The Decline of the West*, trans. Charles Francis Atkinson (New York: Alfred A. Knopf, 1962), pp. 362–78. In his "organic" theory, which is not based upon such definite biological considerations as this one, Spengler calls the two-century interval referred to "The period of the Contending States," after the Chinese historical phenomenon. The Chinese period (Chan Kuo) lasted from 480 to 221 B.C. The comparable period in the Hellenic civilization, from Alexander the Great to Julius Cæsar, lasted from 336 to 46 B.C. Napoleon's accession to power was in 1799, which would point to the Western civilization's "Cæsar" some time in the twenty-first century, under Spengler's theory.

for "maze-brightness" peaked at only 19 to 24 errors after seven generations.)[13]

Seven human generations represent about the time the United States has existed as a nation. But public assistance is a comparatively recent thing in this country, and non-insurance types of public welfare payments at the end of 1967 were being made to only about 4½ per cent of the population; minor, compared to the 30 per cent or more of the population of Rome drawing the dole in Cæsar's time. It is highly doubtful that public welfare, *per se*, has affected the American population genetically to any significant extent so far.

Public welfare, however, like urbanization, is as much a symptom as a cause of a regressive trend toward a closed society. I believe that if the United States had started out as a closed society and had succeeded in remaining so for seven generations, it would be a thoroughly totalitarian nation today and probably the dominant power in a world empire. But it started out as an open society—one in which individuals must decide many things for themselves[14]—and remained an outstanding example of an open society at least until World War I.

In the open society, the fertility differential of Table 3 should not exist, theoretically; and there is some evidence that it did not in early America. American society has always permitted a great deal of vertical mobility; this allows (although other social factors do not always encourage) natural abilities to manifest themselves in economic and professional achievement. Large families at the higher professional and economic levels were as common as at lower levels during this country's earlier history, and children born at the higher levels had a higher expectation of survival. The fertility differential of 1960 was thus, to some degree, reversed under early American social conditions.

[13] Howard H. Kendler, *Basic Psychology* (New York: Meredith, 1963), p. 623.
[14] Karl R. Popper, *The Open Society and Its Enemies*, p. 173.

In an open society, collectivist impulses are subordinate to the individual necessity of dealing with an environment outside the regulatory framework of the *Masse*. In early America, except in the cities and towns, mere distance from one's neighbors and the difficulty of communication were isolating factors for pioneer families. Even in the largest cities, technological and cultural advantages common in urban Europe at that time were precisely as far away as Europe.

Under such circumstances, the primary requirement for survival in the face of environmental exigencies was possession of individual intelligence and ingenuity. "Society" could not be called on to help in an emergency, because "society" was too far away. Even in the small cities, society was a rather loose framework, less accessible to the individual's call for assistance than were his and his neighbors' abilities. The result was a selective premium favoring *H. individualis*, a further selection operating upon people who had already undergone a stern selective process in migrating to this country.

The psychology of the closed society, on the other hand, is that of collective security. Such an orientation was necessary to *H. socialis* under primitive conditions, and departures from it became possible only when technology and cultural exchange had developed to the stage that the environment would not surely overwhelm the individual. The highly civilized society, such as the Roman Empire and the modern West, faces problems that are primarily internal, rather than external—problems of population density, distribution of resources, communication, and the like—but they are problems which, again, require collective solution. The more complex a society becomes, the less self-sufficient the individual becomes and the more he must depend upon a social organization over which he has little or no personal control to guarantee his livelihood.

The price the individual pays for such protection by society is conformity to certain approved patterns of action and behavior. Society has to demand such conformity, because collective programs must be planned on predictable (statistical) factors, and the individualistic non-conformist interferes with predictability. Here we find the real economic, political, and philosophical reason for the egalitarian orientation: identical units are treated more easily arithmetically.

The respects in which such a role for the individual resembles the role of the immature child in a family are apparent. The child is protected and cared for, because he cannot protect and care for himself. In return, a certain conformity is demanded of him, necessarily, and departures from it are punished even as they are punished in society. Familial protection and conformity are intended to be temporary, of course, a preparation for subsequent individual independence, but sometimes they are continued abnormally into the child's adult life. When this happens, the resultant psychological effect is much the same as that manifested by the individual in a protective and conformist society.

Appropriately, there is a correlation—seen in later Athens and Rome as well as in the modern United States—between assumption by society of the protective and corrective role, and the decline of the family as an institution. Society has robbed the family of its normal role. Attempts to restore the importance of the family by encouraging its "socialization"—greater integration into community life—quite naturally have just the opposite effect from that intended. Such efforts rob the family of its peculiar integrity and tend to push it back to a primitive status in which the child was the property of "the community soul-ideology."[15] The breakdown of the family, with the causally related assumption of a protective role by society, represents a regression toward the primitive *Masse*. Society—the *Masse*—becomes, in effect, a monstrously swollen, authoritative family, within which adult children feel, think and act, as should be expected, childishly.

When the necessary inner organization of a society has become so complex that it must treat its adult members as its chil-

[15] Otto Rank, *The Myth of the Birth of the Hero and Other Writings*, ed. Philip Freund (Vintage ed., New York: Vintage Books, 1959), p. 299.

dren, rewarding them for conformity and punishing them for any dissent, it has reverted to a closed society, even though it is no longer primitive in technology and available knowledge. The metropolitan environment, for economic and administrative reasons, tends to become a closed society. Despite the widespread assumption that "democracy" and "open society" are synonymous terms, a democracy may approach the closed society more nearly than does an aristocracy. How large a proportion of the *Masse* participates in determining its regulation is of less definitive importance than how rigid that regulation is.

What happens to the creative minority, *H. individualis*, when a society "closes up"? Toynbee says in several contexts that the creative minority degenerates into a "dominant minority" (which is uncreative), without ever really suggesting a reason for the degeneration; and at one spot he suggests that the creative minority has just disappeared from the society's ruling element and reappears in a rebellious proletariat. I would say that the latter suggestion is closer to the truth, in that *H. individualis* in a closed society often finds himself rebelling on behalf of disadvantaged groups against "the establishment." But I think that what really happens is that *H. individualis* is repressed and destroyed as an effective influence in the society by the resurgence of *H. socialis* in an environment which seems, superficially, to be natural to him. This process operates in several ways.

First, the technological complexity required by densely populated metropolitan areas, as well as the social characteristics of these populations, demands close social organization. For the sake of efficiency, in one area after another, this organization tends to devolve into a hierarchical structure. A hierarchical structure is natural to *H. socialis*; *H. individualis* suffers through his inability to adapt to it.

Second, to accomplish one's personal objectives in the closed social context, it is necessary to deal less with a non-human, natural environment than with other humans at strategic spots in the giant streams of collective action. The "other-directedness" which Riesman has seen as representative of the changing American character[16] is a more valuable survival trait than objective knowledge or creative ability. Other-directedness, again, is a psychological function of the collective ego which guides *H. socialis.*

Third, *H. socialis* is inclined to accept the protective-restrictive qualities of the closed social environment as natural and God-given, just as the savage accepts his particular natural environment, and to act in full confidence of their permanence. *H. individualis*, seeing it against a less social and more objective background, is more dubious. Sensing its unnaturalness and precariousness, he patterns his actions against a background of underlying anxiety.

This anxiety may be far more important to the 1960 fertility differential than either such cultural factors as a differential knowledge of contraceptive methods or a hypothetical decline in actual fecundity such as Spencer proposed. The devastating effect of a temporary state of anxiety upon the performance of the individual sexual act is well known, and it extends to chronic anxiety states. The differential effect upon fertility between *H. socialis* and *H. individualis* could be profound.

Fourth, the crowded environment is distasteful to *H. individualis* by definition. Lack of economic opportunity prevents him from retreating to a less crowded rural environment. Lack of "other-directedness" inhibits his economic ability to isolate himself and his family otherwise. Both social and economic pressures insistently demand that he "integrate" himself with the crowded community. The psychological (and possibly endocrinological) effects of this crowded environment dictate the only retreat left to him: retreat from the species, retreat from reproduction.[17]

H. individualis tends to become a dwindling elite without

[16] David Riesman, Nathan Glazer, and Reuel Denney, *The Lonely Crowd* (Anchor ed., New York: Doubleday, 1953), pp. 34–38.
[17] Cf. *The Decline of the American Male*, by the editors of *Look Magazine* (New York: Random House, 1958), p. 22.

power, increasingly disliked and mistrusted by the majority, leaving the society's maintenance and the cream of its dubious advantages to the fattening population of *H. socialis*. At this point, civilization has failed. *H. socialis* has succeeded in converting it back into the primal *Masse* natural to him, at a higher technological level.

As such a powerless elite, *H. individualis* may still contribute to the civilized society, for a time. But his influence gradually disappears, too. Toynbee's "dominant minority" of this period is composed of *H. socialis*; the "creative minority" has not been converted into it, by either a cultural or a biological process, but has simply withdrawn from society.

CHAPTER FIFTEEN

WHERE IGNORANT ARMIES CLASH BY NIGHT

*The first panacea for a mismanaged nation is
inflation of the currency; the second is war. Both
bring a temporary prosperity; both bring a permanent ruin.*

—ERNEST HEMINGWAY: *Notes on the Next War*

AFTER MOSES HAD LED THE ISRAELITES to the borders of the Promised Land, they were able to get along without him. It is not unreasonable to suggest that, once *H. individualis* has made the contributions necessary to the establishment of civilization, *H. socialis* can dispense with him, and society may actually be better off for not having to put up with his disturbing influence any longer.

The suggestion that this actually will happen in the world as a whole has been put forward brilliantly by Seidenberg. He theorizes that individualism is only a phenomenon of a transitional period during which man moves from dependence primarily on instinct to the triumph of intelligence, and when the transition is complete man will sink back into collectivism as complete as that of his prehistoric phase.[1]

I disagree with Seidenberg's conclusions, on the basis of my conviction that collectivism and intelligence are, ultimately, incompatible. A collectivism enforced by either technological or political compulsion is basically unstable, the repression of an explosive human force; therefore, to maintain the "icy fixity" which Seidenberg foresees for the "posthistoric" age, collectivism would have to be a resumption of the "natural collectivism"

[1] Roderick Seidenberg, *Posthistoric Man* (Chapel Hill: University of North Carolina Press, 1950; Beacon paperback ed., Boston: Beacon Press, 1957).

that held man's societies together instinctively through hundreds of prehistoric millennia. I believe that this would require elimination of all creative intelligence, which is fundamentally non-conformist and revolutionary. Elimination of creative intelligence would result in an eventual reduction of the technological level to the paleolithic stage; such a reduction, in turn, would make dense populations and extensive political groupings impossible, and man would merely return to a prehistoric stage, both biologically and socially. In other words, *H. socialis* cannot dispense with *H. individualis* if he is to retain the latter's gifts; civilization is an artificial product which requires a creative approach for its maintenance as well as for its original development.[2]

Seidenberg's observation of a broad trend toward collectivism at a level of intelligent organization rather than simple instinct, although probably projected too far, is not incorrect, however. The dissipation of *H. individualis* as an effective component in a civilized society logically foretells the society's decline to a lower level of social existence, but this decline runs its course normally in the context of a highly sophisticated collectivism.

There are both visible and invisible reasons for the onset of collectivism. Some of the invisible reasons have already been outlined, but others need to be mentioned in connection with the visible process, which is largely a matter of administrative and political effort to preserve the civilization and stave off its decay.

As has been indicated, *H. socialis* tends to take the benefits of society for granted, as in the primal *Masse*. He knows that his labor has been involved in developing these benefits, but he is less aware of the intangible conceptual and organizational contribution of *H. individualis*. As he gradually succeeds to control of a society, *H. socialis* becomes impatient of the arduous

---

[2] Cf. José Ortega y Gasset, *La Rebelión de las masas* (Madrid: Espasa-Calpe, S. A., 1937), pp. 65ff., 128–29; Jacques Barzun, *The House of Intellect* (Torchbook ed., New York: Harper & Row, 1961), *passim*.

process involved in the production of its benefits; he is like an heir whose patrimony returns an adequate but modest interest, but who casts covetous eyes on the richness of the principal. The *H. socialis* element which adopts this attitude is not merely Toynbee's "internal proletariat," such as the Negro minority and organized labor in the United States, but includes also a significant portion of Toynbee's "dominant minority"—such as Chambers of Commerce which do everything they can to make already swollen cities even bigger.

The impatience of both elements of *H. socialis* is expressed in an exploitive attitude. The workman no longer takes pride in the quality of his workmanship but cares only about the size of his paycheck; management is no longer interested in the quality of its product as long as it can command a market by monopoly or persuasive advertising. The money economy typical of this social period creates a false prosperity, because the economic pressures of the exploitive attitude push both wages and prices upward. Since money is only a symbol, these could balance each other, but the invisible net loss to the society, which leaches away its productive capital, is the deterioration of the human contribution as expressed in the debasement of products. Ayn Rand

An exploitive attitude is not a rarity on the human scene, but when it colors the entire fabric of a complexly organized society, it arouses further collective instincts—particularly the basic instinct to combine forces to gain one's ends and protect oneself. The natural groupings within the society solidify and exert their collective strength against each other. Thus, in the modern context we find giant business combines, giant labor unions, Black Power, dedicated ideological organizations. When one of these groups exerts its collective strength or becomes embroiled in a struggle with another, the reaction of the total *Masse* is evoked, to prevent the breakdown of the social structure. Moral disapproval and public opinion, which are more effective than force in the small social context, have little effect in a large society which assents in fact to an exploitive attitude. The only arbiter both powerful enough and impartial enough to deal with repeated assaults upon social stability by its subsidiary groups is the government.

So enters the state into the picture. The state is not the monarchy that represents a land-holding aristocracy, nor the merchant principiate, nor the parliamentary government of a diverse people. It is the Roman Empire backed by the swords of the legions; the Han Empire woven with the writing brushes of its civil service; the Third Reich enforcing its will with the Gestapo and the SS; or an American nation that depends increasingly upon the decisions of the federal executive to resolve sudden crises of war and peace.

We may not have seen the most extreme form of collectivism possible for a modern state, even in Nazi Germany and Communist China, but the totalitarian state represents the most extreme form of collectivism possible to the civilized human society. In its most benevolent aspect, such as during the reign of Augustus Cæsar, the state strives to revive the innocent "natural collectivism" of the primitive *Masse*, with its group pride and loyalty and its ideals of nobility and dedication to the common welfare. But this the state cannot do, because the elements of its human composition are heterogeneous and often antagonistic to one another, and, even more important, the centralization of government has not solved the society's fundamental problem. This problem remains the relative increase of those who depend blindly upon society for guidance or livelihood and the relative decrease of those who contribute intelligently to society's ability to guide and provide. The civilized state, then, must preserve social stability by force or the threat of force; this requires additional regulation and regimentation, which demand further increases in governmental bureaucracy, and the bureaucracy itself becomes one more non-productive, non-creative element in the fundamental problem.

As a society which is losing the guidance of its *H. individualis* element moves toward the stage of the centralized and regulatory state, it does not take an expert sociologist to realize that something is going wrong. An ill-defined anxiety, an increasing restlessness, a sense of impending emergency, spread through the land. Protest movements may take the form of the Oriental mystery cults of the Roman Empire, the Taoist "Red Eyebrows" and other secret societies of Han China, or the hippies and John Birchers of modern America. They are all protests against contemporary social values, which are deemed to have gone awry.

Such an atmosphere of anxiety and foreboding is fertile soil for intrinsically psychopathic personalities, which Lindner saw as afflicting modern Western society in an increasing flood.[3] These personalities, according to Lindner, are characterized by immaturity, or the inability to endure any delay between desire and consummation. The interval necessary for dealing with reality is ignored, and its elimination by violence is attempted, thus carrying the exploitive attitude to its extreme. This "spoiled child" personality[4] is fostered by an unnatural extension of the protected infantile period, whether by an overprotective family or an overprotective society, and some of the same cultural factors contributing to the fertility differential previously discussed also contribute to an increase in these psychopathic tendencies.

It is characteristic of this type of psychopathic personality to believe fanatically that one simple act of violence—an assassination, a coup, the use of an atomic bomb—can wipe out all of the frustrations that are felt but not clearly understood. When a considerable element of such personalities has accumulated, such as the Freikorps bands of pre-Hitler Germany and the bloodthirsty viewers of the Roman gladiatorial spectacles, they can be polarized as an effective nucleus for the rise of some charismatic leader figure. Now, the leader figure, as contrasted with the creative individualist, is a particular personality type who achieves social dominance because he conforms psychologically to the requirements of an integral—and vacant—niche

[3] Robert Lindner, *Must You Conform?* (Black Cat ed., New York: Grove Press, 1961), pp. 99–115; Robert Lindner, *Prescription for Rebellion* (Evergreen ed., New York: Grove Press, 1962), pp. 173–94.
[4] Cf. José Ortega y Gasset, *La Rebelión de las masas*, pp. 65–66, 77.

in the *Masse* at this stage. This is the position of the authoritative and all-powerful "father." He is enough like his followers to know what they want, which is the simple solution; and he offers it to them, along with the absolute authoritativeness that instills a sense of security in them.

The description of the leader figure demonstrates that he is not *H. individualis*, but *H. socialis*; therefore, he really has no creative solutions to offer. Yet, when the collective power of the *Masse* in its consummate unity is put into his hands, he must use it to provide the solutions he promised or lose the power and status he sought. The rationality of the leader's response probably depends on both the individual and the social situation. Both Hitler and Ch'in Shih Huang Ti staged book-burnings and programs against intellectuals; but Hitler launched "the thousand-year Reich" on a course that led to swift destruction, whereas Ch'in, like the first Cæsars, was able to organize a society at a lower level of technology and population density that allowed the succeeding empire to endure for several centuries.

But, whether the course of the state runs swiftly or slowly and whether it lasts only for the lifetime of one "emperor" or many, it is the same course. The process of unification and organization which solves its immediate crisis saddles the society with an even more burdensome bureaucracy; the non-productive regulatory framework of government becomes engorged with a significant percentage of the society's population. The load borne by the productive element of the society increases, and a growing (also non-productive) police or semi-military force is required to maintain order. Sooner or later—and usually to some degree from the very beginning—resort is had to the final "solution," military adventure.

Military activity is a most tempting recourse for the leader saddled with the problems of an unsound but powerful state, because it offers an immediate, sweeping solution to all of the problems. The fact that the solution is not only merely a stop-gap measure but probably will exacerbate the problems eventually, if recognized at all, is of less concern to the leader than the fact that it is readily available. The leader can set a disciplined military force in motion with a wave of his hand and thereby derive numerous social advantages, both psychological and economic, at once.

Psychologically, warfare arouses some of the strongest instincts of *H. socialis* on behalf of the *Masse*. Although one of the most aggressive of animals, man is naturally cooperative within the social framework, probably by virtue of one of the behavioral mechanisms observed by Lorenz and others in other social animals;[5] but his cooperative orientation applies only within his own *Masse*. Everything beyond the *Masse* is "the stranger" and, potentially, an enemy. Through countless millennia before he became human, man learned a dual lesson, on pain of death, which is that one must cooperate within the *Masse* and keep it strong, and that the *Masse* must be aggressive toward that beyond it. Hardin states that the species which is most successful finds itself to be its own principal enemy, because intraspecific competition becomes more important than interspecific competition;[6] and as man became supreme among animals, he had to relearn his lesson, that he must fight for survival, collectively, against other *Massen* composed of other men. Warfare tends to evoke blind, altruistic loyalty to the *Masse* and unifies it more thoroughly for the leader's convenience than any other means at his disposal.

Resort to warfare provides the state with greater moral justification for restrictiveness and regimentation, for those who dis-

---

[5] E. g., Konrad Lorenz, *Das sogenannte Böse* (Wien: Dr. G. Borotha-Schoeler Verlag, 1963), pp. 89–195; Konrad Lorenz, *Evolution and Modification of Behavior* (Chicago: University of Chicago Press, 1965), p. 20; Konrad Lorenz, *Er redete mit dem Vieh, den Vögeln und den Fischen* (München: Deutscher Taschenbuch Verlag GmbH & Co. KG, 1966), pp. 115–28; Adolf Portmann, *Das Tier als soziales Wesen* (Zürich: Rhein-Verlag, 1953), pp. 305–38; Robert Ardrey, *The Territorial Imperative* (New York: Atheneum, 1966), pp. 289–305.

[6] Garrett Hardin, *Nature and Man's Fate* (Mentor ed., New York: New American Library, 1961), p. 220.

sent from the unified program set out by the leader can be accused of disloyalty to the nation. The plea that a crisis exists can be used to excuse official arbitrariness and brutality, suspension of civil rights, oppressive taxation, and many other actions which might mobilize protest in normal times.

From an economic standpoint, the usefulness of a war status to a leader-dominated state is also considerable. In addition to the excuse it offers for heavier taxation, it permits the government to stabilize the economy by freezing wages and prices and to suppress labor disputes "in the national interest." Such strong-arm measures can be accomplished without creating too much disgruntlement, because a full-throttle military industry, supported by taxation, means new profits for management and full employment for labor; in this manner, Hitler "solved" Germany's economic woes.

The preceding analysis of the descent of a civilized society into ultimately disastrous militarism, occurring when its *H. individualis* element has dissipated and *H. socialis* applies his instinctual talents to its guidance, applies generally to those societies of the past that have followed a well-defined course. Among them are ancient China through the Han Dynasty; the Hellenic civilization through the Roman Empire; and, with some variations, the ancient Egyptian, Babylonian-Assyrian, and Persian empires. But it should be apparent, too, that various nations of the modern West, including the United States, already have embarked on the same general course.

Cook's analysis of the American "warfare state,"[7] while weakened by a "leftist" bias, evokes a striking comparison to the historical effects of the long-entrenched German military hegemony. The influence of a professional military clique upon governmental policy and its alliance with a great industrial complex are reminiscent of the Prussian officer class and the German cartels. In his farewell address as President, Dwight D. Eisenhower warned that "the conjunction of an immense mili-

[7] Fred J. Cook, *The Warfare State* (New York: Macmillan, 1962), *passim*.

tary establishment and a large arms industry is new in the American experience. . . . We must not fail to comprehend its grave implications. . . . The potential for the disastrous rise of misplaced political power exists and will persist."

There is also a valid comparison to developments in imperial Rome. There, men of wealth allied themselves to the military as a support for their power, until at last the legions realized their own strength and seized control, making and destroying emperors at will. In this country, a large percentage of the nation's collective wealth has been placed at the *Masse's* disposal through taxation. The original theory of this process was that this concentrated wealth then would be distributed for general social benefits. Social elements controlling much of the industrial and technological complex, however, find gaining access *Boeing* to this reservoir of collected wealth easier than continued economic expansion in a free market. They ally themselves with a military element seeking its own perpetuation and aggrandizement and support propaganda efforts to keep the voting population fearful for the national security. In this way, they are able to tap the rich sources of national taxation through "defense contracts." Only a few extremist individuals among either the military or industrial groups could be accused truthfully of deliberately promoting totalitarianism, for most are honest advocates of free enterprise in the American tradition; but they are "practical"—and they are prisoners of the society's exploitive orientation.

The funneling of manpower and technology into military industry, and the training of young men for military service, resolve an unemployment problem created by population increase and technological sophistication. But they result in such a national dependence upon a military economy that return to a normal peacetime economy would be disastrous.

The inescapable peril lies in the alternatives facing American society. Increasing dependence upon a military economy leads eventually to utilization of the military machine to test weapons and techniques, to "clear stockpiles," to keep the economy moving forward. Abandonment of the military economy is likely to result in such economic chaos—to say nothing of genuine danger from other *Massen* in the One World of today—that extremist elements of the society are able to seize control.

This is the beginning of the last stage of the *Masse* which has become urbanized, excessively organized, and protective, and, as a result, proletarianized. Rome was only one element of Hellenic civilization, as the United States is but a part of Western civilization, but Rome traversed the last stage more slowly because its technology was at a lower level.

Because of its organization and the concentration of its resources, the declining *Masse* may achieve striking initial success in its wars of desperation. Eventually, however, the process of deterioration within its own body assures that the outer forces which it has evoked will destroy it.

The historical collapse of civilized societies under assaults by barbarians is generally looked upon as the destruction of a superior society by an inferior one. Admittedly, barbarism falls far short of a satisfactory human social stage, and the urbanized, highly organized society is much farther along the historical path of civilized development. But there is ample reason to suggest that the urbanized, highly organized society represents a development *further beyond* the most satisfactory social stage than barbarism is *behind* it.

Barbarism is a genetically and socially higher stage, a more individualistic stage, than the savagery of the primal *Masse*. Genetically and socially, the declining urbanized society approaches savagery, at a more complex technological level. Its conquest by barbarism represents an event of positive evolutionary selection.

CHAPTER SIXTEEN

MAN IN TRANSITION

*We face the question, is that being to
whom the future belongs to be called man, as
previously, or something else?*

—Nicolas Berdyaev: *The Fate of Man in the Modern World*

I F THIS STUDY POSSESSES ANY MERIT, Ortega's "revolt of the masses" is not merely the interesting fantasy of a displaced aristocrat but the contemporary phase of a historical struggle between two basic types of man. Social man struggles incessantly to re-establish his age-old hegemony; individual man battles for survival.

The outcome of this struggle may well determine whether we, as a species, participate in the evolutionary future or take the road of the trilobites and the dinosaurs, yielding our privileges and our responsibilities to some furry, bright-eyed creature that even now lurks outside the edifice of our pride. It certainly will determine how our children and their children live, if that means anything to us.

No individual can avoid participation as a combatant in this struggle, and no individual can avoid the possibility, whether or not he is aware of the fact, that his contribution to one side or the other will be determinative. Whether he stands or compromises on any issue, of course, determines whether he has struck a blow against the enemy; but the matter is not so simple. What is "right," in this case, is relative, because what is unquestionably and morally right for *H. socialis* may be disastrous to *H. individualis*, and vice versa; therefore, the individual's determination of what is "right," upon which he either stands or compromises, also determines whether he has chosen the side of *H. individualis* or *H. socialis* in the struggle.

The struggle is made almost insolubly complex by the fact that no one of us is a combatant just on one side or on the other. Each of us is a divided being. We are our own battlefields, upon which we fight the most deadly and clever of all possible adversaries. For we are our own adversaries, our own fifth columns, and each of us inevitably fights now upon one side and now upon the other.

This, then, is one rationale for man's existence *as an individual*. Even though it begs ultimate social justification, it offers him some meaning that society cannot give him but that he must give to society. Let me sum up briefly the various arguments that have brought us to this position.

In order to avoid semantic connotations of other phrases that may be more descriptive, a "self-affirming imperative" has been set forth as a fundamental drive common to all life. Without postulating some fundamental drive of this nature—not conscious or purposive, but derived from the distinctive physio-chemical structure of the living organism—it is difficult to see how life's local reversal of entropy could continue.

In terms of this phrase, any society is a "coaction for affirmation"—cooperation toward a common affirmative goal. Social motivations, like individual motivations, are psychological phenomena. Although shaped in detail by environment, they take their general form from physiological structure. This structure is inherited according to Mendelian genetic laws, and it is subject to the action of natural selection.

Psychological phenomena, both social and individual, are thus subject to alteration by biological evolution, as well as by culture. A cultural environment is an artificial environment which, like the natural environment, exerts selective pressures toward particular courses of biological development.

A cultural environment is an *expression* of man's psychic potential and, derivatively, of his biological nature. It is also a contributing cause to its further development, because man alters his environment to suit his needs more than does any other animal.

The difference between the cultural environments of the Stone Age and historical civilization indicates a biologically based psychological difference in the people who lived in and partly created these environments. It is reasonable to assume that this difference represents a continuation of the evolutionary process which brought about previous biological changes in the human stem, such as that from *H. erectus* to *H. sapiens*.

Civilization and civilized social forms are results of creative acts of the human mind in discovering new solutions to environmental problems. Such psychological processes would have suffered severe selective disadvantage from the conformity and traditionalism enforced by the primitive social group. We may assume, then, that biological evolution has moved away from "instinctive" sociality toward greater individualism.

In evolutionary terms, the human historical period is extremely short for the development or alteration of a major species characteristic, even though man's control of his environment accelerates selective forces. An incipient *H. individualis* could hardly have replaced *H. socialis* in the human genetic system in such a period, as long as any survival advantage still accrued to sociality—as it obviously has. Therefore, we may consider the historical period one of evolutionary transition, or at least one in which sociality and individualism are both present in a variable and unstable mixture in the human psyche.

The *process* of a civilized society represents an interaction between the components of that mixture. The more individualistic elements of a society find original solutions to its problems, which lead it to a higher and higher level of civilization, and the more social majority adopts the new cultural elements by the social mechanism of mimesis. Historical civilized societies have followed a process of rise and fall that is noticeably regular, although probably not predictable. We may postulate that, if a civilization's rise is related positively to the presence of an adequate creative (individualistic) element, its decline is related to the decrease, either absolutely or relatively, of such an element.

The simplest conclusion to draw is that, beyond a certain point of its usual development, a civilized society ceases to be an environment selectively advantageous to human individualism and becomes an environment selectively disadvantageous to it. The fundamentally social element of the population is then incapable of dealing with the problems of an environment initiated by a more individualistic type of man. For example, the improvement of environmental conditions which accompanies civilization permits an increase in numbers and density of population, but population density beyond a certain point is detrimental to individualism *per se* and instead favors closer adaptation to sociality.

Individualism is related positively to creativity, and creativity is related positively to intelligence. The social factors militating against individualism and creativity are ultimately those that place a low value on intelligence in comparison to conformity, adaptation, and various other "social virtues."

The establishment of libertarian democracy in order to free individuals from social tyranny has led, at least in the major cases of ancient Greece and the modern United States, to the development of egalitarian democracy, which tends to throw out its creative minority along with oppressive minorities. A possible, even probable, result of this development is eventual resort to a totalitarian state in which the will of the majority is expressed and largely shaped by a single leader or ruling clique.

The focus of the civilized society in urban centers is more efficient for both economic and cultural activities, which are important adjuncts to an environment favoring individualism. But urban growth beyond a certain point brings with it the anti-individualistic factors associated with population density.

Urban concentration of population is at least partly involved in a modern fertility differential (in the United States) which penalizes creative intelligence.

The stereotype of the individualist as an utterly selfish person is largely an invention of modern, collectivist-oriented psychology. The causes to which creative non-conformists commit themselves constitute one item of evidence for the view that the intelligent individualist is more naturally humanitarian than the average.[1] When such humanitarianism is translated into collective action in a civilized society, however, it creates a "protectionism" which permits survival without the individual responsibility required under more stringent conditions. This protectionism then exerts a selective factor favoring social dependence over individualistic independence.

I believe that the foregoing synthesis justifies advancing the following historical theorem: *The antagonism between the individual and society is so fundamental that a high level of sociality and a high level of individual intelligence are incompatible in terms of humanity's survival as a species.*

This fundamental antagonism has become discernible with exceptional clarity in the modern West because the supra-social doctrine of Christianity (arising coincidentally with the decline of the Roman world) and subsequent scientific rationalism created a psychological atmosphere in which individualism could express itself as never before. Society, utilizing the creative products of individualism, has simultaneously gained more effective weapons for the suppression of individualism than ever before.

Both historical example and cause-and-effect extrapolation indicate that the eventual consequences of the interaction of sociality and individualism at such an unprecedentedly high level are inevitable and disastrous. E. g., the secrets of atomic power were unlocked through the exercise of an extraordinarily high level of creative intelligence, but their subsequent appropriation to the aims of man's social instincts threatens to destroy civilization, if not humanity itself. More to the point, if of less

---

[1] Jacob W. Getzels and Philip W. Jackson, *Creativity and Intelligence* (New York: John Wiley & Sons, 1962), pp. 158ff., state that "high creative" and "high moral" groups of students share traits which are the reverse of those shared by "high IQ" and "high adjusted" groups.

obvious concern, some of the secrets of the mind—the very wellsprings of both sociality and individualism—have been revealed by the individualistic application of creative intelligence and are being utilized, quite expectably, for such social purposes as "brainwashing" and "psychological engineering."

This is a good juncture (and high time, one might say) to take sides on a question at least as old as Zeno. Should not society be subordinate to the individual, serving only for his convenience instead of maintaining a role superior to and restrictive of the individual? This is, of course, a choice between the terms of the historical theorem stated above, between a high level of sociality and a high level of individual intelligence.

Let me express the conviction first that most, if not all, of today's pressing social problems arise from the single fact that civilized society does not represent a solid advance over primitive society except in fragmentary aspects. *H. socialis* cannot be other than true to his nature; when he gains control of a society, he crams the new wine of a biologically advanced, more individualistic and creative breed of man into the old bottles of primitive social instincts and essentially primitive social forms —with predictable results. Today's contending nations are no more than primitive *Massen*, magnified technologically to the nth degree. They are long outdated, long outgrown by the men confined to them. Unfortunately, a *Pax Americana*, a *Pax Communistica*, a *Pax Nationum Unitum*—whatever a world-wide federation might turn out to be—would not represent an in-depth resolution of causes but rather the same old primitive, collective solution, magnified to an even higher degree. The *Pax Romana* was a period not only of security and prosperity but of frequent tyranny, increasing taxation, and growing power of the legions. It was the prelude to collapse. And the "humanitarian imperialism" of today demands the philosophical conformity of nations as well as of individuals.

If man is to survive, I believe that his choice lies between the suppression of all individualism, reduction of his biological level of creative intelligence to a "safe" point, and reversion to a simpler, more primitive level of technology, on the one hand, and an advance to a looser, less social form of living, on the other.

I consider the latter course to be preferable. What the characteristics of such a form of human existence would be, I would not venture to predict. Its prerequisites probably would include population reduction, deurbanization, and major reorientation of almost every human social concept. At the stage reached by Western civilization today, I shall go so far as to say that I do not believe its attainment is likely without a world-wide social catastrophe comparable in its effects to the collapse of imperial Rome.

Of course, whether the world reverts to primitive socialism or advances (with or without an accompanying social collapse) to a higher human level is an alternative intimately dependent upon the long-term prospects of that embattled rebel, the individualist. Currently his position is the uncomfortable one of a decreasing minority in a socially oriented world. I believe, however, that the chances are rather good that his particular "breed" will win through in the end.

The great world population increase of the last two centuries, in response to an increase in available resources, is precisely in accord with Malthusian theory. We would do well to repeat Darwin's intellectual step when confronted with Malthusian theory; he applied it to the evidence of evolution and derived the theory of natural selection. When population increase follows upon a resource increase, the gene pool of the population is expanded. A greater variety of genetic recombination and an increased incidence of mutation, in an environment that is, by definition, comparatively bland, permit greater variability in the population. When resource limits are reached, or when the environment subsequently contracts, natural selection exerts severe pressure upon the population. Those best equipped to meet this pressure survive and reproduce; those least well equipped are eliminated.

This would be the completely cyclical process implied in

Malthusian theory except for one fact: the increased genetic recombination and mutations may have produced a type better equipped for dealing with the environment than any in the previous population. This type will increase relatively in the population as a result of natural selection. Relative constriction of the environment also may force elements of the population to migrate, and the elements that migrate are likely to be of a different type from those that remain.

Discussion of natural selection in these terms brings to mind naturally the picture of impending catastrophe, in which the population will be decimated and only the strong (presumably including a healthy cadre of *H. individualis*) will survive. What may be overlooked is that *H. individualis* is already in the throes of that catastrophe; he is already undergoing severe natural selection, because his net fertility rate has been reduced below the replacement level by the competition of *H. socialis* in the contemporary environment. As may have occurred more than once in the past, this selective pressure theoretically should strengthen the *H. individualis* element qualitatively, instead of just reducing or eliminating it, because a low net fertility rate does not necessarily mean a uniformly low fertility rate. Wide individual differences in fertility are the rule; some individuals do not reproduce at all, while others more than replace themselves. That portion of the *H. individualis* element which fails (from the evolutionary viewpoint of *H. individualis*) includes both those who do not reproduce themselves and those who are so weak in *H. individualis* traits that they are absorbed into the growing *H. socialis* majority. Those who succeed are the most individualistic portion of *H. individualis*; they either successfully resist the social pressures against their reproduction or escape the dilemma by migrating to a more favorable environment.

There is some evidence that migration by *H. individualis* has been an important phenomenon during the declines of civilized *Massen* in the past. In addition to the Jewish Diaspora under

Roman pressure, we may cite the dispersion of Greek intellectuals from Athens, sometimes through exile; of early American colonists from Europe, often to escape religious conformity; and of intellectuals from Germany before, during, and after World War II.

The successful survivors of *H. individualis*—both those who remain but are able to resist social pressure against their reproduction, and those who migrate—constitute the kernel of a new social process, serving as a creative minority for those elements of *H. socialis* who survive the depopulation accompanying the collapse of the old *Masse*.

It is sufficiently encouraging that there have not only been cycles of rise and fall of civilization in history, but apparently a net increase in individualism and its influence from one historical civilization to its successors. Western philosophy may not represent an advance over the great Hellenic philosophers in intuitive analysis of the principles of existence, but it rests upon a sounder scientific foundation. Above all, Western thought has sought more earnestly for the meaning of the individual (as opposed to just "man") than any other.

This may be scant comfort to the individualist living in a period when he feels the highest civilized values slipping from beneath him, mediocrity and conformity closing in all around him, and Armageddon on the horizon. Nevertheless, the true individualist is freer from his time than other men. Reality dictates that he live in *some* time, and there is no escape from that. The individualist must deal with some form of society as the environment in which he seeks to achieve his personal objectives, and there is no escape from that either. But these are limitations that apply to all men; and, since his objectives are presumably individualistic, he is not bound by the further limitation that applies to most men—the necessity of justifying these objectives socially.

As difficult as his lot may seem to him at times, the individualist is in the enviable position of being closer than most men to the answer to that fundamental question posed by Huxley: "What are people for?"[2] The answer cannot be that "people are for society." That is circular reasoning, a self-canceling equation. People cannot be for society as an ultimate end, because society was created for people in the first place. Unless some third factor is admitted to the equation on faith, the only answer left is that "people are for themselves."

No humane rationalism can fill the philosophical gap left in the Western world by the abdication of suprasocial religion without recognizing this answer. Nor do I believe that the way will be found at last to a better, freer, and more dignified mode of human existence through well-intentioned altruism and collective planning, but only through the interaction of intelligent people being "for themselves."

The conscientious individualist cannot do better than be "for himself," honestly and earnestly, answering the primitive reproaches of his collective ego with Polonius' advice to Laertes:

> This above all,—to thine ownself be true;
> And it must follow, as the night the day,
> Thou canst not then be false to any man.

[2] Julian S. Huxley, "The Age of Overbreed," *Playboy Magazine*, Jan., 1965, p. 180.

APPENDIX 1: ADLERIAN PSYCHOLOGY AND
ENVIRONMENTALIST DOGMA

Alfred Adler's "Individual Psychology" provides one of those foci from which one can trace, along numerous radiating threads, one of the most influential systems of modern Western thought. This system represents an expectable intellectual process of the present phase of Western civilization, an attempt to rationalize as progressive and hopeful the current regression toward the herd society of the prehuman *Masse*. It represents an aspect of Ortega's "proletarianization," in that mediocrity, having been exposed to fundamental new ideas in psychology and biology, fails to assimilate them and reinterprets their superficial content in essentially the same platitudes that existed before these ideas appeared.

Adler's choice of the title "Individual Psychology" is almost a perfect example of what Orwell called "newspeak" in *1984*, for his psychological ideal for man appears to be *Gemeinschaftsgefühl*,[1] translated as "social feeling." Freud[2] remarks on this inconsistency, which he suggests charitably may be a "product of embarrassment."

Adler's "will to power"—the goal of "superiority . . . power . . . the conquest of others"—he portrays as a negative feeling, resulting from the child's feeling of inferiority because he is smaller than adults.[3] In his view, it should be overcome by

---

[1] Alfred Adler, *Understanding Human Nature*, trans. W. Béran Wolfe, M. D. (1st ed.; Greenwich, Conn.: Fawcett, 1961), pp. 38, 60, 71, 82, 85, 223–24.

[2] Sigmund Freud, *New Introductory Lectures on Psycho-Analysis*, trans. W. J. H. Sprott (New York: W. W. Norton, 1933), p. 192.

[3] Adler, *Understanding Human Nature*, pp. 39–40.

167

proper adjustment to *Gemeinschaftsgefühl*.[4] Its difference from the Nietzschean concept is thus apparent.

Adler indicates very strongly that he conceives of no inherent component in personality.[5] Although he contradicts this stand later by speaking of "inborn social feeling,"[6] he is quite frank in giving us one of the major sources of this attitude—the materialistic social teachings of Marx and Engels.[7]

Adler's *Understanding Human Nature* may be compared legitimately with Freud's *Neue Folge*. Both originated in a series of lectures, and both give general pictures of the authors' respective systems. In *Neue Folge*, Freud delivers a brief, dry, and telling criticism of his former pupil's system.[8] He calls it "parasitic," he accuses it of being built on a questionable platitude, he implies that it is no more than a nostrum. Perhaps the most significant item in Freud's criticism is his remark[9] on the popularity of the Adlerian system in America. Indeed, in this country Adler's environmentalistic thesis of adjustment to society has so adulterated Freudian theory in professional practice that "inferiority complex" and "overcompensation" are popularly believed to be Freudian terms.

The popularity of the Adlerian approach in America has the same general significance as Adler's attribution of his debt to Marx and Engels: the environmentalist dogma of human personality development. This dogma in its Adlerian aspect is popular in this country for the same reason that, in its Marxian aspect, it is popular in Russia. A people that has dispensed with the philosophy of a guiding hereditary aristocracy needs an anti-hereditarian rationale to bolster its confidence that it is taking the right course.

This environmentalist dogma is synonymous, of course, with

[4] *Ibid.*, p. 224.
[5] *Ibid.*, pp. 31, 223.
[6] *Ibid.*, p. 60.
[7] *Ibid.*, pp. 34–35.
[8] Freud, *New Introductory Lectures*, pp. 192–95.
[9] *Ibid.*, p. 192.

the egalitarian ethic, which is adhered to by the same peoples for the same reason. The only manner, ultimately, in which an egalitarian ethic can be justified is through the environmentalist dogma.

APPENDIX 2: THE SOCIAL "ALARM REACTION"

One of the early comparisons of the human *Masse* to a multicellular organism was by Trotter.[1] Such a comparison has been made subsequently by those varying so widely in points of departure as Toynbee,[2] Fromm,[3] and Ouspensky.[4]

A human or other higher animal body is composed of separate cells, each with a distinct life of its own, but all specialized and interdependent. The analogists see the individual members of a human society as cells of the superorganism, the *Masse*. It has been suggested, by Russell[5] among others, that this marks a major evolutionary advance. Such an orientation leads to the inevitable conclusion that the social insects are a higher evolutionary form of life than man, because they attained this evolutionary advance much earlier and have carried it much farther. The analogists themselves would do well to complete the analogy before drawing social conclusions from it.

Simpson[6] has warned legitimately against going too far with

[1] Sigmund Freud, *Group Psychology and the Analysis of the Ego*, trans. James Strachey (New York: Bantam Books, 1960), p. 25.

[2] Arnold J. Toynbee, *A Study of History* (Galaxy ed., New York: Oxford University Press, 1962), I, 44–45, 51, 461–64.

[3] Erich Fromm, *May Man Prevail?* (Anchor ed., New York: Doubleday, 1961), p. 3.

[4] P. D. Ouspensky, *Tertium Organum*, trans. Nicholas Bessaraboff and Claude Bragdon (New York: Alfred A. Knopf, 1922), p. 202; P. D. Ouspensky, *A New Model of the Universe* (New York: Alfred A. Knopf, 1943), pp. 49–51.

[5] Bertrand Russell, "The Expanding Mental Universe," *Adventures of the Mind from The Saturday Evening Post* (Vintage ed., New York: Random House, 1961), p. 303.

[6] George Gaylord Simpson, *The Meaning of Evolution* (New Haven: Yale University Press, 1949), pp. 305–307.

such an analogy. He notes its pre-evolutionary derivation from Comte and takes the opposite view, that evolution has moved in the direction of increasing individualization.

The flux by which a multicellular organism maintains itself consists of a multitude of asynchronous and independent biological processes. Only when the organism is affected by a state of deprivation or accumulation are these physiological processes synchronized through a psychological state of need, mobilizing the organism as a whole. The objective of the course of action then imposed by this psychological state of need is, not the maintenance of this synchronization, but relief of the situation, permitting the demobilization of the organic processes and their return to the state of asynchronous and independent activity.

There is a general reaction of the highly complex multicellular organism known as the "general adaptation syndrome." This term describes the organism's general utilization of energy to adapt itself to "stress"—an inclusive term that refers to demands of the environment upon the organism. When the stress is such that it exhausts the organism's adaptive energy, the general adaptation syndrome (GAS) runs out, and the organism dies.

Many of modern civilized man's physiological troubles, such as widespread hypertension and its products, have been found to result from an organic "over-adaptation," which mobilizes the body's defenses in an "alarm reaction."[7] It has been suggested that degenerative diseases in general are a result of this alarm reaction (AR), maintained over a prolonged period. The alarm reaction represents a more complete, more intense, and usually more prolonged mobilization and synchronization of the independent and asynchronous elements of the multicellular organism than its response to simple deprivation or accumulation. It is a physiological response to a more pressing need.

The physiological course of the AR in the organism, when

[7] P. C. Constantinides and Niall Carey, "The Alarm Reaction," in *Scientific American Reader* (New York: Simon & Schuster, 1953), pp. 395–402.

prolonged, is instructive. The initial phase brings reduction in the organism's resources, as they are mobilized in the service of the AR. There is a second phase, or "resistance phase," in which these responses rise once more to normal or even higher levels, and the organism's state seems almost one of super health. But this phase is not permanent; it is followed by a stage of exhaustion, which ends in the death of the organism.

Let us apply the analogy specifically. As Ortega[8] notes, the imperial state created by the Julii and the Claudii was a much more efficient social machine than the old republican Rome, but its decay began with its inception. The Roman "AR" may be said to have set in with the Punic Wars and the empire to have represented the "resistance phase" of apparent super health, which ended in exhaustion and death.

APPENDIX 3: THE COLLECTIVE EGO

The concept of the collective ego may be outlined briefly as follows:

The large mammalian brain in relation to body size is related directly and biologically to the characteristically mammalian period of parental care of the young. During this period, learning occurs in the young, its general amount and importance to survival varying with the species. This, as Mayr[1] points out, represents a trend away from the "closed" program of genetic information (generally termed "instinct") to an "open" program whereby new information can be incorporated.

In the social mammals particularly and in man above all, as Mayr[2] points out, not only the capacity for learning is involved but the readiness to accept authority. The young child must

---

[8] José Ortega y Gasset, *La Rebelión de las masas* (Madrid: Espasa-Calpe, S. A., 1937), p. 105.
[1] Ernst Mayr, *Animal Species and Evolution* (Cambridge: Harvard University Press, 1963), p. 636.
[2] *Ibid.*

accept the authority of its elders in order to learn more quickly and efficiently than by trial and error and in order to "learn how to learn."

These characteristics, of necessity, rest upon a physiological structure of brain and nervous system, which is inherited with the same genetic accuracy as other physiological traits. Inherited in the same way is a biological "clock" of development, apparently involving the endocrine system. This biological clock determines, in the individual, the schedule of "imprinting," the periods at which various complexes of traits are learned by mimesis. E. g., at a certain period, ducks will adopt a human as a parental figure to follow, if the human appears at that time instead of the real mother. During a certain period a child normally develops basic language, and if not exposed to it during that time, it can learn to speak later only with great difficulty.

The collective ego is the term used here for the complex of inherent *impulses* to utilize this capacity for learning by imitating others, who are recognized as being of one's own kind (members of one's own *Masse*) through association (both in the actual and the psychological sense). It extends further than that, however. It also covers the complex of motivations to find one's place in the social context (to determine which members of the *Masse* are "authoritative" and thus to be learned from, and to what extent) and to join with other members of the *Masse* in utilizing cooperatively what has been learned authoritatively.

The primary function of the collective ego is, in the interest of the learning process, to direct the mimetic process toward recognized authority. A secondary function is to check the accuracy of one's own learning process by comparing it and adjusting it to that which has been learned by others at one's own level in the *Masse*, through the same mimetic process directed to the same recognized authority.

Freud rightly insisted on the importance of the leader figure in group psychology. The members of the *Masse* find their sense of identity with each other as a result of possessing the same mimetic relationship toward the same leader: as Freud stated it,[3] all substituting the same object for their ego ideal. This "leader figure" may be temporary or permanent, real or abstract.

This secondary focus upon a joint leader is, of course, a derivation from the primary individual focus upon the figure of authority, who must always be initially a parent or someone who stands in the role of a parent. The leader figure, as Freud points out, is primarily a father-surrogate.

As contrasted with the collective ego, the superego is derived directly and individually from this child-parent relationship. Other authoritative figures may intrude into this superego later, but they must conform to it rather than altering it substantially. The superego thus attains a more "individualistic" character than the collective ego. It at least reflects the contemporary values of the culture, and to some degree that of the individual parent and his sub-*Masse* within the culture, whereas the collective ego reflects basic, generalized complexes common to all human cultures.

A word may be said here about development in this context of the ego, which characterizes *H. individualis*. In some respects the superego militates against the ego and restricts it in collective terms. In other respects the superego assists the ego in its development in opposition to the collective ego, by introducing the differential factors of the particular culture and the particular parental image into the motivations of the collective ego that it was developed to express.

The ego may be said in one sense to represent assignment of the leader figure role to oneself. Dependence on the authoritativeness of an outside leader figure is thus abandoned, and this can occur only when one feels, for one reason or another, that one's own assessment of reality is superior to that offered by someone else. In the primitive-type social group, this is possible —except to a limited extent—only to the dominant figure, the

[3] Sigmund Freud, *Group Psychology and the Analysis of the Ego*, trans. James Strachey (New York: Bantam Books, 1960), pp. 60–61.

apex, of the *Masse*; but his consequent procreative advantage within the *Masse* has the genetic effect of increasing the ratio of its physiological foundations in succeeding generations. The permanence of this genetic effect in the *Masse* then depends upon whether the *Masse*'s environment selectively favors dependence upon the collective ego or the ego.

APPENDIX 4: THE AMERICAN BIRTH RATE DIFFERENTIAL

The 1940 U. S. Census report was the first that gave a breakdown of the number of children born to mothers of various educational levels, on which a theoretical correlation of IQ rating and a projection of this correlation into subsequent generations could be made. Robert C. Cook, Theodosius Dobzhansky, and others have referred to these 1940 census figures and have placed slightly varying interpretations upon them. It will be instructive here to set forth these 1940 statistics and carry out a projection from them such as that which has been carried out on the basis of 1960 figures.

TABLE 5

AVERAGE NUMBER OF CHILDREN BORN TO NATIVE WHITE WOMEN
OF VARIOUS EDUCATIONAL LEVELS: 1940

Schooling completed	Number of women, aged 45–49 years	Children born
None	31,720	3.95
1–4 years, elementary	148,440	4.33
5–6 years, elementary	270,960	3.74
7–8 years, elementary	1,038,220	2.78
1–3 years, high school	455,440	2.37
4 years, high school	417,260	1.75
1–3 years, college	184,000	1.71
4 or more years, college	112,540	1.23

The first thing we notice when we compare Table 5 with Table 3 (see above, p. 133), the similar statistics from the 1960 census, is that the number of children born to the 1960 group was smaller at the lower educational levels and slightly larger at the higher educational levels than for the 1940 group. Apparently, the fertility differential has leveled off during this twenty-year period. As a matter of fact, on the basis of this trend, the Population Reference Bureau[1] calls the fertility differential "substantially smaller."

When we make the same sort of projection in Table 6 that we did in Table 4 (see above, p. 134), the 1940 results are: the initial population has increased by 175 per cent in a century's span; population of below 80 IQ has increased from 8.9 per cent to 30.2 per cent; population of 120 IQ and above has decreased from 8.9 per cent to 1.4 per cent. The median IQ level in this 1940 projection decreases from 100 points to 89 points in four generations—only two points lower than in the 1960 projection.

TABLE 6

EXTRAPOLATION OF DIFFERENTIAL FERTILITY RATE, 1940

IQ Rating	Generations			
	1st	2nd	3rd	4th
Below 60	63,440	125,294	247,456	488,726
60–76	296,880	642,745	1,391,545	3,192,697
77–85	541,920	913,390	1,708,039	3,012,697
86–102	2,076,440	2,886,252	4,011,890	5,576,527
103–108	910,880	1,079,393	1,279,082	1,515,712
109–117	834,520	730,205	638,930	559,064
118–126	368,000	314,640	269,017	230,010
Above 126	225,080	138,424	75,131	46,206
Totals	5,317,160	6,830,343	9,621,110	14,621,639

Thus, the apparent change in the fertility differential between 1940 and 1960 is deceptive. *The actual differential, on the basis of equated IQ level, has changed very little.*

In attempting to determine why the apparent change in the differential is greater than the actual change, comparing Table 6 (1940 projection) to Table 4 (1960 projection), the first thing

[1] *Population Bulletin*, XX, No. 5 (Sept., 1964), 136–37.

we notice is that the IQ equation with educational levels differs. This is because both equations were figured on the Wechsler distribution of the total population in each case, on the basis of a 100 IQ median.

The implication is that the population of Tables 3 and 4 (1960) reflects a higher educational level of all intelligence levels than that of Tables 5 and 6 (1940). The 1940 population was born from 1891 to 1895 and was educated, roughly, in the period from 1898 to 1917; the 1960 population was born from 1911 to 1915 and educated from 1918 to 1937. The implication is supported by historical fact, for more people at all levels of intelligence did receive more education generally in the period just after World War I than in the period just before.

With such a social trend, the fertility differential between educational levels actually could decrease noticeably without greatly affecting the differential between equated IQ levels, and this apparently is what has happened.

Now, the 1960 population was born from 1911 to 1915, while the child-bearing period of the 1940 population extended, roughly, from 1909 to 1935. Thus, although the twenty-year span does not represent a complete generation, many of the 1960 population are the early children of the 1940 population; most of the others are later children of an earlier population.

This being true, we should expect to see the results of the 1940 fertility differential—a lowering of the median IQ level —reflected, *to a certain degree but not completely*, in the composition of the 1960 population. It would be difficult to estimate the extent of such results, but for comparative purposes, let us superimpose the total results upon the 1960 population.

An analysis of Table 6 will show us that the 1940 fertility differential should have resulted in a four-point reduction of the median IQ level in a single generation. Therefore, we shall set the median IQ level of the 1960 population (Table 4) at 96 points instead of 100 and project it to the third generation, roughly comparable to the fourth generation of the 1940 population (Table 6).

Taking the same IQ levels on which we drew projections from Table 6 (1940) above, we find from this projection that the median IQ level in the third generation of the 1960 population would drop to 90 points (only *one* point above the comparable fourth-generation projection of the 1940 population). Those below 80 IQ in this 1960 projection increase to 28.5 per cent in the third generation (compared to 30.2 per cent in the fourth-generation projection of the 1940 population), and those of 120 IQ and above decrease to 3.3 per cent (compared to 1.4 per cent in the fourth-generation projection of the 1940 population). These figures correspond rather closely to theory, since an entire generation is not encompassed by the span between the two censuses.

An "initial" projection (on the basis of an original 100 IQ median) of the comparable 1950 census figures shows a slightly different pattern, but with the same general results: below 80 IQ increases from 8.9 per cent to 20.7 per cent in four generations, 120 IQ and above decreases from 8.9 per cent to 1.2 per cent, and the median IQ level drops from 100 points to 88.

A word about methods: The IQ equation with educational level was reached by applying the Wechsler IQ distribution curve to the total first-generation population in each case. This curve, based on 100 IQ median, establishes 50 per cent of the population between 90 and 109 IQ; 16.1 per cent each from 80 to 89 IQ and from 110 to 119 IQ; 6.7 per cent each from 70 to 79 IQ and from 120 to 129 IQ; and 2.2 per cent each below 70 IQ and 130 IQ and above. The rest was a straight projection of each group on the basis of the differential fertility rate, assuming both parents to be at the same IQ level and assuming that each generation would be divided evenly between the sexes.

APPENDIX 5: THE CITY AS A HOSTILE ENVIRONMENT

Exploitation of human and natural resources by Rome probably was responsible for the deterioration of its primary productive areas, the Italian Campagna and North Africa. The consequences of exploitation by the modern West at a higher technological level are increasingly evident. Some related facts may be cited:[1]

1. Excessive noise tends to increase blood pressure, contribute to the development of gastric ulcers, and overstimulate adrenal glands. Exposure to 90 decibels or more can flush the skin, constrict stomach muscles, and shorten tempers. Noise levels reach more than 100 decibels on New York sidewalks, in some subways, and on highways frequented by trucks and buses.

2. Death rates from coronary heart disease are higher (37 per cent for males; 46 per cent for females) in metropolitan than in non-metropolitan areas, and they vary directly with the degree of urbanization. Death rates for tuberculosis, pneumonia, diabetes, and cirrhosis of the liver are also higher in metropolitan areas.

3. A solution of only .005 per cent benzpyrene painted on the skin of experimental mice for ten months produced cancer in 80 per cent of them. A pack-a-day cigaret smoker inhales about 60 micrograms of benzpyrene a year. From smoke and motor exhaust gases, a *non-smoker* in Detroit inhales nearly 80 micrograms, in Birmingham, Ala., 150 micrograms, and in London 320 micrograms. The death rate for male *non-smokers* from lung cancer has been found to be from nine to eleven times higher in communities of 50,000 or more population than in rural areas.

4. A Cornell University study of 1,700 non-Puerto Rican, white adults between the ages of twenty and fifty-nine living in midtown Manhattan found four out of five with symptoms of psychiatric disorders and about one out of four with neuroses severe enough to disrupt their daily lives. This compares to approximately one of every ten Americans in all age groups suffering from mental illness severe enough to require treatment —in itself a rather high rate to be considered socially "healthy." By contrast, an intensive study of nineteen Hutterite communi-

[1] From Lewis Herber, *Crisis in Our Cities* (Englewood Cliffs, N. J.: Prentice-Hall, 1965).

ties (although different methods of evaluating mental illness were used) showed fewer than three out of 100 suffering from mental illness.

5. Dr. Luther L. Terry, U. S. Surgeon General, states that pollution of rivers, streams, and lakes has increased six-fold in 60 years and is still rising.

6. The U. S. Soil Conservation Service states that more than 17 million acres of good farmland were converted to non-agricultural purposes, mostly urbanization, in the past fifteen years, and an additional 27 million acres will be so converted in the next decade.

Of about 80 major groundwater reservoirs in California, nearly 25 per cent were seriously affected by 1950, as a result of excessive water use; and there were similar reports from Maryland, New Jersey, and Rhode Island.

Such facts give some weight to Herber's observation[2] that there is considerable evidence that cultural decay goes hand in hand with the development of giant cities.

[2] *Ibid.*, pp. 3–4.

ARCHETYPE. A term from Jungian psychology: primordial, symbolic, and universal images in the human psyche.

Australopithecinæ. "Southern ape-men." A prehuman type, remains of which have been found in South Africa, which may or may not have been in the direct human ancestral line.

Berdache. The institution of the homosexual "man-woman" among North American Indians.

BOTHNIAN ICE ADVANCE. The last of four minor halts or readvances of the northern European ice sheet during the retreat closing the Würm glacial period; the others being the Brandenburgian, the Pomeranian, and the Scanian. The Bothnian occurred about 10,000 to 8000 B.C.

CENOZOIC (or Cainozoic) ERA. The last 70 million years, the period of "recent life," such as mammals and modern plants.

COACTION FOR AFFIRMATION. Cooperation toward a goal that satisfies the self-affirming imperative (*q.v.*), to some degree for both or all of the cooperating individuals. Intent is implied, but not necessarily conscious intent. The implication of intent covers both the psychological motivations of man and higher animals and biological tendencies toward organization at lower levels of life.

COLLECTIVE EGO. A term proposed here to describe that portion of the human psyche which is ubiquitous and establishes similar, species-wide reactions to social motivations.

COLLECTIVE UNCONSCIOUS. A term from Jungian psychology: that part of the psyche which has not been repressed but has never entered consciousness, and is, therefore, hereditary; composed primarily of archetypes, or instinctive patterns of behavior.

CONSCIOUS. A term from Freudian psychology: that portion of the psyche which is, at the time, conscious. Differentiated from the preconscious, which contains those unconscious elements that are latent and can easily become conscious; and from the unconscious, which comprises mental processes that must be assumed because they are not accessible directly to awareness.

CREATIVE MINORITY. A term adopted by but not originated by Toynbee, referring to the minority element of a society which, although it may not be dominant, is influential in contributing creative ideas beneficial to the society.

CRÔ-MAGNON MAN. The human type whose remains have been found in the Dordogne region of France, dating from 35,000 to 40,000 years ago.

EGO (*Ich*). A term from Freudian psychology: the coherent organization of mental processes to which consciousness is attached.

EPISTATIC INTERACTION. In Mendelian heredity, the hiding or modification of one character by another superimposed upon it, the two not being allelomorphs.

GENOTYPE. The actual (as opposed to the manifested) genetic structure of an individual.

Gestalt. A German word meaning "form" or "shape." It has a particular meaning in the psychological terminology of Wolfgang Köhler, referring to the tendency of the mind to perceive and comprehend in terms of a totality of form and shape, rather than atomistically.

Homo erectus. The smaller-brained immediate evolutionary predecessor to large-brained "modern" man (*Homo sapiens*). *Homo erectus* includes Pithecanthropus and Sinanthropus.

Homo individualis. A term used here to refer to the type of human who, by inherent predisposition, is oriented primarily to an individualistic approach to reality, rather than a social approach. Also, populations, and population elements composed predominantly of this type of human.

Homo socialis. As contrasted to *Homo individualis*, a term used here to describe the type of human who, by inherent predisposition, is oriented primarily to a social approach to reality.

181

Also, populations and population elements dominated by this type of human.

ID (*Es*). A term from Freudian psychology: the primal and unconscious element of the psyche which is the reservoir and wellspring of desires and basic motivations.

IDENTIFICATION REACTION. A term utilized by Korzybski to describe "short-circuited" mental responses, in which the mind treats as identical all occurrences of a given word or symbol.

MACROMUTATION. Evolution by major jumps, characterized by the sudden appearance of new types, as opposed to gradual and almost undiscernible change.

Masse. A German word meaning crowd, or mass of people, which applies as well to both formal and informal collections of individuals. Erich Neumann, in *Ursprungsgeschichte des Bewusstseins*, differentiates between the primitive *Gruppe*, bound together by natural ties, and the modern *Masse*, bound by artificial ties, and thus between the *Gruppenmensch* (group-man) and *Massenmensch* (mass-man). *Masse* is used in this context indiscriminately for both.

MESOZOIC ERA. The period of "middle life" preceding the Cenozoic era, lasting from 200 million to 70 million years ago.

MIMESIS. Literally, mimicry; a form of imitation. The term is used here primarily as used by Toynbee: as the adoption of already existing cultural elements. The usage here, however, goes beyond Toynbee's purely historical usage and includes the psychological tendency to adopt pre-existing cultural elements instead of creating new ones.

MUTATION. Alteration in the structure of a gene.

NEANDERTHAL MAN. A human type preceding the Crô-Magnon in Europe and existing from Würm I about 70,000 years ago to the beginning of the Göttweig interstadial period about 40,000 years ago.

NEOLITHIC REVOLUTION. "New Stone" revolution. The cultural and economic alteration of the base of human social existence from the paleolithic hunting cultures to a settled, agricultural mode of life, characterized by the manufacture of carefully worked and polished stone tools.

PALEOLITHIC CULTURE. The human culture of the "Old Stone Age" before the neolithic revolution, typified by hunting and food-gathering societies.

PHENOTYPE. The total physical, mental, and emotional manifestation of an individual as a result of interaction between his genotype and his environment.

PLEIOTROPIC. An adjective descriptive of multiple effects of a single gene, that is, its tendency to influence several different phenotypic characteristics.

POLYGENES. Genes that act jointly to control a single characteristic.

PROSTASIA. A social order characterized by domineering aggressiveness; a "peck order" in which differentiation of status in a hierarchy is the rule.

RISS GLACIAL PERIOD. The next-to-last major period of glaciation, preceding the Würm. It is equated generally with the Illinoisian of North America. One estimate is that the Riss lasted roughly from 325,000 to 225,000 years ago.

SANGAMON INTERGLACIAL PERIOD. The period between the Illinoisian and Wisconsin Ice Ages in North America. Roughly equivalent to the Riss-Würm interglacial period in Europe.

SELF-AFFIRMING IMPERATIVE. The tendency of the living organism to preserve and express its identity in contrast to the environment.

SUPEREGO (*über-Ich*). A term from Freudian psychology: the idealized representation of parental authority in the psyche.

SURFACE-TO-VOLUME RATIO. The ratio between the surface of an organism, through which the materials necessary for life must be absorbed, and the organism's volume, which must be supplied adequately with these materials. Its significance is that the volume is cubed each time the surface is squared, thus setting an upper size limit on the effective utilization of certain types of assimilative structure in organisms.

SWANSCOMBE MAN. A human type whose remains were found in Swanscombe, England, dating back to 250,000 or more years ago, which Coon assigns to the grade *H. sapiens*, rather than *H. erectus*. Most other anthropologists disagree with Coon in this.

Tabula Rasa. "Clean slate"; a term applied to the proposal by some psychologists and anthropologists that the mental apparatus of the human is initially a complete blank and acquires the totality of its characteristics as a result of being "written on" by the impact of the environment.

UNCONSCIOUS. A term from Freudian psychology: that portion of the psyche of which we cannot be directly aware but the existence of which we must assume.

WÜRM GLACIAL PERIOD. The last major glacial period, lasting from approximately 70,000 to approximately 10,000 years ago. Equated roughly with the Wisconsin Ice Age in North America.

Adler, Alfred. *The Individual Psychology of Alfred Adler*, ed. Heinz L. and Rowena R. Ansbacher. New York: Basic Books, 1956; Torchbook ed., New York: Harper & Row, 1964.

——. *Understanding Human Nature*, trans. W. Béran Wolfe, M.D., Greenwich, Conn.: Fawcett Publications, 1961.

Adorno, T. W., *et al. The Authoritarian Personality*. New York: Harper & Bros., 1950.

Allport, Gordon W. *Becoming*. New Haven: Yale University Press, 1955.

Ansbacher, Heinz L. "Ego Psychology and Alfred Adler." *Social Casework*, May, 1964.

——, and Rowena R. Ansbacher, eds. *The Individual Psychology of Alfred Adler*, Torchbook ed., New York: Harper & Row, 1964.

Ardrey, Robert. *African Genesis*. New York: Atheneum, 1961.

——. *The Territorial Imperative*. New York: Atheneum, 1966.

Aristotle. "Politics," in *On Man and the Universe*, trans. Benjamin Jowett. Classics Club ed., Roslyn, N.Y.: Walter J. Black, 1943.

Ashley-Montagu, M. F. *Human Heredity*. New York: World Publishing Co., 1959; Mentor ed., New York: New American Library, 1960.

——. *Man: His First Million Years*. Mentor ed., New York: New American Library, 1958.

——. *Man in Process*. New York: World Publishing Co., 1961; Mentor ed., New York: New American Library, 1962.

Asimov, Isaac. *Fact and Fancy*. New York: Doubleday, 1962; Worlds of Science ed., New York: Pyramid, 1963.

——. *The Wellsprings of Life*. New York: Abelard-Schuman, Ltd., 1960; Mentor ed., New York: New American Library, 1961.

Bailey, Thomas A. *The American Pageant.* Boston: D. C. Heath & Co., 1956.

Barnett, S. A. *Instinct and Intelligence.* Englewood Cliffs, N. J.: Prentice-Hall, Inc., 1967.

Barrett, William. *Irrational Man.* New York: Doubleday, 1958.

Barzun, Jacques. *The House of Intellect.* New York: Harper & Row, 1959; Torchbook ed., New York: Harper & Row, 1961.

Bastian, Hartmut. *And Then Came Man.* New York: Viking, 1964.

Bates, Marston. *Expanding Population in a Shrinking World.* New York: American Library Association, 1963.

———. *The Forest and the Sea.* New York: Random House, 1960; Signet ed., New York: New American Library, 1961.

Beadle, George W. "The New Genetics: The Threads of Life," in *The Encyclopædia Britannica Book of the Year, 1964.* Chicago.

Benedict, Ruth. *Patterns of Culture.* New York: Houghton Mifflin, 1934; Pelican ed., New York: Penguin Books, 1946.

Berdyaev, Nicholas. *The Fate of Man in the Modern World.* Ann Arbor: University of Michigan Press, 1935; Ann Arbor Paperback ed., 1961.

Bergson, Henri. *Creative Evolution,* trans. Arthur Mitchell. Modern Library ed., New York: Random House, 1944.

———. *The Two Sources of Morality and Religion,* trans. R. Ashley Audra and Cloudesley Brereton. New York: Henry Holt & Co., 1935; Anchor ed., New York: Doubleday, 1954.

Berrill, N. J. *Man's Emerging Mind.* Apollo ed., New York: Dodd, Mead & Co., 1955.

Bibby, Geoffrey. *Four Thousand Years Ago.* New York: Alfred A. Knopf, 1961.

Boak, Arthur E. R. *A History of Rome to 565 A. D.* New York: Macmillan, 1955.

Bohm, Ewald. "Jealousy," in Vol. I, *The Encyclopedia of Sexual Behavior,* ed. Albert Ellis and Albert Abarbanel. New York: Hawthorn Books, Inc., 1961.

Bolitho, William. *Twelve Against the Gods.* New York: Simon &

Schuster, 1929; Red Seal ed., New York: Modern Age, 1937.

Bresler, Jack B., ed. *Human Ecology*. Reading, Mass.: Addison-Wesley, 1966.

Brooks, Van Wyck. *The Ordeal of Mark Twain*. New York: E. P. Dutton, 1920; Meridian ed., New York: Meridian Books, 1955.

Buettner-Janusch, John. *Origins of Man*. New York: John Wiley & Sons, 1966.

Bullock, Alan. *Hitler: a Study in Tyranny*. New York: Harper & Bros., 1953; Bantam ed., New York: Bantam Books, 1961.

Burch, Guy Irving, and Elmer Pendell. *Human Breeding and Survival*. Pelican ed., New York: Penguin Books, 1947.

Burn, A. R. *Alexander and the Hellenistic Empire*. London: English Universities Press, Ltd., 1947.

Cain, A. J. *Animal Species and Their Evolution*. London: Hutchinson & Co., Ltd., 1954; Torchbook ed., New York: Harper & Bros., 1960.

Calder, Ritchie. *After the Seventh Day*. New York: Simon and Schuster, 1961.

Calhoun, John B. "Population Density and Social Pathology." *Scientific American*, February, 1962.

Camus, Albert. *The Rebel*. New York: Alfred A. Knopf, 1956.

Carrighar, Sally. *Wild Heritage*. Boston: Houghton Mifflin, 1965.

Carrington, Richard. *A Million Years of Man*. Mentor ed., New York: New American Library, 1964.

Cassirer, Ernst. *Language and Myth*, trans. Susanne K. Langer. Dover ed., New York: Harper & Bros., 1946.

———. *The Myth of the State*. New Haven: Yale University Press, 1946.

Chauvin, Rémy. *Tiere unter Tieren*. Frankfurt am Main: Fischer Bücherei GmbH, 1967.

Constantinides, P. C., and Niall Carey. "The Alarm Reaction," in *Scientific American Reader*. New York: Simon and Schuster, 1953.

Cook, Fred J. *The Warfare State*. New York: Macmillan, 1962.

Cook, Robert C. *Human Fertility: The Modern Dilemma.* New York: William Sloane Associates, 1951.

Coon, Carleton S. *The Living Races of Man.* New York: Alfred A. Knopf, 1965.

———. *The Origin of Races.* New York: Alfred A. Knopf, 1962.

———. *The Story of Man.* 2nd ed. New York: Alfred A. Knopf, 1962.

Cummings, Lewis V. *Alexander the Great.* Boston: Houghton Mifflin Co., 1940.

Cuneo, Ernest. *Science and History.* New York: Duell, Sloan and Pearce, 1963.

Darwin, Charles Galton. *The Next Million Years,* Dolphin ed., New York: Doubleday, 1952.

Day, Clarence. *This Simian World.* New York: Alfred A. Knopf, 1936.

De Chardin, Teilhard. *The Future of Man,* trans. Norman Denny. New York: Harper & Row, 1964.

———. *The Phenomenon of Man,* trans. Bernard Wall. Torchbook ed., New York: Harper & Bros., 1961.

Dingwall, Eric John. *The American Woman.* New York: Rinehart & Co., 1956.

Dobzhansky, Theodosius. *The Biological Basis of Human Freedom.* New York: Columbia University Press, 1956; Columbia Paperback ed., 1960.

———. *Evolution, Genetics, and Man.* New York: John Wiley & Sons, 1955.

———. *Heredity and the Nature of Man.* Signet Science Library ed., New York: New American Library, 1966.

———. *Mankind Evolving.* New Haven: Yale University Press, 1962.

Dubos, René. *Man Adapting.* New Haven: Yale University Press, 1965.

Dunbar, Carl O. *Historical Geology.* New York: John Wiley & Sons, 1949.

Dunn, L. C., and Theodosius H. Dobzhansky. *Heredity, Race*

and Society. Mentor ed., New York: New American Library, 1946.

Du Noüy, LeComte. *Human Destiny*. Signet ed., New York: New American Library, 1949.

Einstein, Albert. *Mein Weltbild*. Frankfurt am Main: Verlag Ullstein GmbH, 1962.

Eiseley, Loren. "An Evolutionist Looks at Modern Man," in *Adventures of the Mind from The Saturday Evening Post*, ed. Richard Thruelsen and John Kobler. Vintage ed., New York: Random House, 1961.

————. *The Immense Journey*. Vintage ed., New York: Random House, 1957.

Eisler, Robert. *Man into Wolf*. New York: Philosophical Library, 1952.

Ellis, Albert. *The American Sexual Tragedy*. New York: Twayne, 1954.

Estabrooks, George H. *Hypnotism*. New York: E. P. Dutton & Co., 1957.

Fairservis, Walter A., Jr. *The Origins of Oriental Civilization*. New York: New American Library, 1959.

Feuer, Lewis S. *The Scientific Intellectual*. New York: Basic Books, 1963.

Ford, Clellan S., and Frank A. Beach. *Patterns of Sexual Behavior*. New York: Harper & Bros., 1951.

Frazer, Sir James George. *The Golden Bough*. 12 vols., including aftermath and supplement. London: Macmillan & Co., Ltd., 1911.

Freud, Sigmund. *Abriss der Psychoanalyse*. Frankfurt am Main: Fischer Bücherei KG, 1965.

————. *Civilization and Its Discontents*, trans. James Strachey. College ed., New York: W. W. Norton, 1961.

————. *On Creativity and the Unconscious*. New York: Harper & Bros., 1958.

————. *The Ego and the Id*, trans. Joan Riviere, rev. and ed. James Strachey. New York: W. W. Norton, 1962.

————. *Group Psychology and the Analysis of the Ego*, trans. James Strachey. New York: Bantam Books, 1960.

————. *Moses and Monotheism*, trans. Katherine Jones. New York: Alfred A. Knopf, 1939; Vintage ed., New York: Vintage Books, 1959.

————. *New Introductory Lectures on Psycho-Analysis*, trans. W. J. H. Sprott. New York: W. W. Norton, 1933.

————. *Totem and Taboo*, trans. A. A. Brill. Modern Library ed., New York: Random House, 1918.

————. *Die Traumdeutung*. Frankfurt am Main: Fischer Bücherei KG, 1962.

Fromm, Erich. *The Forgotten Language*. Grove Press ed., New York: Rinehart & Co., 1951.

————. *May Man Prevail?* Anchor ed., New York: Doubleday, 1961.

Furnas, C. C. *The Next Hundred Years*. New York: Reynal & Hitchcock, 1936.

Galton, Sir Francis. "Classification of Men According to Their Natural Gifts," in *The World of Mathematics*, Vol. II. New York: Simon and Schuster, 1956.

Gause, G. F. *The Struggle for Existence*. Baltimore: Williams & Wilkins Co., 1934.

Geddes, Donald Porter, and Enid Curie, eds. *About the Kinsey Report*. Signet ed., New York: New American Library, 1948.

Getzels, Jacob W., and Philip W. Jackson. *Creativity and Intelligence*. New York: John Wiley & Sons, 1962.

Gibbon, Edward. *The Decline and Fall of the Roman Empire*, abridged by Moses Hadas. 1st ed. Greenwich, Conn.: Fawcett, 1964.

Glover, Edward. *Freud or Jung?* New York: W. W. Norton & Co., 1956; Meridian ed., New York: W. W. Norton, 1960.

Goldstein, Kurt. *Human Nature in the Light of Psychopathology*. Cambridge: Harvard University Press, 1940.

Granet, Marcel. *Chinese Civilization*. New York: Meridian, 1958.

Grinker, Roy R., ed. *Toward a Unified Theory of Human Be-*

havior. New York: Basic Books, 1956.

Groddeck, Georg Walther. *The Book of the It,* trans. V. M. E. Collins. Vintage ed., New York: Random House, 1961.

Gropius, Walter. "The Curse of Conformity," in *Adventures of the Mind from The Saturday Evening Post,* ed. Richard Thruelsen and John Kobler. Vintage ed., New York: Random House, 1961.

Guignebert, Charles. *Jesus,* trans. S. H. Hooks. New York: University Books, 1956.

Hadas, Moses. *A History of Rome.* New York: Doubleday, 1956.

Haldane, J. B. S. "Genesis of Life," in *The Earth and Its Atmosphere,* ed. D. R. Bates. New York: Basic Books, 1957.

Hall, Edward T. *The Silent Language.* New York: Doubleday, 1959.

Hamilton, Edith. *The Greek Way to Western Civilization.* New York: W. W. Norton & Co., 1930; Mentor ed., New York: New American Library, 1948.

Hardin, Garrett. *Nature and Man's Fate.* Mentor ed., New York: New American Library, 1961.

————. *Population, Evolution, & Birth Control.* San Francisco: W. H. Freeman & Co., 1964.

Hawkes, Jacquetta. "Prehistory," Part I, *History of Mankind.* UNESCO; New York: Harper & Row, 1963.

Hayakawa, Samuel Ichiye. "How Words Change Our Lives," in *Adventures of the Mind from The Saturday Evening Post,* ed. Richard Thruelsen and John Kobler. New York: Vintage Books, 1960.

Heberer, Gerhard, Gottfriend Kurth, and Ilse Schwidetsky, Hrsg. *Das Fischer Lexikon: Anthropologie.* Frankfurt am Main: Fischer Bücherei KG, 1959.

Heilbroner, Robert L. *The Future as History.* Evergreen ed., New York: Grove Press, 1961.

Heisenberg, Werner. *Physik und Philosophie.* Frankfurt am Main: Verlag Ullstein GmbH, 1963.

Herber, Lewis. *Crisis in Our Cities.* Englewood Cliffs, N. J.: Prentice-Hall, Inc., 1965.

Hicks, John D., and George B. Mowry. *A Short History of American Democracy*. Boston: Houghton Mifflin, 1956.

Hitler, Adolf. *Mein Kampf*. New York: Reynal & Hitchcock, 1941.

Hoagland, Hudson. "The Elements of Life," in *An Outline of Man's Knowledge of the Modern World*, ed. Lyman Bryson. New York: McGraw-Hill, 1960.

————. "Cybernetics of Population Control," in *Human Ecology*, ed. Jack B. Bresler. Reading, Mass.: Addison-Wesley, 1966.

Hoffer, Eric. *The True Believer*. New York: Harper & Bros., 1951.

Hofstätter, Peter R., Hrsg. *Das Fischer Lexikon: Psychologie*. Frankfurt am Main: Fischer Bücherei KG, 1957.

Hubback, Eva M. *The Population of Britain*. London: Penguin, 1947.

Hubbard, L. Ron. *Dianetics*. New York: Hermitage House, 1950.

Hughes, H. Stuart. *Consciousness and Society*. New York: Alfred A. Knopf, 1958.

Hulse, Frederick S. *The Human Species*. New York: Random House, 1963.

Huntington, Ellsworth. *Civilization and Climate*. New Haven: Yale University Press, 1915.

————. *The Human Habitat*. New York: W. W. Norton, 1963.

————. *Mainsprings of Civilization*. Mentor ed., New York: New American Library, 1959.

Huxley, Julian S. "The Age of Overbreed." *Playboy*, January, 1965.

————. *Evolution in Action*. New York: Harper & Bros., 1953; Mentor ed., New York: New American Library, 1957.

————. *Knowledge, Morality, & Destiny*. Mentor ed., New York: New American Library, 1960.

Jacobi, Jolande. *The Psychology of C. G. Jung*, trans. Ralph Manheim. London: Routledge and Kegan Paul, Ltd., 1942.

Jacobs, Jane. *The Death and Life of Great American Cities*. Vintage ed., New York: Random House, 1961.

Jones, Ernest. *The Life and Work of Sigmund Freud*. 3 vols. New York: Basic Books, 1961.

Jung, C. G. *Aion*, Bollingen Series XX. New York: Pantheon, 1959.

———. *Antwort auf Hiob*. Zürich: Rascher Verlag, 1961.

———. *The Archetypes and the Collective Unconscious*, trans. R. F. C. Hull, Bollingen Series XX. New York: Pantheon, 1959.

———. *Die Bedeutung des Vaters für das Schicksal des Einzelnen*. Zürich: Rascher Verlag, 1949.

———. *The Structure and Dynamics of the Psyche*, Bollingen Series XX. New York: Pantheon, 1960.

———. *Symbols of Transformation*, Bollingen Series XX. New York: Pantheon, 1956.

Kahn, Herman. *On Thermonuclear War*. Princeton: Princeton University Press, 1960.

———, and Anthony J. Wiener. *The Year 2000*. New York: Macmillan, 1967.

Kaufmann, Walter. *From Shakespeare to Existentialism*. Anchor ed., New York: Doubleday & Co., 1960.

———. *Nietzsche*. Princeton: Princeton University Press, 1950.

Kendler, Howard H. *Basic Psychology*. New York: Meredith, 1963.

Kenner, Hugh. "Don't Send Johnny to College." *The Saturday Evening Post*, November 14, 1964.

Kimble, Gregory A., and Norman Garmezy. *Principles of General Psychology*. New York: The Ronald Press, 1963.

Kluckhohn, Clyde. *Mirror for Man*. 1st ed. New York: Fawcett World Library, 1960.

Köhler, Wolfgang. *Dynamics in Psychology*. Evergreen ed., New York: Grove Press, 1960.

———. *Gestalt Psychology*. Mentor ed., New York: New American Library, 1959.

———. *The Mentality of Apes*. 2nd rev. ed., trans. Ella Winter. Vintage ed., New York: Random House, 1959.

Kramer, Samuel Noah. *History Begins at Sumer*. Anchor ed., New York: Doubleday, 1959.

Krutch, Joseph Wood. *The Measure of Man*. New York: Bobbs-Merrill, 1954.

Kuiper, Gerard P., ed. *The Atmospheres of the Earth and Planets*. Chicago: University of Chicago Press, 1949.

Kulischer, Eugene M. *Europe on the Move*. New York: Columbia University Press, 1948.

La Barre, Weston. *The Human Animal*. Chicago: University of Chicago Press, 1955.

Lamb, Harold. *Alexander of Macedon*. New York: Bantam Books, 1946.

———. *Genghis Khan*. Infantry Journal ed., New York: Penguin, 1942.

Lane, Frederic C., Eric F. Goldman, and Erling M. Hunt. *The World's History*. New York: Harcourt, Brace and Co., 1947.

Langer, Susanne K. *Philosophy in a New Key*. Cambridge: Harvard University Press, 1942.

Langer, William L. *The Diplomacy of Imperialism, 1890–1902*. New York: Alfred A. Knopf, 1935.

Lattimore, Owen and Eleanor. *The Making of Modern China*. New York: W. W. Norton & Co., 1944.

Leakey, L. S. B. *Adam's Ancestors*. London: Methuen & Co., Ltd., 1934; Torchbook ed., New York: Harper & Bros., 1960.

———. *The Progress and Evolution of Man in Africa*. London: Oxford University Press, 1961.

Le Bon, Gustave. *The Crowd*. Compass ed., New York: Viking Press, 1960.

Leiser, Erwin. *"Mein Kampf."* Frankfurt am Main: Fischer Bücherei KG, 1962.

Levi-Strauss, Claude. *The Savage Mind*. Chicago: University of Chicago Press, 1966.

Lévy-Bruhl, Lucien. *Primitive Mentality*, trans. Lilian A. Clare. Boston: Beacon Press, 1966.

Lilly, John C. *Man and Dolphin*. New York: Doubleday, 1961.

Lindner, Robert. *Must You Conform?* Black Cat ed., New York: Grove Press, 1961.

———. *Prescription for Rebellion.* Evergreen ed., New York: Grove Press, 1962.

Lindsay, Jack. *A Short History of Culture.* 1st. ed. Greenwich, Conn.: Fawcett, 1966.

Linton, Ralph. *The Tree of Culture.* New York: Alfred A. Knopf, 1955.

Look Magazine, The editors. *The Decline of the American Male.* New York: Random House, 1958.

Lorenz, Konrad. *Evolution and Modification of Behavior.* Chicago: University of Chicago Press, 1965.

———. *Er redete mit dem Vieh, den Vögeln und den Fischen.* 7. Aufl. München: Deutscher Taschenbuch Verlag GmbH & Co. KG, 1966.

———. *So kam der Mensch auf den Hund.* 2. Aufl. München: Deutscher Taschenbuch Verlag GmbH & Co. KG, 1966.

———. *Das sogenannte Böse.* Wien: Dr. G. Borotha-Schoeler Verlag, 1963.

———. *Über tierisches und menschliches Verhalten.* München: R. Piper & Co. Verlag, 1965.

Malthus, Thomas Robert. *An Essay on the Principle of Population.* London: J. M. Dent & Sons, Ltd., 1798; Modern Library ed., New York: Random House, 1960.

Marx, Karl. *Capital,* trans. Samuel Moore and Edward Aveling. Modern Library ed., New York: Charles H. Kerr & Co., 1906.

Matthew, William Diller. *Climate and Evolution.* New York: New York Academy of Sciences, 1939.

Mayr, Ernst. *Animal Species and Evolution.* Cambridge: Harvard University Press, 1963.

McKenzie, R. D. "The Rise of Metropolitan Communities," in *Recent Social Trends in the United States.* Report of the President's Research Committee on Social Trends. New York: Whittlesey House, 1934.

Mead, Margaret, ed. *Cultural Patterns and Technical Change.*

New York: UNESCO, 1955; Mentor ed., New York: New American Library, 1955.

Medawar, P. B. *The Future of Man.* Mentor ed., New York: New American Library, 1961.

———. *The Uniqueness of the Individual.* New York: Basic Books, 1957.

Meigs, Cornelia. *The Violent Men.* New York: Macmillan, 1949.

Menninger, Karl. *Man Against Himself.* New York: Harcourt, Brace & Co., 1938.

———. *The Vital Balance.* New York: Viking Press, 1963.

Meyer, Heinrich. *Was Bleibt.* Stuttgart: Hans E. Günther Verlag, 1966.

Mill, John Stuart. *On Liberty.* Gateway ed., Chicago: Henry Regnery, 1955.

Muller, Herbert J. *The Loom of History.* New York: Harper & Bros., 1958; Mentor ed., New York: New American Library, 1961.

———. *The Uses of the Past.* London: Oxford University Press, 1952; Mentor ed., New York: New American Library, 1956.

Mumford, Lewis. *The City in History.* New York: Harcourt, Brace & World, 1961.

Myrdal, Gunnar. *Beyond the Welfare State.* New Haven: Yale University Press, 1960.

Needham, Joseph. *Science and Civilisation in China.* Cambridge: Cambridge University Press, 1954–56. Vols. I and II.

Neumann, Erich. *Ursprungsgeschichte des Bewusstseins.* Zürich: Rascher Verlag, 1949.

Niebuhr, Reinhold. *The Irony of American History.* New York: Charles Scribner's Sons, 1952.

Nietzsche, Friedrich W. *Also Sprach Zarathustra.* Stuttgart: Alfred Kröner Verlag, 1960.

———. *Der Wille zur Macht.* Stuttgart: Alfred Kröner Verlag, 1959.

Ogburn, William F. "The Family and Its Functions," in *Recent Social Trends in the United States.* Report of the President's

Research Committee on Social Trends. New York: Whittlesey House, 1934.

Ortega y Gasset, José. *The Dehumanization of Art and Other Writings on Art and Culture.* Anchor ed., Garden City, N. Y.: Doubleday, 1956.

——. *España invertebrada.* Madrid: Revista de Occidente, S.A., 1959.

——. *History as a System.* New York: W. W. Norton, 1962.

——. *Man and Crisis.* New York: W. W. Norton, 1958.

——. *Man and People.* New York: W. W. Norton, 1957.

——. *The Modern Theme,* trans. James Clough. Torchbook ed., New York: Harper & Bros., 1961.

——. *La Rebelión de las masas.* Madrid: Espasa-Calpe, S.A., 1937.

Orwell, George. *1984.* New York: Harcourt, Brace & Co., 1949.

Ouspensky, Peter Demianovich. *A New Model of the Universe.* New York: Alfred A. Knopf, 1943.

——. *Tertium Organum,* trans. Nicholas Bessaraboff and Claude Bragdon. New York: Alfred A. Knopf, 1922.

Packard, Vance. *The Hidden Persuaders.* New York: David McKay, 1957.

Pendell, Elmer. *The Next Civilization.* Dallas: Royal, 1960.

Pfeiffer, John. *The Human Brain.* New York: Harper & Bros., 1955; Worlds of Science ed., New York: Pyramid, 1962.

Piaget, Jean. *Psychology of Intelligence.* International Library ed., Paterson, N. J.: Littlefield, Adams, 1963.

Plutarch. *Selected Lives and Essays.* Roslyn, N. Y.: Walter J. Black, 1951.

Popper, Karl R. *The Open Society and Its Enemies.* Torchbook ed., New York: Harper & Row, 1963.

Population Bulletin. Population Reference Bureau, Inc., Washington. Vol. XXI, No. 4 (October, 1965).

Portmann, Adolf. *Biologische Fragmente zu einer Lehre vom Menschen,* 2. Aufl. Basel: Benno Schwabe & Co. Verlag, 1951.

——. "Die Evolution des Menschen im Werk von Teilhard de

Chardin," in Ernst Benz, *Der Übermensch*. Zürich: Rhein-Verlag, 1961.

————. *Das Tier als soziales Wesen*. Zürich: Rhein-Verlag, 1953.

Quiring, Heinrich. *Heraklit*. Berlin: Walter de Gruyter & Co., 1959.

Raman, T. A. *Report on India*. New York: Oxford University Press, 1943; Fighting Forces ed., Washington: The Infantry Journal, 1944.

Rank, Otto. *The Myth of the Birth of the Hero and Other Writings*, ed. Philip Freund. Vintage ed., New York: Vintage Books, 1959.

Rapaport, David. *Organization and Pathology of Thought*. New York: Columbia University Press, 1951.

Rauschning, Hermann. *The Revolution of Nihilism*. New York: Longmans, Green & Co., 1939.

Renouvin, Pierre. *Histoire des relations internationales*. Paris: Hachette, 1955.

Riesman, David. *Individualism Reconsidered*. New York: Doubleday & Co., 1954.

————, Nathan Glazer, and Reuel Denney. *The Lonely Crowd*. New Haven: Yale University Press, 1950; Anchor ed., New York: Doubleday & Co., 1953.

Robinson, C. E. *Hellas*. Beacon paperback ed., Boston: Beacon Press, 1955.

Russell, Bertrand. *Authority and the Individual*. Boston: Beacon Press, 1960.

————. "The Expanding Mental Universe," in *Adventures of the Mind from The Saturday Evening Post*, ed. Richard Thruelsen and John Kobler. Vintage ed., New York: Random House, 1961.

Santillana, Giorgio de. *The Origins of Scientific Thought*. Mentor ed., New York: New American Library, 1961.

Sarton, George. *A History of Science*. Vols. I and II. Cambridge: Harvard University Press, 1952–59.

Scheinfeld, Amram. *The Basic Facts of Human Heredity*. New York: Washington Square, 1961.

Schlesinger, Arthur M., Jr. "The Decline of Heroes," in *Adventures of the Mind from The Saturday Evening Post*, ed. Richard Thruelsen and John Kobler. Vintage ed., New York: Random House, 1961.

Schmitt, Bernadotte E. *The Origins of the First World War.* London: The Historical Association, 1958.

Schweitzer, Albert. *The Philosophy of Civilization*, trans. C. T. Campion. New York: Macmillan, 1960.

――――. *The Psychiatric Study of Jesus*, trans. Charles R. Joy. Boston: Beacon Press, 1948.

Seidenberg, Roderick. *Posthistoric Man.* Chapel Hill: University of North Carolina Press, 1950; Beacon paperback ed., Boston: Beacon Press, 1957.

Seton-Thompson, Ernest. *Lives of the Hunted.* New York: Charles Scribner's Sons, 1901.

Shapley, Harlow. *The View from a Distant Star.* New York: Basic Books, 1963.

Shirer, William L. *The Rise and Fall of the Third Reich.* New York: Simon and Schuster, 1959.

Shklovskii, I. S., and Carl Sagan. *Intelligent Life in the Universe.* San Francisco: Holden-Day, Inc., 1966.

Silverberg, Robert. *Lost Cities and Vanished Civilizations.* Philadelphia: Chilton, 1962; Bantam ed., New York: Bantam Books, 1963.

Simpson, George Gaylord. *The Meaning of Evolution.* New Haven: Yale University Press, 1949.

Singer, Charles, *et al.*, eds. *A History of Technology.* Vols. I–IV. New York: Oxford University Press, 1954–58.

Sinnott, Edmund W. *The Biology of the Spirit.* New York: Viking Press, 1951.

――――. *Cell & Psyche.* Chapel Hill: University of North Carolina Press, 1950; Torchbook ed., New York: Harper & Bros., 1961.

Skinner, B. F. *The Behavior of Organisms.* New York: Appleton-Century, 1938.

――――. *Walden Two.* New York: Macmillan, 1948.

Slijper, E. J. *Whales*, trans. A. J. Pomerans. New York: Basic Books, 1962.

Smith, Homer W. *From Fish to Philosopher*. New York: Doubleday, 1961.

————. *Man and His Gods*. New York: Grosset & Dunlap, 1952.

Snow, C. P. *The Two Cultures: and a Second Look*. New York: Cambridge University Press, 1963.

Spatz, Hugo. "Gedanken über die Zunkunft des Menschenhirns und die Idee vom Übermenschen," in Ernst Benz, ed., *Der Übermensch*. Zürich: Rhein-Verlag, 1961.

Spengler, Oswald. *The Decline of the West*, 1 vol. abridgement, trans. Charles Francis Atkinson. New York: Alfred A. Knopf, 1962.

Sperry, R. W. "Neurology and the Mind-Brain Problem." *American Scientist*, April, 1952.

Stumpf, Samuel Enoch. *Socrates to Sartre*. New York: McGraw-Hill, 1966.

Sydenstricker, Edgar. "The Vitality of the American People," in *Recent Social Trends in the United States*. Report of the President's Research Committee on Social Trends. New York: Whittlesey House, 1934.

Talmon, J. L. *The Origins of Totalitarian Democracy*. New York: Praeger, 1960.

Tarn, W. W. *Hellenistic Civilisation*. New York: St. Martin's Press, 1952.

Taylor, Edmond. *The Fall of the Dynasties*. New York: Doubleday, 1963.

Terman, L. M., ed. *Genetic Studies of Genius*. Stanford, Cal.: Stanford University Press, 1925.

Thompson, Warren S. *Population Problems*. New York: McGraw-Hill, 1953.

————, and P. K. Whelpton. "The Population of the Nation," in *Recent Social Trends in the United States*. Report of the President's Research Committee on Social Trends. New York: Whittlesey House, 1934.

Thomson, Sir J. Arthur. *Riddles of Science.* 1st ed. Greenwich, Conn.: Fawcett, 1962.

Tocqueville, Alexis de. *Democracy in America.* Mentor ed., New York: New American Library, 1956.

Torrance, E. Paul. *Guiding Creative Talent.* Englewood Cliffs, N. J.: Prentice-Hall, 1962.

Toynbee, Arnold J. *Greek Civilization and Character.* Mentor ed., New York: New American Library, 1953.

————. *A Study of History,* 12 vols. London: Oxford University Press, 1934–62; Galaxy ed., New York: Oxford University Press, 1962–63.

Trotter, W. *Instincts of the Herd in Peace and War.* London: T. F. Unwin, Ltd., 1916.

Udall, Stewart L. *The Quiet Crisis.* Avon ed., New York: Avon Books, 1963.

Van Der Post, Laurens. *The Heart of the Hunter.* New York: William Morrow & Co., 1961.

Van Loon, Hendrik. *The Story of Mankind.* Cardinal ed., New York: Pocket Books, 1953.

Veblen, Thorstein. *The Theory of the Leisure Class.* Modern Library ed., New York: Random House, 1934.

Velikovsky, Immanuel. *Ages in Chaos.* New York: Doubleday, 1952.

Viaud, Gaston. *Intelligence: Its Evolution and Forms,* trans. A. J. Pomerans. Science Today ed., New York: Harper & Bros., 1960.

Weidenreich, Franz. *Apes, Giants, and Man.* Chicago: University of Chicago Press, 1946.

Wells, H. G. *The Outline of History,* 2 vols. New York: Doubleday, 1949.

Whorf, Benjamin Lee. *Language, Thought, and Reality.* Cambridge: The Technology Press of Massachusetts Institute of Technology, 1956.

Williams, Roger J. *Biochemical Individuality.* New York: John Wiley & Sons, 1956.

Whyte, Lancelot Law. *The Next Development in Man.* Mentor ed., New York: New American Library, 1950.

Wylie, Philip. *Generation of Vipers.* New York: Rinehart, 1942.

Wynne-Edwards, V. C. *Animal Dispersion in Relation to Social Behavior.* New York: Hafner, 1962.

Achæans, 90
Adler, Alfred, 8, 167–68
Africa, 66, 77, 85, 103, 124, 178, 180
Aggressiveness, 9, 21–22, 153
Agriculture, 24, 69–71, 89, 117, 119–21, 124, 182
Alarm reaction, 170
Alexander the Great, 3, 89, 111
Allport, Gordon W., 6, 9
Amenhotep IV: see Ikhnaton
America, 77, 88, 141–42, 150–51, 154, 168, 183–84
Americans, 97, 112, 117, 141, 145, 151, 154–55, 165, 178
Anarchy, 12
Anaxagoras, 111
Anaximander, 88
Anemia, sickle cell, 124
Animal, 30, 35; domesticated animal, 24; individual (non-social) animal, 14, 116; man as a social animal, 12, 20, 24, 44–45, 47–48, 53, 68, 116, 138, 153, 171; social animal, 9, 12–14, 19, 21, 24, 39, 60, 116, 153, 171
Anthropology, 24, 184
Anxiety, 145, 151
Aquinas, St. Thomas, 7
Archetype, 40, 180
Ardrey, Robert, 41
Aristocracy, 61, 90, 104, 108, 111, 113, 118–20, 130, 144, 150, 168
Aristotle, 7, 92, 113
Armageddon, 165
Aryans, 79, 89–91, 94, 110
Ashley-Montagu, M. F., 43
Asia, 66, 69, 77, 85, 103
Assyria, 91
Astronomy, 125
Athens, 88, 92, 110–13, 118–19, 121, 125, 137, 143, 165
Attica, 88, 90, 118; see also Greece
Australopithecus, 17, 20, 23, 29, 32, 34, 42, 66, 75, 180
Authoritarianism, 86, 143, 150, 152, 155, 160

Babylon, 3–4, 89–90, 125
Babylonia, 46, 91, 154; see also Empire, Babylonian-Assyrian
Bagehot, W., 66
Barbarians, 91–92, 156
Barbarism, 79–80, 156
Bathurst Island, 139
Behavior, 14, 16, 38, 40–41; adaptive behavior, 39; animal behavior, 76; maternal behavior, 128; pathological behavior, 83, 86, 127, 151–52; patterns of behavior, 9, 39–41, 44, 50, 84, 153, 180; role behavior, 20, 38–39, 42; social behavior, 16, 18–20, 39–40, 50, 73, 82–83, 138
Belshazzar, 3
Belshazzar's Feast, 3–4
Bergson, Henri, 33
Berlin, 126
Berrill, N. J., 20
Biology, 34, 167
Birch, John, Society, 151
Birmingham, Ala., 178
Birth: birth-death differential, 26; birth rate, 128–29, 131, 133, 174; human birth process, 18
Black Power, 149
Bohemianism, 49
Bourgeoisie, 118
Brain, 17–18, 28, 41, 44, 56, 58, 67, 87, 138, 171–72
Britain, 88
British, 78, 108
Britons, 51
Buddha, 88
Buettner-Janusch, John, 65

Cæsar, 96, 152; Augustus Cæsar, 150; Julius Cæsar, 130, 137, 141
"Cæsarism," 140
Calhoun, John B., 82–84, 128
California, 179
Cannon, Walter B., 42
Carrighar, Sally, 83–84
Carrington, Richard, 60

Carthage, 125
Caspian Sea, 67, 69–70
Caucasus, 90
Cenozoic era, 16, 180, 182
Census Report, U. S., 132–33, 135, 174, 177
Chamber of Commerce, 149
Ch'angan, 120, 126
Chan Kuo (Warring States), 119, 125; see also China
Chardin, Teilhard de, 7
Chicago, 129
Children's Bureau, 129
Chimpanzee, 7, 13, 17
Ch'in Dynasty, 119, 152; see also China
Ch'in Shih Huang Ti, 119, 152
China, 46, 77, 88–89, 119–21, 125, 150–52, 154; Chan Kuo (Warring States), 119, 125; Ch'in Dynasty, 119, 152; Han Dynasty, 119–21, 126, 150–51, 154; Hsia Kingdom, 91; "Hundred schools," philosophy, 88, 125; San Kuo (Three Kingdoms), 121; Shang Dynasty, 90–91
Christian, John, 82
Christianity, 88, 161
Chromosome, 7
City, 3–4, 63, 72, 74, 83, 85, 91, 115–18, 120–23, 125–29, 136, 142, 144–45, 149, 160, 177, 179; advantages of city, 71–72, 116, 118, 160; city as environment, 116–17, 126–27, 178–79; city slums, 83; disadvantages of city, 117, 121–22, 125–28, 144–45, 160, 178–79; see also Civilization, urban; Metropolis; Urbanization
City-state, 123
Civilization, 4, 24, 46, 48, 51–52, 55, 59, 63, 91, 103, 112, 114–15, 117, 121–23, 126, 139, 146–48, 159–62; agrarian civilization, 122; biological theories of civilization, 26; civilization and individualism, 49, 160; civilization as environment, 27, 160; cycles in civilization, 4, 24, 46, 55, 72, 159, 162–63, 165; decline of civilization, 4, 47–48, 86, 115, 122, 148, 154, 156, 164; origin of civilization, 25, 27, 29; urban civilization, 69, 71, 89, 122

Civilizations: according to Toynbee, 48–51; American, 52; Arabic, 49; Far Eastern, 49; Hellenic, 49, 52, 91–92, 110, 112, 125, 154, 156; Huang-ho (Sinic, Chinese), 25, 46, 70, 89, 91, 108, 125; Indian (Hindu), 46, 49, 52, 91; Indus (Indic), 25, 46, 49, 70, 89, 91; Iranic, 49, 89, 91; Mayan, 25, 49, 51; Mexic, 49; Nile (Egyptian, Egyptiac), 25, 46, 49, 52, 70, 89; Orthodox Christian, 49; Peruvean (Andean), 25, 49; Syriac, 49; Tigris-Euphrates (Sumeric), 25, 49, 89, 91; Western, 25, 46, 49, 51, 53, 87, 90–91, 98, 102, 112, 123, 125, 136–37, 142, 151, 154, 156, 161, 163, 167, 178; Yucatec, 49
Climate, 30–31, 52, 66, 70, 90, 110, 117
"Coaction for affirmation," 15, 45, 64, 100–1, 158, 180
Collective ego, 42–45, 57, 60, 70–71, 101, 111, 145, 166, 171–74, 180
Collective unconscious, 40, 43, 180
Collectivism, 12–13, 17, 35, 71, 84, 92, 139, 142, 147–48, 150
Colorado River, 9
Communism, 71, 84, 138, 150
Communists, 97
Competition, 9–10, 13–14, 30–31, 68–71, 100, 153, 164; group competition, 14–15, 22, 69, 77
Comte, Auguste, 170
Conformity, 17, 31, 37, 50, 57, 64, 86, 89, 101, 104, 114, 118, 123, 142–44, 159–60, 162, 165
Confucius, 88
"Conspiracy together for power," 15
Constitutional Convention of 1787, 112
Cook, Fred J., 154
Cook, Robert C., 135, 174
Coon, Carleton S., 22–23, 82–83, 184
Cooperation, 9, 13–15, 71, 84, 153, 158, 180
Countryside, 117–18, 121, 128; see also Environment, rural
Creativity, 31, 36–37, 47, 57–58, 83, 86, 92, 110, 116, 122, 131–32, 145, 148, 160–62
Crô-Magnon man, 67, 87, 181–82

Crowding, 82–83, 130, 145
Cultural accumulation, theory of, 25, 27
Cybernetics, 42
Cyrus the Great, 88; *see also* Persia

Daniel, 4
Darius the Great, 3; *see also* Persia
Darwin, Charles, 52, 163
Da Vinci, Leonardo, 51
Death, 27; birth-death differential, 26; death rate, 178; *see also* Mortality
Deevey, E. S., 75
Democracy, 85, 89, 106, 108–14, 119, 144, 160
Determinism, 10
Detroit, 178
Dinosaur, 157
Disease, 27, 124, 178
Dobzhansky, Theodosius, 98, 136, 174
Dog, 18
Dominance, 31, 60, 63, 83, 86, 104, 151, 173
Durkheim, E., 38

Economics, 5, 143–45
Economy: military, 155–56; money, 149; peacetime, 155
Education, Scottish Council for Research in, 135
Educational level, 131–34, 174–77
Egalitarianism, 97–106, 108, 113–14, 143, 160, 169
Ego, 42–45, 70, 173–74, 181
Ego ideal, 43, 173
Egypt, 49, 62, 89–91, 94, 103, 154; *see also* Empire, Egyptian
Einstein, Albert, 130
Eisenhower, Dwight D., 154
Elam, 91
Elite: *see* Aristocracy; Minority
Emerson, Alfred E., 14
Emerson, Ralph Waldo, 128, 130
Empire: Babylonian-Assyrian, 154; Egyptian, 154; Han (China), 121, 150–52, 154; Persian, 154; Roman, 76, 92, 122, 130, 136–37, 142, 150–52, 154–55, 163, 171; world, 141
Energy, 170; open energy system, 8; solar energy, 7
Engels, Friedrich, 168
England, 120, 125–26, 184

Entelechy, 7
Environment, 8, 10, 14, 26–27, 29–32, 35–36, 39, 45, 51–54, 59, 61–71, 80–81, 84, 89, 100, 104, 107–8, 110, 115–17, 124, 139, 142, 144–45, 158–59, 163–64, 183; artificial environment, 126, 158; rural environment, 118, 121–22, 125, 145; social environment, 14, 18, 27, 35, 42, 44, 53–54, 64, 80, 85, 89, 95, 109, 114, 118, 145, 158, 160, 165; urban (metropolitan) environment, 122, 125–26, 128, 144; *see also* City; Countryside; Metropolis; Society as environment
Epistatic interaction, 10, 181
Equality, 106–8, 114; biological equality, 98; ethical equality, 98–100, 113; legal equality, 98–100, 113
"Establishment, the," 144
Euphrates River, 3, 71
Europe, 66, 74, 77, 88, 102, 125–26, 142, 165, 182
Evolution, 6, 9–10, 13, 16–17, 23, 26, 28, 32, 34, 41, 45–47, 52, 64, 68–69, 83, 87, 157–59, 163, 169; Lamarckian theory of evolution, 52
Exploitation, attitude of, 149

Fairservis, Walter A., Jr., 91
Family, 10, 20–21, 139, 143; size of family and educational level, 132–33
Farmer: *see* Peasant
Fascism, 84
Fecundity, 129, 145
Federalists, 97
Fertility, 79–80; fertility differential, 80, 86, 132–35, 140–41, 145, 151, 160, 164, 174–77
Food, 22, 76, 78–79, 81–82, 128; food-gathering, 29, 183
France, 125–26, 181
Freedom: *see* Liberty
Free will, 10
Freikorps, 151
French, 97
Freud, Sigmund, 18, 38, 42–43, 91, 167–68, 172–73
Fromm, Erich, 169

Galileo, 64
Gauls, 51

Gene, 10, 48, 65, 67, 77–79, 88, 91, 124, 158, 174, 182; human gene pool, 139, 159, 163; *see also* Chromosome; Mutation; Selection, natural

General adaptation syndrome, 170

Genius, 47, 49

Genotype, 53, 70, 78, 181, 183; *see also* Gene

Germany, 79–80, 84, 123, 125–26, 150–52, 154, 165

Gestalt, 16, 40, 42, 181

Gestapo, 150

Getzels, Jacob W., 36–37, 57–58, 131

Gini, Corrado, 129

Goal, 6–8, 14–15, 158, 180; "primary goal," 6

Goethe, Johann Wolfgang von, 80

Goldstein, Kurt, 8

Gorilla, 18

Goths, 121

Göttweig interstadial period, 67, 182

Government, 5, 112, 137, 140, 144, 150, 152, 154; *see also* Majority rule; Minority rule; State, the

Gracchus, Tiberius, 119–20

Grain: grain dole, 137; grain economy, 24–25

Grand Canyon, 9

Grasslands, 89, 91, 94

Greece, 46, 61, 74, 86, 88, 92, 110, 118, 121, 123, 128, 130, 160; *see also* Athens; Civilization, Hellenic

Greeks, 78, 93–95, 110–11, 137, 165

Green, T. H., 138

"Group consciousness," 138

Hamilton, Alexander, 112

Han Dynasty (China), 119–21, 126, 150–51, 154; *see also* China; Empire, Han (China)

Hannibal, 119

Happiness, 5–6

Hardin, Garrett, 68, 153

Hatti, 91; *see also* Hittites

Hebb, D. O., 39

Heilbroner, Robert L., 102

Hellas: *see* Greece

Hemingway, Ernest, 130

Heraclitus, 88, 110

Herber, Lewis, 179

Herd: animal, 138; human, 167; prehuman, 138

Hero, 51, 61

Heterostasis, 42

Hierarchy, 60, 62, 71–72, 83–86, 100–1, 113, 116, 144, 183; *see also* Prostasia

"Hippies," 151

History, 5, 35, 136, 157, 159, 165

Hitler, Adolf, 151–52, 154

Hittites, 90, 110; *see also* Hatti

Homeostasis, 14, 42; group homeostasis, 19

Homo erectus, 22–23, 28–29, 32, 65, 159, 184

Homo faber, 33

Homo individualis, 32–38, 41, 44, 47–48, 53, 55, 59, 61–66, 70–71, 74, 77–80, 82, 85–86, 88–89, 113–18, 121–23, 125–26, 130–32, 135–36, 139, 142, 144–48, 150, 152, 154, 157, 159, 164–65, 173, 181

Homo sapiens, 22–25, 27–29, 32–34, 42, 44–45, 65–66, 159, 181, 184

Homo socialis, 33–38, 44, 47, 53, 59–60, 63–65, 71, 75, 79, 82, 84, 86, 113–16, 121–23, 130, 138, 142, 144–49, 152–54, 157, 159, 162, 164–65, 181

Hoover Report, 129

Hsia Kingdom, 91; *see also* China

Hsiangyang, 120, 126

Humanitarianism, 161–62

"Hundred schools," philosophy, 88, 125; *see also* China

Hunting, 20–22, 29, 63, 66–67, 69, 71, 75, 79, 84, 124–25, 138, 182–83

Huntington, Ellsworth, 52–53, 81, 84, 90, 110, 112

Hutterites, 178

Huxley, Julian S., 166

Hyksos, 90, 94

Id, 43, 182

Ikhnaton, 62, 91

Imhotep, 49

Imitation, 19–20, 172, 182

Imprinting, 20, 39–41, 172

Independence, Declaration of, 97

India, 46, 51, 81, 88–90

Indians, American, 180; Ramah Navajo, 133

Individual, 4–5, 10, 13–14, 29, 38–39, 42, 44, 47, 60, 63–65, 68, 71–72, 84, 95, 97, 100, 114, 116–17, 138, 142–43, 157–58, 165–66, 183; creative individual, 33, 48, 50, 52, 69, 84, 88, 101, 110, 113, 122, 151, 159; individual and collectivism, 5; individual and environment, 53, 115, 142; individual and society, 5–6, 11, 13, 15, 38, 64, 86, 93, 97, 109, 116, 138–39, 141–43, 158, 161–63, 165; individual assurance, 60–61; uniqueness of the individual, 10

Individualism, 12, 31–32, 35, 37–38, 49–51, 66–69, 72, 81, 85–86, 92–95, 100–1, 104, 110–11, 122, 147, 159–62, 165; creative individualism, 31–32, 48, 50–52, 72–73, 88, 92, 101–2, 110, 123, 159, 162; economic individualism, 49; individualism and civilization, 49, 92, 159; sentimental individualism, 49; "submerged" individualism, 122

"Individualistic revolution," 87–92
Individualization, 64
Indo-European: see Aryan
Industrialism, 49, 77
Inequality, 103–4
Insects: fruitfly, 82; mosquito, *Anopheles gambia*, 124; moth, *Biston betularia*, 81; social insects, 16, 39, 46, 169
Instinct, 18, 39, 41, 84, 147–48, 159, 162, 171, 180
Intelligence, 29, 36–37, 56–58, 108, 110, 112–13, 131–32, 140, 142, 147–48, 160–62, 176
Ionia, 88, 90, 123, 125; see also Greece
IQ, 36–37, 56–58, 108, 131–35, 174–77
Irish, 78
Irrigation, 25
Islam, 88
Israel, 88
Israelites, 147
Italy, 84, 119–20, 123, 125, 178

Jackson, Andrew, 97
Jackson, Philip W., 36–37, 57–58, 131
Jefferson, Thomas, 97, 112
Jericho, 70
Jerusalem, 94

Jesus, 95–96
Jews, 51, 91–95, 164
Job, 94
Josephus, 94
Judaism, 88
Jung, C. G., 40, 43
Junkers, 80
Justice, 93–96, 98, 100
Juvenal, 137

Kassites, 90
Kiser, Clyde V., 129
Köhler, Wolfgang, 13, 181
Korzybski, Alfred, 182
Kulischer, Eugene M., 79

Labor unions, 149
Laertes, 166
Land grants, public, 137
Language, 41, 139, 172
Law, 95; English sheep law, 120; Roman land law, 119–20
Leader figure, 17, 60–61, 114, 152–54, 160, 172–73
Learning, 18–20, 29, 38–39, 57, 59, 84, 171–72
Lehrmann, D. S., 39
Lemmings, 127
Libertarianism, 97, 100–1, 105–7, 113–14, 160
Liberty, 97, 101, 104, 107, 118
Lindner, Robert, 151
Linton, Ralph, 90
Locke, John, 55
London, 125–26, 128, 178
Lorenz, Konrad, 9, 17, 19–20, 35, 39–40, 153
Lucan, 136

Macromutation, 10, 23, 182; see also Mutation, genetic
Mahavira, 88
Majority, 5, 48, 107–8, 113, 146, 159, 164; majority rule, 106–9, 112–13, 160; tyranny of the majority, 106, 114
Malaria, 124
Malthus, Thomas Robert, 76, 163
Malthusian theory, 163–64
Man, 6–7, 9, 21, 26, 28–29, 33, 47, 147, 162, 171; "common man," 5; historical man, 35, 147, 157; "mass

Man (*cont.*), man," 74, 138, 150–52, 156, 182; modern man, 28; nature of man, 4, 12–13, 24, 28, 35, 46, 126, 153, 157, 162; primitive man, 5, 28, 45; "uncommon man," 5, 162; Western man, 4

Marx, Karl, 97, 120, 168

Maryland, 179

Masses, 74, 112, 118, 120, 140, 144, 149, 156, 167; "revolt of the masses," 5, 157

Mathematics, 125

Mayr, Ernst, 56, 171

Medawar, P. B., 56, 132, 136

Medes, 3, 110

Mediterranean Sea, 66, 70, 78

Melville Island, 139

Menninger, Karl, 42

Mesolithic period, 30

Mesozoic era, 16, 182

Metropolis, 125, 136, 144, 178; *see also* City; Civilization, urban; Urbanization

Middle Ages, 76, 95, 123, 125; "Greek Middle Ages," 88

Middle East, 88

Migration, 31, 78–80, 85, 90, 128, 164–65

Miletos, 92

Military: activity, 152–53; economy, 155–56; expenditure, 137; industry, 154; *see also* Warfare

Mimesis, 19–20, 24, 29–31, 38, 48, 58–60, 62, 64, 67, 70, 79, 84, 86, 122, 159, 172–73, 182

Minority, 47, 107–9, 145–46, 160, 163; creative minority, 33, 48–51, 53, 55, 57–59, 61–62, 78–79, 86, 89, 115, 118, 123, 130–31, 136, 144, 146, 160, 165, 181; dominant minority, 107, 109, 112, 114, 144, 146, 149, 160; minority rule, 106–9, 112, 160; Negro minority, 149

Mobility, vertical, 107–8, 141

Molds, slime, 13

Mongols, 79, 89, 91

Morality, 11, 67, 94–95, 157

Mortality, infant, 128

Moses, 91, 147

"Motivated activity," 6

Motivation, 6, 8–9, 15, 22, 42, 45, 58, 104, 158, 172, 180, 182

Mouse, 128, 178

Mumford, Lewis, 72, 111

Mutation, genetic, 10, 26, 28–30, 32–33, 39, 64–66, 70, 81, 163–64, 182

Mystery cult, 151

"Napoleonism," 140

National Socialism (Nazi), 84, 150, 152, 154

Neanderthal Man, 66–68, 138, 182

Negro, 149

Neocortex, 41

Neolithic: culture, 71–72, 182; period, 32; revolution, 25–26, 30, 63, 65, 67, 69–70, 72, 76–77, 84, 87, 102, 182–83

Neumann, Erich, 182

New Jersey, 179

New York, 129, 178

Nietzsche, Friedrich Wilhelm, 8, 15

1984, 5, 167

Nomadism, 85

Nomads, 91

Orangutan, 18

Organism, 8–9, 13–16, 39, 183; multicellular organism, 13–16, 169–70; "social organism," 169; unicellular organism, 13

Ortega y Gasset, José, 5, 8, 74, 86, 93, 136, 138, 157, 167, 171

Orwell, George, 5, 167

"Other-directedness," 144–45

Ouspensky, P. D., 169

Outhit, M. C., 134

Ozymandias, 136

Pacific, the, 103

Paleocortex, 41

Paleolithic: culture, 24–25, 47, 69, 71–72, 75–76, 84, 113, 183; period, 23, 27, 29, 46, 64–66, 72; psychology, 29, 71–72; society, 21, 139, 148

Paleontology, 22–23

Paris, 126

Parsees, 51

Parsons, Talcott, 16, 38

Patrician: *see* Aristocracy

Pax: Americana, 162; *Communistica*, 162; *Nationum Unitum*, 162; *Romana*, 162

Peasant, 118–21, 125

Peloponnesian War, 121
Pendell, Elmer, 56
Pericles, 111, 137
Persia, 46, 88, 89, 91, 154; *see also* Empire, Persian
Persian Gulf, 70
Persians, 110
Phenotype, 53, 65, 183
Philip of Macedon, 121
Philosophy: Hellenic, 165; "Hundred schools," 88, 125; Western, 165
Physics, 47
Piaget, Jean, 16, 19–20, 41
Pilate, Pontius, 96
Pindar, 110
Pithecanthropus, 181
Pittsburgh, 129
Plato, 92
Pleiotropy, 10, 183
Pleistocene, 124, 138
Politics, 5, 143, 147
Polonius, 166
Polybius, 74, 86, 128
Polygenes, 10, 183
Popper, Karl R., 55, 84, 138
Population, 38, 47–48, 68–69, 71, 74–77, 79–81, 84, 102, 109, 113, 122, 125, 127–29, 135, 141, 144, 174–77, 182; population control, 76; population decrease, 74, 81, 86, 119, 128–30, 135, 163–64, 175; population density, 74–75, 78, 81–83, 85–86, 90, 116, 120–22, 124, 127–29, 142, 144, 148, 152, 160; population increase, 74, 76–78, 81, 86, 103–4, 117, 119–20, 132–34, 160, 163, 175; world population, 30, 75–77, 163
Population Reference Bureau, 175
Portmann, Adolf, 12, 40
Preferential treatment, principle of, 99–101, 104; *see also* Aristocracy; Minority rule
Proletariat: *see* Masses
Prometheus, 64
Promised Land, 147
"Propriate striving," 9
Prostasia, 85, 183; *see also* Hierarchy
Prussia, 80, 154; *see also* Germany
Psametik, 89
Psyche, 12, 37–38, 40, 42–43, 180, 182–84

Psychology, 5–6, 143, 145, 160–61, 167–68, 184; Adlerian psychology, 167–68; American psychology, 6, 168; analytical psychology, 40, 42; Behaviorist psychology, 6, 39, 56; European psychology, 6; Freudian psychology, 42–43, 168, 172–73, 180–84; herd psychology, 138, 142, 150; human psychology, 23, 26, 29, 32, 143, 145, 158; Jungian psychology, 40, 43, 180; Lockean and Leibnitzian traditions in psychology, 6–8, 56
Psychosis, 127, 151
Public welfare: *see* Welfare, public
Public works, 137
Punic Wars, 119, 130, 171
Puritans, 112
Purpose, 6–7
Pythagoras, 88

Rabbit, 128
Rats, 16, 21, 57, 82–84, 128, 140
Rebellion, 4–5, 8, 29, 144, 163; *see also* Masses, revolt of
"Red Eyebrows," 151
Reich, Third, 150, 152, 154; *see also* Germany; Hitler, Adolf; National Socialism
"Releaser," 39–41
Religion, 4, 62, 67, 94–95, 98, 106, 165–66
Renaissance, 125
Republicans, 97
Revolution: American, 97; French, 97, 137–38; Industrial, 77; Russian, 97; technological, 102
Rhode Island, 179
Riesman, David, 145
Riss glacial period, 27, 29, 66, 183
Robinson, James Harvey, 47
Romans, 94, 112, 151, 165
Rome, 46, 49, 51, 76, 92, 112, 119–22, 125, 128, 130, 136, 141, 143, 151, 154, 156, 161, 163, 171, 177; *see also* Empire, Roman
Russell, Bertrand, 169
Russia, 100, 168

Sadler, Michael Thomas, 129
Saint-Just, Antoine de, 137
Samos, 88

San Kuo (Three Kingdoms), 121; *see also* China

Schiller, Johann Christoph Friedrich von, 80

Schutzstaffel (SS), 150

Schweitzer, Albert, 8

Science, 4, 34, 161

Scotland, 135

Security, 138, 142, 152, 162

Seidenberg, Roderick, 35, 147–48

Selection: natural, 10, 14, 26, 27–28, 31, 34, 45, 53, 64, 70, 78, 80–82, 109, 112, 127, 136, 139, 142, 156, 158–60, 163–64, 174; sexual, 10, 134, 138–39

"Self-actualization," 8

"Self-affirming imperative," 9, 11–13, 15, 45, 158, 180, 183

Semi-species, 33

Semites, 79, 90

Seneca, 136

Sex, 15, 18–19, 31, 82–83, 99, 145

Shang Dynasty, 90–91; *see also* China

Sheep, 18

Shelley, Percy B., 136

Simpson, George Gaylord, 36, 64, 169

Sinanthropus, 138, 181

Skinner, B. F., 5

Slave, 118–19

"Social feeling" (*Gemeinschaftsgefühl*), 167

Sociality, 12–14, 16, 18, 22–23, 29, 31–32, 35, 59, 100, 159–62

Society, 12–16, 21, 44, 60–62, 142–44, 146–47, 149–50, 152, 158, 161–62, 166; Cherokee society, 51; "closed society," 84, 113, 138–39, 141–42, 144–45; Dahomey society, 50; Dobuan society, 50; forms of society, 46, 48, 63–64, 66, 72, 79, 83, 150–51, 162; Iroquois society, 50–51; Kwakiutl society, 50; "open society," 84, 141–42, 144; "primitive society," 29, 42, 46, 48, 50–51, 63, 84, 100–1, 122, 136, 138–39, 143, 146, 150, 156, 159, 162, 167, 173, 183; Seminole society, 50; society and the individual, 5–6, 11, 62, 138–39, 142–45, 158–59, 161–62, 166; society as environment, 18, 21, 27, 42, 53, 63–64, 84–85, 143–

Society (*cont.*), 45, 158–60, 165; *see also* Civilizations; Environment, social

Sociology, 5, 150

Socrates, 111

Soil Conservation Service, U. S., 179

Sparta, 128

Spatz, Hugo, 41

Spencer, Herbert, 145

Spengler, Oswald, 4, 140

"Spoiled child" personality, 151

State, the, 150, 154, 160

Steinheim man, 22

Stress, 170

Sumer (Sumeria), 46, 89–91, 125

Superego, 38, 43, 173, 183

Survival, 139, 141–42, 153, 157, 159, 161, 163, 171; survival pressures, 27, 136, 139; survival value, 22, 28–29, 42, 145

Swanscombe man, 22, 63, 184

Symbiosis, 9

Tabula rasa, 6, 56, 184

Tasmanians, 77

Technology, 27, 46, 51, 125, 128, 136, 142, 144, 147, 152, 156, 162–63

Teleology, 7

Terman, L. M., 131

Territoriality, 22, 31

Terry, Dr. Luther L., 179

Thales, 88

Thermal Maximum, 90

Thompson, Warren S., 128–29

Three Kingdoms: *see* San Kuo; China

Timocracy, 120

Tiwi, 139

Torrance, E. Paul, 131

Totalitarianism: *see* Authoritarianism

Town, 117–18, 121–22, 142

Toynbee, Arnold, 4, 20, 33, 48–51, 55, 90–91, 119, 121–22, 144, 146, 149, 169, 181–82

Trilobite, 157

Trotter, W., 169

Tryon, R. C., 57, 140

Twins, 56

Tyranny, 5, 114, 160, 162; tyranny of the majority, 106, 114; *see also* Authoritarianism

United States, 60, 100, 102, 106, 112–

United States (*cont.*), 13, 126, 128–29, 141, 143, 149, 154, 156, 160
Urbanization, 121, 125–26, 128, 130, 136, 141, 156, 160, 178; *see also* City; Civilization, urban; Metropolis

Valens, 121
Value, 6, 11, 44, 151, 158, 165, 173
Viaud, Gaston, 33
Victorianism, 95
Vienna, 125

Walden Two, 5
Wales, 126
War, 22, 76, 80, 111, 123, 150, 153–54, 156; *see also* Aggressiveness; Military
"Warfare State," 154
Warring States: *see* Chan Kuo; China
Watson, J. B., 56

Wechsler distribution, 132, 134, 176–77
Weiss, Paul A., 13, 15
Welfare, public, 111, 137, 139–41; welfare state, 112, 138
Wen, 120
Weyl, Hermann, 47
Whorf, Benjamin Lee, 41
Wiener, Norbert, 42
Williams, Roger J., 58, 98
"Will to Live," 8
"Will to Power," 8, 15, 167–68
World War I, 141, 176; World War II, 165
Würm glacial period, 27, 30–31, 65–69, 75, 139, 180, 182–84

Yeomanry: *see* Peasant

Zeno, 162
Zoroaster, 88

Epistle to the Babylonians was set on the Linotype in eleven point Caledonia with two-point spacing between the lines. Foundry Lombardic was selected for display.

The book was designed by Jim Billingsley, composed and printed by Heritage Printers, Inc., and bound by the Becktold Company. The paper on which this book was printed is designed for an effective life of at least three hundred years.

UNIVERSITY OF TENNESSEE PRESS

KNOXVILLE